TO RALPH GARBER
Dean, Faculty of Social Work
University of Toronto, 1977-89
Mentor, Colleague, Friend

ACKNOWLEDGEMENTS

The authors wish to thank the following people and organisations whose generous contributions have made the publication of this book possible. The publication of this work commemorates the 80th anniversary of the Faculty of Social Work, University of Toronto, celebrated in October 1994.

FOR ST. CHRISTOPHER HOUSE, Executive Director Gordon Morwood, in tribute to the pioneers in community work whose innovation, leadership and commitment continue to fuel the vision for responsive community service.

BILL STERN, in memory of Lon Lawson, a crusader for social justice who devoted his life to caring for people.

JEAN PALMER, in memory of Florence Philpott, friend and social work colleague.

FACULTY OF SOCIAL WORK, UNIVERSITY OF TORONTO, The Ralph Garber Community Initiatives Fund.

and

For University Settlement House, Executive Director Kevin Lee; The Flavelle Foundation; and the following individuals

June Flavelle Barrett, Lois Becker, John Haddad, Mae Harman, Professor Elspeth Latimer, Charlotte Maher, Sylvia Miller, Dr. Helen Morley, Ruth Mott, Professor Ben Zion Shapiro, Helen Sutcliffe and Paul Zarnke.

TABLE OF CONTENTS

PART 3 — ASSESSMENTS AND CONCLUSIONS
ALLAN IRVING, HARRIET PARSONS
AND DONALD BELLAMY

PREFACE

This book began life in 1974 as a project for Harriet Parsons who had recently retired from her position as a public relations and continuing education consultant to the Metropolitan Toronto Library Board. The idea came a year earlier from her friend Rae Abernathy who was a long-time worker in the Canadian YWCA. Abernathy told her about the fascinating archival material she had discovered while sorting out the Central Neighbourhood House files as her retirement project. And so the decision was made to write a book on University Settlement, Central Neighbourhood House and St. Christopher House, the three original Toronto settlements that have survived into the late twentieth century.

Born in Mount Morris, New York, in 1903, Harriet came to Canada in 1907 with her father, the late Professor Arthur Leonard Parsons, who joined the Department of Mineralogy at the University of Toronto. Harriet's interest in the social settlements began during her high school years at Toronto's Harbord Collegiate when she read Jane Addams' *Twenty Years at Hull House*. Later, Harriet worked as a volunteer at University Settlement and was also familiar with the work of St. Christopher House. She obtained a B.A. from Wellesley College in 1925 specializing in economics. The highlight of her college career was the course entitled *Social Ideals in English Letters* with one of the great pioneers of the American settlement movement Vida Scudder.

From 1926-31 Harriet was a general reporter for the *Cleveland Plain Dealer*, and from 1931-33 she was on the editorial staff of *Canadian Content*, an early attempt at a Canadian newsmagazine. During 1933-42 she worked as a freelance journalist for Canadian magazines, chiefly *Saturday Night, Canadian*

Home Journal and *Maclean's*. She wrote about social and economic topics such as the role of women in public affairs, slum housing, youth problems, penal reform, education and Canada's involvement in overseas trade. During this time Harriet also conducted evening classes in journalism for the Department of Extension at the University of Toronto.

In 1942 Harriet joined the staff of the Consumer Branch, Wartime Prices and Trade Board in Ottawa, as coordinator of women's work in Ontario. Later, she became National Education Secretary working with national women's organizations across Canada. From 1945-50 she served as economics and taxation convener for the National Council of Women of Canada. She was one of the founders of the Consumers' Association of Canada, the peacetime organization which, in 1947, succeeded the Consumer Branch of the Wartime Prices and Trade Board. In 1947-48 she was the field secretary of the new Consumers' Association of Canada.

Between 1948-56 she continued to carry out research and to write on Canadian topics such as post-war economic conditions in the Maritimes, the iron and steel industry and emergency housing. In 1957 Harriet became the first full-time Publications and Information Officer with the Toronto Public Libraries where she remained until 1968. After her first retirement in 1968, she served as public relations and continuing education consultant to the new Metropolitan Toronto Library Board until 1973.

For the last fifteen years of her life Harriet devoted her considerable efforts and talents to this project, and it is with great regret that she did not live to see its publication. Harriet died on 20 January 1989, at the age of 86.

Initially, Harriet's work plan was simply to spend one year in research, another in writing and then allow a third year for final revisions and polishing. By 1976 she had completed a prodigious amount of research on the settlements and compiled detailed, handwritten notes for the entire period 1910-75; in addition, she had also written a few working papers. In 1977 she took time out to write "The Role of J.J. Kelso in the Canadian Settlement Movement," a paper which was used by Andrew Jones and Leonard Rutman in the writing of their biography of Kelso, *In the Children's Aid: J.J. Kelso and Child Welfare in Ontario* (1981). Based on comments about her Kelso paper, Harriet decided to situate her account within a broader social context. To do this she had to read far more of the secondary literature and familiarize herself more thoroughly with the economic, social and multi-cultural aspects of Toronto in the early decades of this century.

In 1979-80 Harriet participated in a doctoral course at the Faculty of Social Work at the University of Toronto given by Professors Ralph Garber and Donald Bellamy who helped her expand the scope to include the experimental forerunners of the Toronto social settlements. On the advice of R.I.K. Davidson of the University of Toronto Press, a second part was to be included to bring the account up to more recent times. Although Harriet had compiled massive amounts of material and research notes on the three settlements up to 1975, she did not feel up to this additional task and turned this section over to Dr. Allan Irving who had recently joined the University of Toronto Faculty of Social Work. With Dr. Irving's major interest in the history of social welfare in Canada, and aided by Parson's research material and interview transcripts, he wrote Part II of the book, which covers 1930-80. Professors Garber and Bellamy continued to offer encouragement to both authors; in addition, Dr. Bellamy helped Harriet complete a number of her chapters and is the book's third author.

The papers of the three settlements are now in the city of Toronto archives and have been reorganized with detailed indexes of the material. All Parson's research material used in the writing of this history can be found in the Parson's collection in the Baldwin Room of the Metropolitan Reference Library or at the Faculty of Social Work at the University of Toronto where access may be obtained by contacting Don Bellamy or Allan Irving. Another valuable resource were the excellent brief histories of several other settlement houses written in 1986 by Patricia J. O'Connor.

It remains to thank people. Dr. Ralph Garber, Dean of the University of Toronto's Faculty of Social Work from 1977 to 1989 spent many hours with Harriet Parsons and later Allan Irving discussing the progress of the book. On a number of occasions his timely interventions kept the project afloat. In 1993 the then Dean of the Faculty of Social Work, Heather Munroe-Blum (now vice-president, research and international relations, University of Toronto) and Ralph Garber generously offered to provide funds from the Ralph Garber Community Initiatives Fund to help with the publication of the book. We have dedicated the book to Ralph Garber. Professor Don Bellamy worked closely with Harriet over a ten-year period and was ever willing to lend a sympathetic ear; he also spent many hours applying his fine editorial skills to Parts I and II. R.I.K. Davidson, at the time social sciences editor at the University of Toronto Press, was instrumental in obtaining a $2500 grant from the Ontario Arts Council to hire doctoral students Mary Parthun (now deceased) and Patricia Daenzer, both of the Faculty of Social Work, who provided excellent research notes for the 1970s. Three MSW students, Irv Kideckel, Ellen Pomer and Pamela A. McCann, produced four research papers in a course with Allan Irving in the 1986-87 academic year. To the great many people who provided help, advice and assistance to Harriet Parsons over the years, a thank you on Harriet's behalf. Appreciation is extended to Carol Seidman, Assistant Dean, Faculty of Social Work, for her enthusiastic support and successful fundraising activities in connection with this publication. Thanks as well to Angela Umbrello of the Faculty of Social Work for her technical wizardry at word processing, her countless excellent suggestions and her cheerfulness in putting up with the eccentricities of the three authors. Without her assistance the diverse parts of this manuscript would never have been brought together. Finally, we would like to thank Brad Lambertus, managing editor of Canadian Scholars' Press, for his many fine suggestions for improving the text and for the long hours he devoted to the manuscript. Working with him was a pleasure.

PART 1

PIONEERS IN THE SLUMS, 1890-1929

Harriet Parsons
with **Donald Bellamy**

Chapter One

How the Social Settlements Came to Canada

Introduction

Toynbee Hall, the first social settlement,opened in London's East End in 1884 and was quickly followed by other settlements in England and Scotland. American visitors to Toynbee Hall in the late 1880s took the idea back to the United States,where it so captured the imagination of social reformers that over one hundred settlement houses were established by the end of the nineteenth century.

Canadians began to explore the movement as early as 1889 and experimented with a few settlement-like institutions in the 1890s. However, the first real Canadian settlement was not founded until 1902 when Sara Libby Carson and her friend Mary Lawson Bell opened the Evangelia Settlement in Toronto's east end. Why was Canada so slow to adopt the settlement idea? The reasons are both simple and complex. The slowness, in part, reflected the less advanced stage of industrial development, the smaller size of cities and the relatively small influx of immigrants before 1900. More complex reasons were to be found in the conflicts between conservative and radical approaches to reform and in the complex weaving of the personalities and principles that interacted to shape social welfare development in urban Canada in the late nineteenth and early twentieth centuries.

The best way to understand the development of the social settlement movement in Canada is to look at the British and American settlement movements, which preceded and inspired the Canadian movement, and to examine the conditions of life and work in the late nineteenth century, especially in Toronto where most of the early exploration of the social settlement movement took place.

THE BRITISH AND AMERICAN SETTLEMENTS

By 1880 London was the largest city in the world with a population of about four million. The growth and prosperity that accompanied the Industrial Revolution was overshadowed by incredibly poor working conditions, the widening gulf between classes, the vast extremes of wealth and poverty, the proliferation of slums in all the large industrial cities and the increasing degradation not only of living conditions but also of the spirit of the poor. England went through more than one hundred years of experimentation with a variety measures — mutual aid societies, workingmen's colleges and cooperatives — designed to combat or ameliorate the adverse effects of industrialization before the social settlement idea evolved, largely through the teachings of the Christian Socialists. These reformers sought to replace the competitive nature on which industrialization was based with the spirit of Christian cooperation and to establish the Kingdom of God on Earth. Inspired by the earlier work of Thomas Carlyle, some of the major thinkers and writers in the late nineteenth century were involved in the Christian Socialist movement. Among them were Charles Kingsley, Matthew Arnold and John Ruskin, all of whom taught either at Oxford or Cambridge.

John Ruskin, a renowned lecturer on art and economics, encouraged his students to get to know the workingman firsthand, to see for themselves the conditions of the poor. In 1867, because of Ruskin's influence, Edward Denison became the first settler in London's East End who aimed to aid the workingman and to bring the area's problems to the attention of the local authorities. A year later Denison and his friend John Richard Green met with Ruskin to suggest that other young university men be invited to form a colony in the East End to carry out the work Denison had been attempting alone. Although this specific proposal never went forward, the idea of a university settlement was born.

TOYNBEE HALL

The man most responsible for making the university settlement house a reality was Rev. Samuel A. Barnett, an Oxford graduate who became the vicar of St. Jude's parish in Whitechapel in 1872 at the request of the Bishop of London. The bishop warned him that this was "the worst parish in my diocese, inhabited mainly by a criminal population and one which has, I fear, been much corrupted by doles." Barnett and his wife Henrietta Rowlands did their best to change conditions in the neighbourhood surrounding the vicarage, but it was uphill work.

In 1875 the Barnetts went to Oxford to tell some of the undergraduates about the poor and invited them to stay in Whitechapel to see the situation firsthand. In the following years Barnett maintained contact with the young men from Oxford and Cambridge, and eventually he recommended that a house be hired where university men could live and study the life and problems of the poor. "A settlement of university men," he wrote, "will do a little to remove the inequalities of life, as the settlers share their best with the poor and learn through feeling how they live." In 1884 Toynbee Hall opened.

It was named in memory of the ardent young social reformer Arnold Toynbee, also a disciple of Ruskin, who lectured at Oxford on the Industrial Revolution. With Toynbee Hall the settlement idea came into practical focus as a place where succeeding generations of university men could take up residence, study the conditions of the poor, devise programs for their education and enjoyment, and attempt to bring about social reform. From the outset, Toynbee Hall was based on broad Christian Socialist principles, to which was added Ruskin's teaching that art must be made "the treasure of the people." Workingmen's clubs, boys' clubs, art exhibits and piano concerts flourished side by side. The key concept was the development of friendship and understanding among people of different classes; charity was always eschewed in favour of helping people to help themselves.

Regardless of the efforts to bridge the class gap, it was evident that the more advantaged, university-educated residents of Toynbee Hall had a special role to play if real social change were to take place. J.A.R. Pimlott, writing about the first fifty years of Toynbee Hall, states that the activities of the residents as citizens "extended from the mere exercise of the vote to participation in local government, from social research to active propaganda in social matters, from the humdrum routine of visiting the poor to the formulation of national schemes for the relief of unemployment and the alleviation of distress." Some residents held paid positions at Toynbee Hall; a few others devoted their whole lives to the East End. But in the early days, the great majority worked in the area west of Whitechapel "as civil servants, in local government, law, medicine, journalism," bringing a wealth of professional expertise as well as social theory to focus on the problems of the poor.

Social research was an integral part of the activities at Toynbee Hall. Charles Booth's monumental study of poverty and its causes among the working-class people of England had its origin in his association with Toynbee Hall's first warden Samuel Barnett, and Toynbee Hall men assisted in the study. Sir William Beveridge began his research on unemployment, which later led to the establishment of employment exchanges, unemployment insurance and the famous Beveridge Report of 1941, when sub-warden of Toynbee Hall from 1903-05. The imperative of social reform was always dominant in the minds of those at Toynbee Hall. Residents became sanitary inspectors, organized a company to build model lodging-houses, promoted the cooperative movement, and actively worked in support of trade unions, even to the extent of organizing strikes and strike relief. As an institution Toynbee Hall generally retained a neutral stand in industrial disputes and political controversies; it acted as a focal point where people of all shades of opinion could meet and discuss problems openly.

Toynbee Hall was also notable as a training ground for future leaders in social work and social reform. One such man, who was to leave a strong impression on Canadian social work training, was E.J. Urwick, the first sub-warden at Toynbee Hall from 1900-03. He became head of the Department of Political Economy at the University of Toronto and from 1927-37 headed its Department of Social Service, which was renamed the Department of Social Science in 1929.

From its inception Toynbee Hall was a secular institution. Samuel Barnett, its chief promoter and first warden though himself a clergyman, felt strongly that the church alone could not cope with the problems of the slums. In a paper which he gave at Oxford in 1883, entitled "Settlements of University Men in Great Towns," Barnett rejected the idea of a college mission as too narrow and stressed the need to "bring the life of the university to bear on the life of the poor, irrespective of church or creed." This pointed to a philosophical difference of opinion between the religious and secular points of view that was to foretell future splits in settlement movements in the United States and Canada. Even during the establishment of Toynbee Hall a heated disagreement arose over the idea of a purely secular settlement. In the end a group of students broke away to establish Oxford House in Bethnal Green to perform both religious and social work.

THE AMERICAN SETTLEMENTS

As in Britain the advent of massive industrial growth in the United States brought sharp contrasts of wealth and poverty, great divisions between labour and capital, and the growth of overcrowded, unsanitary urban slums. By 1890 New York had a population of about 1,500,000 and Chicago had doubled its population from 503,000 in 1880 to 1,047,000. In both cities some 40 per cent of the residents were foreign-born, many of them clustered in ethnic ghettos. The depressions of 1873 and 1883 reduced countless willing workers to abject poverty, adding their miseries to those of the immigrants.

Social welfare, as opposed to outright charity, was still in its infancy when the new social settlements started in the United States. It was a period of social unrest, urban reform and trade union activity. Not surprisingly, a great many new social services and efforts at coordination grew in this environment. The teaching of sociology in universities was an important influence on these developments.

In 1886 the Rev. Stanton Coit founded the first American settlement, the Neighborhood Guild (later renamed University Settlement) on the Lower East Side of New York, after spending three months earlier in the year at Toynbee Hall. He chose the original name Neighbourhood Guild because he felt this expressed the fundamental idea that the institution embodied.

Vida Dutton Scudder, one of the first American women to study at Oxford, had attended lectures by John Ruskin and returned to the United States in 1886 "kindled with the flame of social passion." She began to discuss with friends and colleagues at Smith College (where she obtained her M.A. degree) and at Wellesley College (where she became an instructor in English literature) the possibility of starting a university settlement movement. These discussions led to the formation of the College Settlements Association, which comprised delegates from five of the leading eastern women's colleges. Then, in 1889, the first of the College Settlements was opened at 95 Rivington Street in New York by Vida Scudder and Jean Fine.

By a strange coincidence, the opening of New York's College Settlement took place just two weeks before Hull House, the third social settlement in North America, was opened in Chicago by Jane Addams and Ellen Gates Starr. They too were under the influence of Toynbee Hall, which they had visited a year earlier during a trip to Europe. Chicago's Hull House was to become one of the most famous social settlements in the world, and it had a profound effect on the development of the settlement movement in the United States and Canada.

The sense of being part of great social changes to improve the lot of mankind created feelings of intense excitement and messianic purpose in the early university settlement workers. Three years after she founded Hull House, Jane Addams attended the Ethical Culture Societies' summer school on philanthropy and social progress where she found herself in the company of other settlement pioneers such as New York's Vida Scudder. Jane Addams wrote of her experience at the summer school:

> I doubt if anywhere on the continent that summer could have
> been found a group of people more genuinely interested in

social development or more sincerely convinced that they had
found a clue by which the conditions in crowded cities might
be understood and the agencies for social betterment
developed.

The early American settlements faced many problems. With very few
training facilities and the generally low pay there was a shortage of trained
workers. C.R. Henderson, in *Social Settlements* (1899), outlined some of the
major criticisms of the settlements in this first decade: the youth and
inexperience of most of the workers, the secular nature of the settlements
and the narrow focus of the monastic way of life with early settlements
having either all male or all female residents.

In response to criticism from many churches and missions, which saw
the lack of evangelism as a serious flaw in the secular settlements, a number
of settlements were organized under religious auspices. One of these was
Christodora House, which was founded on the Lower East Side of New York
in 1897 by Sara Libby Carson and Christina I. MacColl, two workers in the
American YWCA movement. It began as a young women's settlement, to
which work for men and boys was later added. Although located in a largely
Jewish neighbourhood, it was avowedly Christian and Christianizing in
character.

THE SETTLEMENT MOVEMENT COMES TO CANADA

Canadians spent nearly 20 years of experimentation with different
versions of this inner city institution before a real settlement was founded.
Evangelia Settlement was opened in 1902 in Toronto by Mary Lawson Bell
and Sara Libby Carson, who had started Christadora House in New York.
Why did it take so long? And when a settlement was started, why was it an
evangelical institution rather than a secular one as the original settlements in
Britain and the United States? Two major parallel sets of forces might account
for what happened.

On the one hand, the socio-economic context hardly favoured the kind
of neighbourhood intervention taken in the other countries. In 1884, as
Toynbee Hall opened its doors to the slum dwellers of London, the city of
Toronto was celebrating its Golden Jubilee. It took 50 years for the city's
population to grow from 9,252 inhabitants in 1834 to over 100,000. Canada's
economy was largely agricultural rather than industrial, and urban problems
were not as pressing in the 1880s and 1890s as they had been for more than a
hundred years in Great Britain and had quickly become in the United States.
There was little motivation to follow the settlement example until non-

English-speaking immigrants began arriving in large numbers around the turn of the century to compete for poorly paid, unskilled labouring jobs and crowded into cities ill-prepared to house them. However, the 1880s were not without social problems. Many community leaders were alarmed about drunkenness and crime in the larger cities. Equally disturbing was the large number of ill-treated, neglected or deserted children. The idea that government ought to make some provision for the relief of the poor encountered heavy resistance. The churches tended "to deplore any encroachment by government upon the sphere of charity," which they had long considered their special preserve. As social problems grew the downtown churches and missions in the larger Canadian cities tried valiantly to meet the needs of their less-fortunate neighbours. The religious, temperance and moral teaching of the churches was combined with judicious charity to the deserving poor.

Not surprisingly, the evangelical churches were determined to protect what they considered to be their domain. Given their ecclesiastical structure, the churches had the administrative capability to open religiously oriented neighbourhood services. Ironically, it was the provision in the inner city of such a service infrastructure by these churches that slowed the development of the social settlement movement in Canada's cities.

CHAPTER TWO

CANADIAN REACTION TO THE SETTLEMENT MOVEMENT

The first exploration by a Canadian of the new settlement movement was probably a visit to Toynbee Hall in 1889 by Presbyterian minister and journalist Rev. J.A. Macdonald.

Macdonald has been described as "a big, burly man with a slight speech impediment lending drama to his very real eloquence." However, it was not his sermons but his journalistic endeavours that were to give him his future, nationwide influence on Canadian religious, social and political thought. In the late 1890s he founded and edited two independent Presbyterian journals, the monthly *Westminster* and the weekly *Presbyterian*. He then became editor-in-chief of the *Toronto Globe*, where he remained for over a decade. Macdonald accepted with some sadness the secular approach taken by the Toynbee Hall settlement, but did not see the necessity for it in the prevailing Canadian conditions. As editor of the *Knox College Monthly*, he recounted his impressions in an article entitled "East London and the Universities Settlement" in the May 1889 issue of the journal:

> The movement is in no way evangelistic. Professedly it is not religious. It is not even Christian except in so far as all true service to man is Christly.... No religious services are held, and the religious argument is not used. All this perplexed me at first, and for this many at a distance, ignorant of the circumstances, will condemn the movement and predict its failure. It may seem that ... the apparent secularism of the effort dooms it. I am not so sceptical now. When one sees the

crowd of outcasts for whom no man cares, one is grateful for any scheme of relief. Anything that will elevate these people and inspire them in the least degree is making for righteousness.

Actually, in Toronto the foundation was already in place for a settlement movement. Two early missions, started by compassionate women as sabbath schools for young boys, were already firmly established with a religious basis and a focus on children: the Dorset Mission and the Fred Victor Mission.

THE DORSET MISSION (LATER THE ST. ANDREW'S INSTITUTE)

In 1870 Isabel Alexander started what came to be known as the Dorset Mission. This mission, which was taken under the wing of St. Andrew's Church in 1877, was the predecessor of St. Andrew's Institute. This move was thanks to Rev. Daniel James MacDonnell, who was to become the guiding spirit of the Dorset Mission. Rev. MacDonnell accepted a call to St. Andrew's Church in Toronto in 1870, at 27 years of age, after completing theological studies at Queen's University in Kingston and Glasgow, Scotland. With MacDonnell's more liberal and open-minded approach to educational programs, night school work began, a penny savings bank was founded and the sabbath school continued. Reform goals were clearly aimed at the individual through moral training, education and thrift. The enrolment in the night school was limited to 40, making it a privilege to attend, and to help them feel independent, pupils were required to pay a five-cent tuition fee.

From the beginning the teachers were not all adherents of St. Andrew's Church. "The project is not a denominational one in any sense," the *Globe* wrote in 1879, "the persons engaged in it being themselves of various forms of religion" (though probably all Protestant).

The night school, under the direction of Hamilton Cassels, an attorney and a member of St. Andrew's Church, became an outstanding success. It was the foundation of the St. Andrew's Institute, which opened in a three-storey building at the corner of Nelson and John streets in 1890. Cassels and John Kay were two of the prominent sponsors responsible for raising $17,152 for the purchase of the land and building. The new building offered fine recreational, educational and meeting facilities in a neighbourhood that once was one of the best in Toronto but now was rapidly becoming a slum. New features included the gymnasium and the swimming baths that provided not only an athletic facility but also a much-needed means of personal cleanliness in a neighbourhood where private baths were scarce.

The main emphasis of the Institute was on teaching and training boys and girls in the three Rs. MacDonnell strongly favoured this approach, as the fathers and mothers might learn from their children. The program for young workingmen was also strengthened. The Young Men's Club began as a Bible class conducted by Emma George, and a MacDonnell Club for men met on Sunday afternoons and was addressed by MacDonnell once a month. A little later an interesting experiment in democratic training started when a committee of nine boys assisted in the management of the night school, "the selection of this committee being made by the boys themselves." A monthly journal, *The Institute Reporter*, was also edited and published by the boys.

MacDonnell was convinced that, with St. Andrew's Church only a few blocks from the institute, the men and women of the district would be encouraged to come to it and "every proposal to hold preaching or devotional services in the institute for them — in effect, to make it a mission church — always met with his firm objection." However, this attitude did not apply to the Sunday school for boys and girls, and the singing of hymns was a regular part of the program at the clubs and gatherings for men and women.

THE FRED VICTOR MISSION

The origins of the Fred Victor Mission can be traced to 1883 when Mary Sheffield became concerned about street waifs in the Jarvis Street area. From small beginnings the sabbath school grew and expanded into a mission serving adults as well as children. Gospel, temperance and other meetings were added along with night schools. At first the work was chiefly among men and boys, with aggressive work done among vagrant and homeless men of the district. A boys' cooking class was included from the early days in the junior department. But in 1892 the first mothers' meeting was held and soon sewing classes were held for girls. The next year the work of the mission was actually moved to four different addresses before a brand new building was opened in 1894.

The handsome building was a gift of Hart A. Massey, philanthropic manufacturer of farm implements, in memory of his youngest son, Fred Victor, who died in 1890 at the age of 22. During his teens Fred Victor had spent several evenings a week at the mission and became very concerned about the conditions of the poor. There was nothing perfunctory about his father's giving the land and building for the mission as a memorial. Under the close direction of Massey one of the best architects of the day, E.J.

Lennox, was engaged to design the building. Massey even seems to have given his personal attention to the development of future programs at the new mission. In a letter to the mission's founder Mary Sheffield, he tactfully suggested that much of the work should be that usually performed by deaconesses. As she was going to Chicago, Massey suggested that she study the work of the training school there. He wrote, "I have no doubt that the evangelical work in connection with Mr. Moody's system is excellent, but I do not think that their training would be so conducive to the work we propose carrying on at the Mission as that of the training school."This indicates that Massey hoped that the institutional program of the new mission — the practical, helping services — would be as important as the religious and evangelical services.

Early in its history the Fred Victor Mission did add a number of useful social services to its basic program of religious services and educational work. Around 1900 the Ladies' Rescue Branch of the Mission Society was organized to aid unfortunate girls. This led to the establishment of the Victor Home for Young Women, which in 1905 received a new home on Jarvis Street from the estate of Hart A. Massey. By 1906 trained nurses were engaged to minister to the poor in their homes. A deaconess regularly met the trains at Union Station, "especially to guard young women coming for the first time to the city from the many nefarious traps that are set for them," and another deaconess visited homes in the neighbourhood. Like most of the other missions Fred Victor distributed food, clothing and fuel. The mission's special work with homeless men led to the provision of free suppers of fresh buns and hot coffee before the Thursday evening meetings in the winter months. Work with children remained of paramount importance and included a Junior Epworth League for boys and girls, industrial classes (primarily manual training and household science), boys and girls clubs, and the continuing sabbath school and Bible classes.

Hart Massey's daughter, Lillian Massey-Treble, gave a decided boost to one of the practical educational services. There had always been cooking and sewing classes and kitchen garden work for the girls. By 1900, through her generosity, the Victor School of Household Science and Arts was established on the fifth floor of the mission. It was renamed the Lillian Massey Normal Training School of Household Science the next year.

Although the mission opened its doors and extended its services to anyone, it was solidly Methodist, drawing its paid and volunteer personnel and its financial support from Methodist benefactors — the Massey family and Methodist churches throughout the city. In 1894 these churches joined together to form the Toronto Missionary Society of the Methodist Church, which was responsible for the vested control and management of the mission's work. By 1900 nearly all the Methodist churches in Toronto were cooperating with the missionary society. Their work went beyond the confines of Fred Victor Mission to include all mission or other Christian work in connection with this denomination in the city. Evangelical efforts now went beyond the doors of the mission in the form of a gospel wagon and cottage meetings that carried the spiritual message to the streets and homes. In later years this all-embracing approach led to the establishment of an Italian mission and sponsorship of a citywide student evangelical campaign in 1909 and 1910.

Beside the support of the Methodist churches, another source of strength for the mission was its close association with Victoria College, the Methodist affiliate of the University of Toronto. The college supplied an unending stream of enthusiastic volunteers; in return, work at the mission had a profound effect on some of the young men who were training for the ministry at Victoria College. They later went on to make outstanding contributions to the development of social work in Canada: notably J.S. Woodsworth, James M. Shaver, Arthur H. Burnett and Frank N. Stapleford.

The Fred Victor Mission did not escape the philosophical tug and pull between the social settlement movement and the religious side of the work. The clubs, classes and social services at the mission were directly influenced by the social settlement movement, and even mission benefactors like the Massey family were keen supporters of the educational, recreational and social service programs. But the resistance to the secular approach led to some ambivalence to its own institutional program. In the 1900 report, six years after the mission had embarked on its expanded program in the new building, the motives for institutional methods were still being carefully evaluated. Such methods, the report states, have value "not only as feeders to the evangelistic services" but have "inestimable value in themselves." That it was thought necessary to make this statement speaks volumes as to the attitude of at least some members of the governing missionary society.

Prior to 1908, the work of Fred Victor Mission appears to have been directed entirely toward the improvement of the individual. The religious side of the work was aimed at saving the individual soul. The hostel for workingmen, the home for unfortunate girls and the home nursing services represented the rescue function. The clubs and classes at the mission were aimed at improving manners, morals, cleanliness, thrift and self-reliance. In 1908, the annual report referred to "the great distress arising from lack of work and consequent poverty," in its concern for the social problem. But even then the solutions were still highly individual; for example, a kindling industry was established to help unemployed men keep their self-respect by chopping wood to earn money instead of receiving charity.

COMPARISON OF THE ST. ANDREW'S INSTITUTE AND FRED VICTOR MISSION

Together the St. Andrew's Institute and Fred Victor Mission provided the poverty-stricken areas west and east of the business core with many facilities and programs associated with social settlements in Great Britain and the United States. Each was equipped with a gymnasium, a large auditorium or meeting room, numerous smaller rooms for classes for young and old of both sexes, a night school and a penny savings bank. In addition, St. Andrew's Institute had swimming baths, a kitchen, a library and an infant classroom. One third of Fred Victor Mission was occupied by Victor House, a full-fledged lodging hostel for 225 men operated by the Central Lodging House Association. The mission itself had added features such as a restaurant, an employment bureau, a baby shelter and a dispensary.

Despite these similarities there were key differences between these two pioneering Canadian institutions and the leading settlements outside the country. The early British and American settlement houses began as new institutions, usually motivated by social reform and free to choose either a secular or a religious route. But St. Andrew's Institute and Fred Victor Mission both originated from missions with a strong evangelical commitment in their work among the poor. However, the degree of religious emphasis differed greatly between them. Fred Victor Mission was aggressively evangelical throughout its early years and devoted fully half its program to religious services and biblical instruction; while the institute remained determined not to be a church mission, as the choice of the word institute implies. Though it kept its Sunday school for the children and maintained a Christian atmosphere in its work, it functioned as an educational institution.

CHAPTER THREE

THE INFLUENCE OF JANE ADDAMS

Jane Addams, who founded the Hull House settlement in Chicago, had no direct influence or involvement in the establishment of any Canadian settlements, but her progressive and innovative ideas sharpened the awareness of several key Canadians, among them John Joseph Kelso and William Lyon Mackenzie King, about the problems of the poor and influenced the early history of social work in Canada. Hull House, located in a neighbourhood near Chicago's stockyards, contained a heterogeneous population of Italians, Germans, Polish and Russian Jews, Bohemians, Canadian French and Irish, and it offered services such as clubs, classes and a gymnasium. In addition, Hull House workers were actively involved in civic affairs; for example, cooperating with women's trade unions to arbitrate in a strike at a knitting factory and sitting on a committee to investigate the sweating system in Chicago's clothing industry. For three successive winters economic conferences between businessmen and workingmen were held, and the Working People's Social Science Club, organized in 1890 by an English workingman, met weekly for talks and discussions on social problems.

Hull House received general approval and support in Chicago. It was well-regarded by other social agencies and gained the intellectual approval of sociologists in the new University of Chicago, which was founded in 1892. At an early stage Hull House contracted a reputation for radicalism. Addams attributed this view chiefly to the Working People's Social Science Club, which discussed controversial subjects such as socialism and the single tax. It was a period, as C.R. Henderson pointed out in *Social Settlements* (1899), when the wealthy were concerned lest the new settlements prove too socialistic, while the radicals criticized them for offering palliatives rather than actual remedies.

Kelso Visits Hull House

One of the most colourful figures in early Canadian social work, John Joseph Kelso, was an early visitor to Hull House. As a boy Kelso had known poverty and had left school early to earn his living as a messenger boy. He entered journalism as a printer's devil and worked his way up to reporter, first in the police court and later at the Ontario Legislature. While a police reporter he had been so appalled at the plight of underprivileged children in the courts and on the streets that he agitated successfully to start organizations to protect children. Kelso saw his efforts culminate in the passage of the Children's Protective Act by the Ontario Legislature in 1893. He was then invited by Sir Oliver Mowat, Liberal premier of the province, to administer the act. He was soon serving as an ambassador-at-large, travelling frequently to conferences and meetings in the United States and Canada, linking the social welfare movements in those two countries.

One of his first trips as a provincial official was to Chicago, during the World's Fair in 1893, when he attended three major conferences including the National Conference of Charities and Corrections. Writing years later in notes for his unfinished memoirs, Kelso recalled that he was "greatly impressed with the value of a neighbourhood settlement house as a preventive and corrective social agency and also as an inspirational centre for the residents of the district. From then on I was determined to bring about settlement work in Toronto, but it was not easy to demonstrate the need."

Mackenzie King Meets Jane Addams

In 1895, only a few weeks after receiving his B.A. degree from the University of Toronto, Mackenzie King heard Addams give an address on the settlement idea at the Pan-American Congress on Education and Religion. The conference brought together some 700 people from the United States, Canada and elsewhere. Jane Addams described the efforts in her neighbourhood to make "the neglected people feel that they are part of the human Christian brotherhood," and the attempts to remedy the "sweating system." She took pains to deny that Hull House was a centre of socialism or single-tax propaganda. King was greatly pleased when she traced the settlement movement back to the social thought and practical work of Arnold Toynbee. "I never listened to an address which I more thoroughly enjoyed," he confided to his diary.

After Jane Addams finished her address, King introduced himself to her, called on her after supper and the next morning met her and Miss Emma George at St. Andrew's Institute. He accompanied them to Broadway Tabernacle where Addams gave a talk on her work at Hull House. "I love Toynbee and I love Miss Addams. I love the work in which the one was and the other is and which I hope soon to be engaged in," he wrote in his diary that Sunday evening, 21 July 1895.

The influence of Toynbee on King's thinking was a rather emotional experience. King particularly liked the way Toynbee related the religious motive to practical measures for social reform. He wrote in his diary: "Tonight I read ... some notes and jottings by Arnold Toynbee. I was simply enraptured by his writings and believe I have at last found a model for my future work in life."

This was a time in King's life when he was going through an inner battle as to the direction his life should take. An eager, earnest young man, King always saw himself as eventually occupying some illustrious position, but what was the best field to enter? On the one hand, being deeply religious, he was attracted to the ministry. On the other hand, his studies had turned his thoughts strongly toward a career as a professor of political economy. Or perhaps he would follow in the footsteps of his mother's famous father, William Lyon Mackenzie, the first mayor of Toronto and leader of the Rebellion of 1837. His meeting with Addams followed his recent study of the suggestions of Arnold Toynbee for a more just society, which may have led him to yet a fourth possible choice, that of social service.

One aftermath of Addams' visit was King's involvement with the Young Men's Club at St. Andrew's Institute the following autumn. He organized a lecture-discussion series on social and labour problems similar to forums at Toynbee Hall and Hull House. King's social studies program for the young workingmen at St. Andrew's Institute, with its airing of controversial issues and conflicting points of view, was a pioneer experiment, and nothing like it occurred again in the Canadian social settlement movement until J.S. Woodsworth started the People's Forum at All People's Mission, Winnipeg, in 1909.

In 1896 King was awarded a fellowship for graduate work at the University of Chicago. He lived for two months at Hull House, where he renewed his acquaintance with Addams and met other pioneers in the social welfare movement including Julia Lathrop, who was conducting a study of charities and relief, and Florence Kelley, a prime mover against the sweating system and an active proponent of better housing for the poor. At the university, King studied both economics and sociology with a major focus on trade unions. He also devoted a great deal of time to studies of the social settlement movement under the guidance of Professor C.R. Henderson, a pioneering teacher of sociology. Later in the year he helped Henderson gather and organize material for the latter's forthcoming book *Social Settlements* (1899), the first comprehensive survey of both British and American social settlement developments.

While staying at Hull House, King got a first-hand, often appalling view of life in the Chicago slums. He wrote two articles about Hull House for Canadian journals: "In Chicago Slums — The Work of Hull House Among the Poor," published in the Toronto *Globe*, 16 January 1897, and "The Story of Hull House," in *The Westminster*, 6 November 1897.Both accounts gave vivid portrayals of the aims and activities of Hull House, stressing the effective action taken to obtain better neighbourhood services and legislation to correct such evils as child labour and sweatshops.

King, however, was astonished and somewhat perturbed that in her speeches Addams invariably stressed *ethical* impulses working towards social reconstruction, rather than coming out plainly on *religious* impulses. It seems he did not fully appreciate the reasons for Addams' insistence on the secular approach to dealing with the problems of such a mixed community.

Immediately after his return home from Chicago, King was engaged as a secretary for local arrangments for the National Conference of Charities and Corrections by the conference's organizer J.J. Kelso. The conference was the occasion for a joyful reunion with his friends from Chicago, especially Jane Addams and C.R. Henderson. During the week King was presented with three possible career choices: Kelso suggested a position as head of a confederation of charities in Canada; Professor Henderson strongly advised King to go into university extension work at Chicago; but, even as he was preparing an application for this post, a letter arrived from a leading economist at Harvard offering him a scholarship. He accepted this offer with alacrity. "A turning point in my life — upward and onward, a new start in life," he wrote in his diary.

However, the influence of his days at Hull House lingered. Before his departure for Harvard, King persuaded the editor of the *Mail and Empire* to let him write a series of three articles on the emerging social problems in Toronto. The topics were the three problems that he had found most disturbing in Chicago: foreign settlements, bad housing and sweatshops. King did not stop there; he went to see an old family friend William Mulock (later Sir William), then postmaster general in the Laurier government. King told him of abhorent conditions he had found on government clothing contracts for letter carriers' uniforms. Impressed, Mulock commissioned him to prepare a report on the conditions and later used King's recommendations as the basis for the Fair Wages Resolution he introduced in the House of Commons.

It was no coincidence then that three years later, while King was in Europe on a travelling fellowship, Mulock cabled an invitation to come to Ottawa as first lieutenant in the new labour department. Although he had been offered a position as instructor of political economy at Harvard University, King decided to accept Mulock's offer — going on to become the first deputy minister of labour in Canada, the minister of labour and finally prime minister of Canada.

After King became deputy minister of labour, Kelso asked him to speak to a social welfare conference in Toronto on the desirability of starting a social settlement modelled on Hull House. King indicated that he felt it would be premature to promote the movement in Canada; however, he did speak on social settlements in crowded centres at the Fifth Canadian Conference of Charities and Corrections in Hamilton in 1902. Kelso seemed to have accepted King's dictum, for the time being, and dropped his campaign for social settlements for another five years, by which time worsening social conditions in Toronto's slums were approaching crisis dimensions. No urgent need was yet seen to launch new secular social centres, to extend the hand of friendship to foreign immigrants or to promote social research and social reform in the slum areas of Canadian cities.

CHAPTER FOUR

EVANGELIA: THE FIRST
CANADIAN SETTLEMENT

In the summer of 1902 Mackenzie King may have seen no urgent need
for social settlements in Canada, but the first Canadian settlement, Evangelia
House, had already been opened the preceding winter by Sara Libby Carson.

SARA LIBBY CARSON, A PIONEERING PROFESSIONAL

Sara Libby Carson was one of the most important figures in determining
the direction of the Canadian settlement movement. Between 1897 and 1918
she organized or re-organized ten social settlements — three in the United
States and seven in Canada. In 1897 she had been a co-founder of Christodora
House in an immigrant neighbourhood on the lower east side of New York
city; then came Evangelia in Toronto in 1902; after that two more settlements
were founded in New York before Carson was brought back to Canada in
1912 to set up a chain of Presbyterian settlements across the country, beginning
with St. Christopher House in Toronto. In 1915 she was invited to re-organize
University Settlement in Toronto. She was also chosen to give the first
courses on settlement work and community work at the department of social
service, which opened at the University of Toronto in 1914.

What kind of person was Sara Libby Carson? What were the chief
influences that shaped her approach to settlement work? She has been
described as "a small, plump dynamo of a woman" who came, "like a
meteor," to the Canada of the 1890s, a woman who possessed charm,
determination, a remarkable ability to organize and "a certain autocracy in
dealing with others." One of her former co-workers recalled her as an autocrat,

but also as a person of warmth and merriment whose serious, intense face "broke so easily into smiles." Little is known of her early life except that she was a Quaker and a graduate of an eastern women's college. Both Carson's religion and her education tended to support her independence and confidence in her own ability to venture into new fields. The Society of Friends was one of the few denominations of the day to accord men and women an equal place in the affairs of the church.

Carson's social work career of more than forty years began in the late 1880s in the American Young Women's Christian Association (YWCA) movement, first with the New York YWCA and later with the national association. Her experience at Christodora House and her long apprenticeship with the YWCA were two significant factors in shaping her social thought and in developing her practice. Sara Libby Carson was one of the travelling field secretaries engaged by the national organization of the American YWCAs who were sent from city to city to conduct "evangelistic meetings and organize club work." Apparently she was still employed by the American YWCA when she made her first visits to the Toronto YWCA in 1897, the same year that she and a friend started Christodora House in New York.

CHRISTODORA HOUSE IN NEW YORK

In June 1897 Sara Carson and Christina I. McColl, another young woman trained in the YWCA, rented a five-room flat, a basement and a room behind a delicatessen shop on the lower east side of New York, in a district largely populated by Germans, Jews and Italians. This was the beginning of Christodora House, which was to become one of the most noted religious settlement houses in the United States. Within two years of its founding, Christodora House moved into a five-storey building of its own, acquired an influential board and developed chapters in many of the women's colleges, such as Smith and Mount Holyoke, to contribute to its support. The Christodora program included a penny bank, a children's playroom, classes on subjects from shirtwaist making to foreign travel, a summer cottage on Staten Island, Sunday evening open suppers, and periodic bargain sales in the basement, "when a half-worn dress could be got for a nickel and a pair of warm stockings for a penny." The religious program offered Bible classes, children's hours and a Sunday afternoon service.

The religious emphasis at Christodora House was a natural corollary to the YWCA background of its founders, but more than that it was a deliberate effort to restore the religious element to what had become a predominantly secular social settlement movement. Reactions to this move were predictably mixed. A New York Hebrew publication offered warnings about the settlement, pointing out what they perceived to be the danger to their faith in the "generous kindness and openly avowed aim of these young Christian women." Social gospellers, on the other hand, tended to see the effectiveness of the Christodora experiment as a triumphant vindication of their belief that religion should underlie and be imbedded in all social service and social reform movements, including the social settlements.

Kate Melville, a visiting Canadian journalist, provided a particularly interesting evaluation of Christodora's religious efforts. Writing in the Presbyterian journal *The Westminster* (1899), she described her impressions:

> Christodora is avowedly and first of all a Christian and Christianizing force. Other settlements near the Jewish quarter, doing excellent social work, have thought it inadvisable to adopt an aggressive Christian platform; but this has been found no deterrent at Christodora, although adding a delicacy and point and a tremendous significance to the work.

Great care was taken by the settlement workers not to offend Hebrew sensibilities — the goal was to belong to God, which covered both Hebrews and Christians. A resident worker said triumphantly: "We have had a larger attendance at our religious meetings this year than at any other time." Margaret Sangster also wrote: "Eighty per cent of the young women and little girls who throng the doors of Christodora are Hebrews and Roman Catholics, but they gladly attend the gospel meetings and crowd into the Bible classes."

With such response to Christodora's aggressive Christian purpose, Carson proceeded with an unshaken conviction of the need for a strong Christian religious ingredient in all social settlement work. Her beliefs had a direct effect on the Canadian settlement movement.

SARA LIBBY CARSON AND THE CANADIAN YWCA

Sara Carson's first visits to the Toronto YWCA were made in 1897, at the invitation of the evangelical committee, to fuel enthusiasm for Bible study and to encourage the formation of a girls' club, a new department for the YWCA. A girls' club was formed immediately to continue the work begun by Carson. The Toronto YWCA, founded in 1873, had a long and impressive record of good works including Bible study and religious services, operation of a boarding home for young women released from prison and a girls' industrial institute for young women working in offices and factories. But all of these services operated from the top down. The sympathetic, upper-middle-class women who composed the board and committees worked for the girls, not with them.

By the time of Carson's visit, however, a change in point of view was developing. The work to be done was now perceived as formative, not reformative, in character, and the YWCA made a "deliberate choice of a positive educational and social type of activity that no other organization offered and which has been essentially the field of the YWCA ever since." The self-governing girls clubs were one way of involving the members in planning their own programs and conducting their own meetings.

At this time the Dominion Council was in a transitional stage. The inspiration for a national organization had come in 1893 when some 60 Canadian women, including many YWCA leaders, attended the Women's Congress held at the Chicago World's Fair. This was quickly followed by an initial conference to form a national YWCA organization for Canada. The first annual meeting of the newly formed Dominion Council met in Ottawa in January 1895 and passed a constitution enabling Canadian YWCAs to join the world YWCA as a separate entity. For a while the new national organization became little more than an administrative convenience, but with the dawn of the new century the Dominion Council adopted a more active role. At the London, Ontario conference in 1900 committees were set up for city and student departments and the appointment of a travelling secretary was discussed. The need for trained leadership was becoming increasingly apparent, so the Dominion Council arranged a four-day conference for association secretaries and workers in Toronto in October 1901. The same year Carson was brought back to Toronto by the Dominion Council of the YWCA as its first general travelling secretary for the city associations, "as she is very helpful in organizing and starting new work."

EVANGELIA: 1902–04

Sara Libby Carson and her friend Mary Lawson Bell from Montreal rented a three-storey brick building at 716 Queen Street East. The downstairs area was converted for settlement activities and stocked with games and children's books to attract the young neighbourhood girls. The upstairs flat became a residence, at first for the two founders but soon for a growing number of resident teachers and trainees. Initially, the settlement was a cooperative venture between the two women and the Dominion Council of the YWCA. The council had established its first national headquarters there and permitted Carson, who was still on salary, to devote much of her time to organizing the settlement. However, there was a difference of opinion between the two in the operation of Evangelia. The Dominion YWCA executive viewed the settlement mainly as a training school for YWCA secretaries. In May 1902 Mrs. T.M. Harris, the national president, spoke enthusiastically of the settlement phase of the work and generally gave the impression that the settlement was under the supervision of the Dominion Association. It seemed inevitable that tension and conflict were bound to arise between a strong-minded leader like Carson and the women of the Dominion executive. By October Carson had resigned from the YWCA to devote herself entirely to settlement work, and the national YWCA headquarters moved from Evangelia.

However, the settlement continued to be affiliated with the Dominion YWCA for another two years. During that time it was generally referred to as the Young Women's Settlement, the aim of which was to serve as a social, educational and religious centre for young women. By 1904, supported by voluntary contributions, the building was fitted with a gymnasium, library, reading-room and assembly hall. There were five resident teachers (of whom two were university graduates, one from Trinity and one from University College) and many other volunteer teachers. There were five clubs at Evangelia, each with about 50 members. Each club conducted its own meetings according to parliamentary procedure and had its own club colours and club song. Three clubs for schoolgirls from six to fourteen years of age met after school. The smaller girls were taught kitchen gardening (general household skills), gymnastic work and physical culture. Girls in the higher grades were taught plain sewing, embroidery and cooking, and they were helped along other educational lines if needed. For the older girls and young women who worked during the day, two clubs met in the evening for instruction in physical culture, cooking, dressmaking, millinery, stenography, "as well as the ordinary subjects of an English education."

An appeal in the University of Toronto's *Varsity* for women students to work as volunteers stated: "It is appalling to think that some of these girls left school about the age of twelve and, after four or five years spent in factories or stores, they have almost forgotten how to read." The same *Varsity* article pointed out that work at the Evangelia Settlement focused on religious and educational work among girls with regular Bible classes but, the article pointed out, "no attempt is made to force direct religious teaching on the girls, as the society works rather through physical and intellectual channels up to the spiritual."

The training at Evangelia was practical rather than theoretical. The young women in training became residents in the settlement. They came to know first hand the conditions in the surrounding neighbourhood and learned skills to organize group activities and to work with individuals of varying ages and backgrounds. They also absorbed, seemingly by osmosis, the atmosphere of dedication to the service of the less fortunate, with its strongly religious motivation. Significantly this training program during Evangelia's first years was an early forerunner of professional training for social work in Canada. It preceded by a dozen years the founding of the department of social service at the University of Toronto which later developed into today's faculty of social work.

EVANGELIA: THE SECOND PERIOD

Sara Carson realized that affluent people must be included and encouraged if Evangelia was to flourish and expand. Chapters were formed in Victoria College, St. Hilda's College (Trinity) and the Association of Graduate Nurses of Toronto. The chapter members came into residence for two weeks each year, "gaining insight into a downtown district, helping with the work and spreading knowledge of the difficulties and the ways in which they are being met."

But the greatest impetus toward the expansion of Evangelia came when wealthy philanthropists, among them Edmund Boyd Osler (later Sir Edmund), Ann and Margaret Laidlaw, and Mrs. H.D. Warren, became interested in the work. At first an advisory committee of moneyed people was formed; this was closely followed by the establishment of an organized board and, in 1906, Evangelia was incorporated.

About the time that Osler, a leading Toronto financier and philanthropist, began to give his support, Evangelia moved to another store with living quarters above: this was a larger building on the south side of Queen Street just east of the Don River Bridge. Eventually three stores were joined to accommodate the growing number of young people attracted to the settlement. The third location of Evangelia was just west of the Don River at the northeast corner of Queen and River streets. Here, in 1907, an impressive three-storey, many-gabled mansion (the former home of William M. Davies, a brickyard owner) was purchased and a modern addition built to provide for a gymnasium and clinic, as well as other activities. The equipment alone cost $40,000 — a large sum in those days. By 1909 the house, valued at $55,000, was free of debt and fully equipped for service.

Earl Grey, the governor-general of Canada, opened the new building on 14 October 1907, enhancing the prestige and public acceptance of Canada's first social settlement. The guest list included some famous names in Ontario and Toronto history. The governor-general was accompanied by the lieutenant-governor of Ontario Sir William Mortimer Clark and Mrs. Clark. Guests included the Ontario premier James P. Whitney; the mayor of Toronto Emerson Coatsworth; and the new president of the University of Toronto Robert A. Falconer. As president of the Evangelia Board, Osler officiated at the ceremonies.

In 1908, with the settlement well-established in a new building and with a capable successor in Edith Ellwood, Carson resigned and returned to settlement work in New York. Co-founder Mary Lawson Bell went to Ottawa where she was involved in the founding of a new settlement patterned on Evangelia. Carson left behind a strong, well-equipped institution with a lively program of clubs, classes, clinic, social events and neighbourly visiting, which set the basic pattern for all future settlements in Canada, whether secular or religious. Edith Ellwood, maintained the strength and sound organization of Evangelia, adding such important services as the playground, the well-baby clinic and the summer camps. When Edith Ellwood married and moved to Ottawa, she was succeeded by Catherine (Kitty) Wright, a warm and friendly person who had much experience in settlement work.

EVANGELIA BREAKS NEW GROUND

Evangelia is credited with opening the first nursery school and the first supervised playground in Toronto. Inspiration for the playground came partly from an address given at Evangelia by Mrs. Humphrey Ward, a well-known English novelist. She had helped found a settlement in London and was an ardent proponent of playgrounds. Evangelia's broad lawns sloping down to the Don River gave ample space for play activities. The first equipment consisted of swings and hammocks and a building was erected containing a shower and deep baths "open to all little people, on payment of one cent dues."

A clinic at Evangelia was established cooperatively with the Toronto General Hospital (then on Gerrard Street East), the Hospital for Sick Children and the Social Service Commission. Eventually the clinic expanded to include a small hospital room for tonsillectomies, a general clinic and a well-baby clinic. Twelve young doctors served voluntarily and several nurses living in the settlement worked in the clinic and attended confinements.

The clubs, classes, religious services and neighbourly visiting of the earlier period continued. The new playground facilities made possible a great extension of sports, games and physical activities. The self-governing clubs trained boys and girls, men and women of all ages in parliamentary procedure. The cooking classes were expanded to include classes for boys as well as girls, and occasionally men. Music and dramatics were added and a

Christmas tree party, with lovely gifts, was a highlight of the year. Religious gatherings were held Sunday evenings after church and provided the added attractions of songs and refreshments. A lunchroom was opened to serve midday dinner to women workers from a nearby laundry. As they served the women their dinners, volunteers from well-to-do homes in Rosedale or Parkdale gained an awareness of the harsh conditions under which many women worked. One of these volunteers, Adeline Wadsworth, wrote: "I can remember even now being very shocked with the conditions of their hands — swollen, red, looking deformed and painful — probably due to the long duration in water, strong soap and lye. Hands that seemed utterly destroyed."

Outdoor activities formed an important part of the program. On summer evenings the well-lighted grounds were used for croquet, sing-songs, concerts and lectures. Garden chairs and tables were set out under the trees, and here ice-cream and cake were served on special occasions. Outings of many kinds were arranged: picnics in Reservoir Park, Centre Island and High Park, boat excursions to Niagara-on-the-Lake and street-car rides around the city for the women's clubs and for the children. Summer camps on Lake Simcoe were opened to provide holidays for members: first at the Sedore Farm near Jackson's Point then at The Gables, a farm near Barrie on Kempenfeldt Bay which was purchased by Sir Edmund Osler in 1912 for Evangelia's use.

At its peak, Evangelia had a daily average of 600 members in attendance, a staff of 12 residents and about 100 volunteers, including the young doctors and nurses in the clinic and the students from the university. Toward the end of the war years, Evangelia went into a tailspin and abruptly closed in 1918. Many reasons have been given for Evangelia's sudden demise: the war itself was drawing off interest from the settlement into war work; the settlement's chief supporter, Sir Edmund Osler, was in failing health; the coal bills were astronomical. In the chaos of Evangelia's closing even the official records of Canada's first settlement house disappeared with only scattered newspaper clippings, YWCA records, some brief statements by Sara Libby Carson and recollections of former staff and volunteers collected half a century later to chart its history.

Until the late 1970s the abandoned building remained a ghostlike presence at the corner of Queen and River streets — the weathered, gold-lettered words *Evangelia Settlement* visible over the three-arched doorway. Eventually it was demolished to make way for the new home of the Toronto Humane Society.

Another YWCA Settlement Falters

In the spring of 1902 the Toronto YWCA gingerly tried to establish social settlement work in The Ward, the polyglot slum area in the heart of downtown Toronto. Without the direction of a strong organizer like Sara Libby Carson, the efforts of the Toronto YWCA faltered. At the June, 1902 meeting of the Toronto board one of the directors, Mrs. Gunther, spoke of the great need of settlement work in the district and gave her audience "an interesting account of her own private efforts among the shiftless and untaught class of young girls and the remarkable and encouraging results." A settlement committee, chaired by Mrs. Gunther, explored the possibilities for organizing such work. They tried to secure space on Terauly Street (now Bay Street) in a room then occupied by the College Street Church Mission, but the whole plan temporarily fell through.

After this debacle Mrs. Gunther suggested that the YWCA start work among the young neighbourhood girls using the facilities for cooking and sewing classes available in the YWCA headquarters on Elm Street. Early in 1903 the settlement held meetings twice a week and a worker was paid to take charge. The Sunbeam Club for little girls drew an average attendance of 20 to its sewing and cooking classes. For the juvenile classes there was a piano, a circulating library and a self-governing club organized "much to the delight of the children." But only two years later what had started out to be a social settlement became a junior section of the YWCA, with programs designed to meet the specific needs of the younger girls and children in the immediate neighbourhood.

CHAPTER FIVE

THE NEW DRIVE FOR
SOCIAL SETTLEMENTS

The chain of events that led to the founding of the new Toronto settlements from 1910–1912 reflected a fascinating interplay of people and movements all pursuing a more or less common goal of enhanced community service and improvement, while embracing differing views as to how best to achieve this end.

ECONOMIC BACKGROUND

During the first decade of the twentieth century Toronto jumped abruptly into a period of the most phenomenal growth Canada had ever experienced. Immigration soared, and for the first time a large proportion of the newcomers did not come from Britain. It was the beginning of a multi-culturalism that was perhaps the most significant new social phenomenon of the first decade of the century. The population growth of the city of Toronto was spectacular; from 1901–1911 the population increased by 82 per cent.

But there was no escape from the problems of poverty, unemployment and slums. Working conditions in Toronto in the early 1900s were generally deplorable. The 60-hour work-week was still common. The average wage of blue-collar workers was actually below the poverty line, and that of white-collar workers only slightly above. Sweatshops in the clothing trades were still prevalent. Trades unions were organizing but were generally weak. Seasonal layoffs in many industries and widespread unemployment during cyclical depressions further reduced real wages. Unemployment insurance was non-existent.

The economic crisis of 1907–1908 did have one good effect: it crystallized the changing attitudes toward poverty that were developing in Toronto. Until then Toronto's more affluent citizens tended to equate poverty with moral failure. Their attitude was largely the outgrowth of a pioneer society in which anyone willing and able to work could always find work, and it was also based on the fear that indiscriminate charity or government relief would create a pauper class.

This shift was mirrored in profoundly changing attitudes toward poverty in Britain and the United States. Charles Booth's monumental study of London's poor showed that poverty extended beyond paupers to the working poor who were living in conditions far below an acceptable standard, and that environmental causes of poverty were quite as important as personal ones. Robert Hunter, head worker at University Settlement, New York, published a book in 1904 which emphasized the need for government to establish and enforce minimum standards. In Toronto, Professor James Mavor made a study of living conditions in 1907–1908.

The new attitudes toward poverty emerged in an Associated Charities' report of the period:

> In our contact with the poor, and in our personal efforts on their behalf, we may discover that they are not wholly to blame for the conditions in which we find them. Sharp commercial practices, industrial depression, wretched homes, unsanitary dwellings, excessive rents, high cost of living, ineffectual laws in dealing with wife deserters, and the general disadvantages the poor have to live under, are responsible for much of the misery which exists today.

SOCIAL SERVICES

There was no shortage of charities, hospitals, orphanages, child welfare societies and correctional institutions in Toronto. What the city lacked was adequate coordination of the various charitable efforts and sufficient social services to address the individual and family problems of the poor and immigrants. In 1909, according to the president of the Associated Charities, there were 244 churches and 55 charitable institutions and organizations in the city. The main channel for general relief was the House of Industry, the city's poorhouse located at the corner of Elm and Elizabeth streets. With grants from the city for outdoor relief it dispensed fuel and food to the needy. The Toronto Relief Society, an organization of women that received a small grant from the city, provided rent, clothing and extras for the sick. The Toronto Relief Office in city hall investigated requests for relief and referred people to the appropriate agency, usually the House of Industry.

The Associated Charities, with board representatives from Protestant, Catholic and Jewish charities, attempted to coordinate this array of charitable organizations. The Associated Charities leaned heavily for financial support on its founder, Goldwin Smith, who contributed $1,000 a year to its upkeep. By 1911, however, it was largely supported by grants from the provincial government and city council.

At this time virtually all the charitable agencies, including the House of Industry, were under private auspices. The city of Toronto assumed as little direct responsibility as possible for the provision of relief or the supervision of charities, although it had a well-developed system of non-statutory grants to private agencies. As the problems of poverty grew the inadequacy of the Associated Charities became obvious. The city finally responded in 1911 by appointing a charities commission to investigate the workings of the various charity organizations. As a result of the commission's recommendations, city council created the Social Service Commission in October, 1912 as a central bureau under civic control to screen all charitable institutions appealing to the city or the public for funds.

HEALTH SERVICES

In the first decade of this century tuberculosis was prevalent in Toronto, and numerous cases of typhoid, smallpox, diphtheria and scarlet fever were reported each year. The infant mortality rate was high — according to a 1911 report one out of every five babies born in Toronto died before reaching its first birthday. The neighbourhoods inhabited by immigrants and other working-class people produced mortality statistics two or three times higher than those of wealthier areas of the city. Prior to 1910 the health services available to care for Toronto's sick included seventeen hospitals, six free dispensaries and various nursing services for the sick poor. All of these were operated under private auspices, though the city made grants to some of them.

Toronto's first board of health was established in 1866 and although the first medical officer of health was appointed in 1883, the department was never given sufficient funding to provide effective health protection. The great breakthrough occurred in 1910 when Dr. Charles J.C.O. Hastings, a physician of considerable experience and a vigorous reformer, was appointed medical health officer.

When Dr. Hastings took up his new position he inherited a department with a 27 cents per capita funding, a staff of 70 and one public health nurse to visit tuberculosis patients in their homes. By 1920 the average expenditure per capita of the department had risen to $1.56 and there were over 500 men and women on the payroll, including 114 public health nurses.

Dr. Hastings' interest in the city's social problems had started some years earlier. As a private physician he was one of the first in Toronto to specialize in obstetrics. Through his daily contact with the city's poor, he became aware of the living conditions of ordinary workers. Hastings' accomplishments in the department of public health were manifold: a modern health department with a first-class bacteriological and chemical laboratory was established, chlorination of the water supply was initiated in 1910, and compulsory pasteurization of milk and cream became a reality in 1914. He waged an ongoing campaign for the prevention of communicable diseases. His wider concern over housing and sanitation, his development of the public health nursing services and his establishment of a special social service division within the department had far-reaching effects on the future public welfare involvements of the city. These services were closely linked with the work of the social settlements between 1910 and 1918.

INTEREST IN SOCIAL SETTLEMENTS AWAKENS

Recognition of the industrial and environmental causes of poverty led to an immense upheaval in Canadian social thought from 1909–1912, with Toronto, Winnipeg and Montreal the focal points for much of the ensuing social reform movement in the country. It was a period of social change when all sorts of ideas were in the air. It was a time when the phrase social welfare was just beginning to supplant the older terms of charity and philanthropy, and the establishment of the newer forms of social service, including the settlements, was an integral aspect of this social change.

Most of the social reform movements that were cresting in Canada from 1907–1914 had had their counterparts in the United States in the late nineteenth century. Although inevitably influenced by the American experience, one of the differences was the greater influence, in fact dominance, of the churches in the development of the social service movement in Canada. The social gospel was the power behind much of the social reform of the time, not only through the Protestant churches but also in the student social movement in the universities and colleges. This power extended to the secular welfare movement where Methodist, Presbyterian, Anglican and Baptist leaders listened to the social gospel being preached from the pulpit on Sundays and carried over a Christian social motivation into their secular institutions.

Catholics and Jews also developed many of their own social services based on religious motivation. It was only in the secular institutions, however, that it was possible for Christian and Jew, Protestant and Catholic to work together for better social conditions and for social services that applied equally to all.

Other forces were also at play. The drive for equal suffrage was gaining momentum, spurred on by such events as the visit to Toronto in 1909 of Emily Pankhurst, the British suffragette leader. The National Council of Women of Canada and local councils of women across the country were linked by committees studying immigration, housing, health, supervised playgrounds for children, domestic science training, career opportunities for women, unemployment relief, protection for workers and organized charity. Canadian women were becoming adept at framing resolutions or briefs to be presented to government bodies and, at the local level, were active in stimulating new social services. When the International Council of Women met in Canada for the first time in 1909, holding its meetings at the University of Toronto, the sessions gave major attention to the expansion of the social services. Jane Addams was one of the speakers, focusing international attention on the settlement movement.

These were the years when the progressive movement in the United States was rising toward its peak. It was a movement instigated largely by social workers like Jane Addams who had served their apprenticeships in the social settlements and realized the futility of their efforts to change the condition of the poor at the local level without comprehensive reforms through the national political process. While a similar social political progressive movement did not emerge in Canada until the 1920s, the dynamic quality of the earlier American movement had an invigorating effect on some of the Canadian social reformers who were involved in the burgeoning Canadian social settlement movement. Two books published about this time also had a profound effect on attitudes and made Canadians more aware of the problems posed by mass immigration and of the need for new kinds of social institutions to help immigrants adjust to their new surroundings.

In 1907 Rev. James Shaver Woodsworth, disenchanted with his work as pastor of an affluent Methodist church in Winnipeg, became superintendent of All Peoples' Mission in the city's north end. He lived among the immigrants, studied their problems and the slum conditions in which they lived, and developed two institutes for the newcomers along social settlement lines. Out of his experiences and observations Woodsworth wrote *Strangers Within Our Gates, or Coming Canadians*, which was published in 1909 by the Missionary Society of the Methodist Church of Canada as a textbook. This was a milestone in awakening the consciences of Canadians to the problems of immigrants. The work was comparable only to Jane Addams' *Twenty Years at Hull House*, published the following year and widely read in Canada, the United States and around the world.

THE KEY PEOPLE IN THE SETTLEMENT MOVEMENT

The three key figures in the Canadian settlement movement — John G. Shearer, Robert A. Falconer and J.J. Kelso — had much in common and knew one another well. Middle-class professionals holding high administrative positions, they were exceptionally able public speakers and writers, and they were Presbyterian. Shearer and Falconer were born in Canada of Scottish origin, and Shearer was essentially an Ontario man — born on a farm in southwestern Ontario, he was educated at the University of Toronto and Knox College and was a practising pastor in western Ontario churches before entering national work. Falconer had a broader range of early experience. Born in Prince Edward Island, he was the son of a Presbyterian minister who went as a missionary to Trinidad where Robert received much of his early education at Queen's Royal College. He won a West Indies scholarship to the University of London where he received his B.A. degree, he then went to the University of Edinburgh for his M.A. and B.D. degrees. On his return to Canada in 1892 he went directly into academic work as lecturer, professor and principal, successively, at the Presbyterian Theological College in Halifax. Kelso differed from the other two leaders in significant ways. Unlike them he was an immigrant to Canada coming as a child with his family from Ireland. In Ireland his father had owned a starch factory which was lost through fire. On arriving in Canada he had difficulty in finding work, and as a result the family experienced real poverty for some years. This led Kelso to leave school at an early age to work, eventually to make a name for himself as a newspaper reporter. Kelso did not receive a university education, but became self-educated through his avid reading.

Falconer became familiar with the work of social settlements in Scottish slums while a student at Edinburgh. Shearer, while a student at the University of Toronto, was impressed by the evangelical work being performed in Toronto's Ward by Jonathan Goforth. But Kelso had gained a personal knowledge of the seamy side of Toronto life through his daily experiences as a police reporter, which made him acutely aware of the plight of poor children, especially the inhuman treatment of juvenile offenders in the courts and of the appalling slum conditions from which most of these children came.

Unlike the women involved in Toronto's first social settlements, Shearer, Falconer and Kelso had no thought of going to live among the city's poor. They approached the social settlement movement as planners, organizers and policy makers working to establish appropriate neighbourhood centres and sitting on their boards, while leaving it to others, mostly younger men and women, to become the residents, the staff and the volunteer workers of the new settlement houses.

In 1908 Dr. Shearer, indefatigable warrior against what he considered to be the forces of evil, ended his seven years of service as general secretary of the Lord's Day Alliance when its campaign for rigid sabbath observance culminated in the passage of the Lord's Day Act by the Parliament of Canada. He immediately turned to new battles for temperance and other moral and social reforms. Opportunities for service in the social gospel reform movement quickly materialized. Appointed executive secretary of the new board of moral and social reform of the Presbyterian Church in Canada in 1907, Shearer called together representatives of the Protestant churches, and of labour and other organizations, to form the Moral and Social Reform Council of Canada, which was later renamed the Social Service Council of Canada. Shearer (Presbyterian) and Rev. T. Albert Moore (Methodist) were chosen as joint secretaries. It was through his position with the Presbyterian Board of Moral and Social Reform that Shearer became a leading figure in the establishment of the chain of Presbyterian settlement houses in the larger Canadian cities, beginning with St. Christopher House in Toronto in 1912.

By coincidence, it was also in 1907 that the 40-year-old Rev. Robert A. Falconer left his position as principal of the Presbyterian Theological College in Halifax to become president of the University of Toronto. Over the next few years Falconer played a leading role in the founding of the University Settlement and in the establishment of the department of social service (now the faculty of social work) at the university.

Also by 1907 J.J. Kelso had revived his interest in starting social settlements in Toronto along the lines of Jane Addams' Hull House. In the years since 1902, when Mackenzie King had indicated that settlements were not yet needed in Canada, Kelso had had other interests to occupy his time: marriage and a family, extension of the children's aid movement, the campaign for juvenile courts in other provinces and promotion of the playgrounds movement. As well, he continued his annual involvement in the meetings of the National Conference of Charities and Corrections in the United States and his influential role in building up the parallel Canadian conference. During this time Kelso had become more and more concerned with the need for trained workers in this field. From 1905 he was in constant contact with students anxious to pursue careers in social welfare.

In the autumn of 1907 Falconer had just arrived in Toronto when Kelso sent him a note with a clipping about social settlements. Kelso followed this up over the next two years by urging Falconer to start some form of social work training at the university and by making a proposal for a social settlement in the Ward under university auspices. As a result of his contacts with Falconer and the students, Kelso actively participated in the founding of both University Settlement and Central Neighbourhood House, and he sat on the boards of both institutions for a number of years. Kelso was also one of the first speakers invited to address the Presbyterian Board of Moral and Social Reform; he served on the board's executive from 1908–1910, years during which that body was considering whether and how to establish social settlements.

THE STUDENT SOCIAL SURVEY

In the spring of 1909 the world-famous British evangelist Gipsy Smith came to Toronto to conduct a series of revival meetings in Massey Hall. In preparation for this mission, Methodist church leaders sent about a dozen students from Victoria College into the congested districts of downtown Toronto "to call at every house, find out, as far as possible, the religious condition and outlook of the people, urge them to attend the meetings in Massey Hall, and then to make a careful report of the conditions they found." The reports of these young men revealed "a state of moral and religious destitution past all belief" and "sanitary conditions of the most horrible kind," worse even than the old-world slums of Whitechapel in London's East End. The students were so disturbed by their findings that they determined to spend their summer vacation in an evangelistic campaign to further study the housing situation in the slum areas. The campaign received the cooperation of the pastors and young people's associations in Methodist churches throughout Toronto. The whole endeavour was coordinated under a special committee of the Methodist City Mission Board, chaired by Rev. S.W. Dean, superintendent of Fred Victor Mission. The students' chairman was J.M. Shaver, then studying for the ministry at Victoria Theological School, who headed up the new Victoria students' society formed for the occasion, the Students' Christian Social Union.

The plan of the campaign had four components: house-to-house visitations in certain designated areas of the downtown districts, collection of information on overcrowding and unsanitary conditions, and presentation of facts to the people in the churches. Funds for the campaign, totalling $2,959, were raised through subscriptions collected in 30 Methodist churches, and through miscellaneous contributions and collections received at tent meetings. A huge white tent, seating 500 people, was erected on the grounds of the Metropolitan Church at Queen and Church streets. Two other tents were provided by the Epworth leagues in the east and west ends of the city. A total of approximately 600 tent meetings, open-air and factory meetings were attended by 37,000 people. On more than 100 occasions the students presented the facts of the city's problems from the church pulpits and to the leagues, and more than 17,000 people were visited in their homes.

For the religious canvass, questionnaires were printed asking about the religious affiliation and church attendance of the householders and roomers at each address in the selected downtown districts, both east and west of Yonge Street. Each student kept a careful record of the responses. In most areas they found very few church members but a considerable number of people who attended church sporadically. When all the results were tabulated the final report stated: "Not over 50 per cent of the people in the downtown sections are in attendance at church anywhere." This finding was the basis of strong pleas for the downtown churches to remain where they were and for uptown people to support them financially "to minister to people who need the church supremely."

The student social survey of slum conditions in downtown Toronto was clearly secondary to the evangelical campaign in the minds of the Methodist church leaders and of most of the students. But the appalling physical environment in which so many of the city's poor were living made a tremendous impact on the students who visited the homes and saw unsavoury and unhealthy conditions they had never dreamt could exist.

One of the keenest members of the student investigating team was Arthur H. Burnett, an Englishman studying theology at Victoria who had worked for several years in the Whitechapel district of London before coming to Canada. He now turned his camera on the equally bad conditions of "squalor, dirt and misery" in Toronto's slums. His photographs of dilapidated houses, yards filled with refuse, narrow lanes, rear dwellings, outdoor privies and children playing in muddy streets began to appear in church journals and other publications. Lantern slides were made from many of his photographs and used to illustrate talks given by himself and others; these pictures conveyed a sense of horror to the comfortable middle-class people in Toronto's churches, clubs and colleges as words could not have done.

The social survey of housing, unsanitary conditions and overcrowding was intensified in the summer of 1910 when Burnett was joined by George P.

Bryce, a theological student at Knox College (Presbyterian). Since Bryce had just returned from a year at the New York School of Philanthropy, today the Columbia University School of Social Work, he was able to compare slum conditions in Toronto with those in the huge American metropolis. He wrote several articles for magazines, illustrated by Burnett's photographs.

The conditions the students discovered were certainly not new. As a police reporter in the 1880s Kelso had observed much the same conditions in the old St. John's Ward and other downtown areas. City residents could see something of the worsening conditions in the lower part of the city as they travelled on the street railway lines that ran through the slum districts, but they saw only the surface. They could not see the rear houses, the filthy lanes and yards, or the overcrowded conditions inside many once respectable workingmen's homes. It was the students who penetrated the lanes and visited the homes; shocked by what they saw, they set about making the public aware of the existing slum situation with an inspired zeal.

The immediate aftermath of the first summer's survey began in the autumn of 1909 when Jim Shaver led a class in city problems at the University of Toronto YMCA. At the university's Victoria College Arthur Burnett was given responsibility for arranging a series of 20 lectures and student conferences on social questions, under the auspices of the Students' Christian Social Union. Highlights of the series were Kelso's address on heredity and environment and President Falconer's concluding talk on the university student and the social problem.

The Students' Christian Social Union remained active for several years, alternating a study of social problems in the winter with students moving out into the field of social service in the summer. Not surprisingly, upon graduation some of the student leaders quickly moved into active promotion of the settlement movement. The social union's first president, Jim Shaver, helped to organize the University Settlement in 1910. Arthur Burnett, the second president, joined his friend George Bryce in becoming a founder and first resident of Central Neighbourhood House in 1911.

THE STUDENT LEADERS

Shaver, Bryce and Burnett were to play outstanding roles in founding two of Toronto's foremost social settlements. At the time of the student social survey, all three were theological students with a strong interest in social problems. Yet, ironically, they were the founders and early workers of Toronto's first, and for many years only, secular social settlements.

Jim Shaver was 33 years old when he headed the Victoria College students' evangelical campaign and social survey. He came to the Faculty of Theology, Victoria University, in the autumn of 1908 and led the student evangelical campaign in the summer of 1909. By the time he received his certificate in the spring of 1910 he had already been chosen to be the first head resident for the new University Settlement to be opened that fall. Shaver's mother had been a Presbyterian, his Lutheran father had converted in a Methodist revival, while Shaver "took his stand for Christ" at a revival meeting when he was 16 years old. Shaver taught school and acted as a lay preacher in eastern Ontario and Quebec during his high school years and continued to preach on Sundays during his five years at Queen's University.

George Pardon Bryce was a member of a notable Canadian family. His father, Dr. Peter Henderson Bryce, was Ontario's medical health officer and then chief medical officer of the immigration services of the federal department of the interior. There was probably no man in Canada in the first decade of this century who had a broader or more intimate knowledge of immigrants coming to Canada. George's uncle, Rev. George Bryce, was a founder of Manitoba College in Winnipeg and, in 1902, a moderator of the Presbyterian Church in Canada. While at Knox College, Bryce became convener of the city missions committee of the University YMCA and wrote the 1908–1909 report that recommended the establishment of a social settlement in downtown Toronto. His awakening interest in social service as a life's work took him to the New York School of Philanthropy in 1909. In the summer of 1910 he returned to Toronto to join Burnett in the social survey of downtown Toronto. The next year he helped found Central Neighbourhood House in the heart of the Ward.

Arthur Henry Burnett, who played such an outstanding role in the student social survey and the subsequent development of social services in Toronto, came to Canada from England where he had worked for five years in the Whitechapel district of London's East End. Burnett spent five years at Victoria College and the faculty of theology. For two of his summer vacations he participated in the student survey of social conditions in downtown Toronto; in his final vacation he made social surveys of Hamilton, Brantford, St. Thomas and Windsor under the direction of Rev. T. Albert Moore of the Methodist department of temperance and moral reform. While at Victoria he was not only instrumental in founding the Students' Christian Social Union, but served on the editorial staff of *Acta Victoriana*, the college journal, with special responsibility for the missionary and religious department. In 1912 he was awarded a scholarship to the New York School of Philanthropy, where he did field work for the Charity Organization Society and lived and worked at Greenwich House, the cooperative social settlement under the direction of Mary Kingsbury Simkhovitch, one of the leaders of the American settlement movement. Burnett's unique contribution to the Canadian social welfare movement was his intimate knowledge of the social and economic conditions both of London and New York, as well as Toronto and other smaller Ontario cities.

CHAPTER SIX

J.J. KELSO: CHARTING THE FUTURE OF CANADIAN SOCIAL WELFARE

By 1909 Kelso's long-held desire to start social settlements in Toronto along the lines of Jane Addams's Hull House took a more active turn. In an interview with the *Toronto Star* he talked about a "communal social centre" established in the city's immigrant section to be managed by university students. In January he represented Canada at the White House Conference on the Care of Dependent Children and met or renewed acquaintance with many luminaries in the American social welfare field: Jane Addams and Lillian D. Wald of settlement house fame; C.R. Henderson, professor of Sociology at the University of Chicago; Dr. Hastings Hart, then with the new Russell Sage Foundation; Dr. Booker T. Washington, the black educator; and Judge Ben B. Lindsey of the juvenile court in Denver, Colorado.

In November, 1909 a University College sophomore, J.R. Mutchmor, approached Kelso with an invitation to address the students on how to prepare for social work careers. This meeting, held in the old university dining hall and attended by 22 students, turned out to be a momentous occasion.The students were so enthused by Kelso's talk that they urged him to put it down in writing. He did this, but it was not published until 1913 when he included it in his 21st annual report as superintendent of neglected and dependent children under the title "Some First Principles of Social Work." This statement set forth Kelso's broad concept of social welfare and the need he saw for professional training for social work, together with a call for the establishment of a social settlement "in every poor district." Kelso's statements vividly expressed the freshness, the excitement, the sense of mission surrounding the new concept of social welfare at the time. Kelso's words reflected an optimistic and solid conviction that these new ideas were going to result in fundamental reforms in society. The statement opened with a challenge to change: "A new note is being sounded in public affairs — one that awakens hope in the breasts of many thousands, who on account perhaps of obscurity and lowly surroundings have not been regarded as entitled to more than a passing regard — it is that of SOCIAL WELFARE — the recognition of the rights of every human being no matter what the condition of birth or material possessions. The spirit of Brotherhood — the desire to spread more generously over our race, the comforts and happinesses of life — is taking possession of the hearts of men, and is manifesting itself in a thousand ways."

In this document Kelso charted much of the future development of Canadian social welfare. He called for a social welfare department in every municipality, nationally organized employment offices, centralized collection of charitable funds, better wages and shorter working hours, a mothers' allowance for widows with small children, a probation system in the criminal courts, and the extension of playgrounds and social settlements to every poor neighbourhood. Kelso knew it would require wise legislation and administration to bring about these reforms, to establish the necessary welfare agencies and to create a trained body of social workers who would be accorded the status of a profession.

In 1909, when Kelso addressed the students, the prevailing attitude toward social work seemed to be that no experience was necessary and that anyone could do it. In support of his plea for a school of philanthropy in Canada, Kelso declared:

> There are of course exceptions to every rule and some men and women have, without special training, made a notable success of their work — good judgment and careful observation have taught them the better way. But to secure the best service an educated class of men and women should be encouraged to devote themselves to the serious study of social problems, and this can best be done in a school of philanthropy affiliated with the university and working in harmony with existing philanthropic movements so that theoretical and practical training may go hand in hand.

Kelso's passion for the goals of social work would not be satisfied with mere scientific training. He wrote: "A prime requisite is that every student should feel the call to social service as imperative as to the ministry or mission field — all heart and no head has characterized many failures heretofore: to substitute all head and no heart would be the greater calamity."

Kelso, who played an important role in the founding of both the University Settlement and Central Neighbourhood House, pointed out that the idea of a social settlement had originated among university men and women "who realized the potency of education and culture in solving some of the intricate social problems that affected the daily life of the poor." He emphasized the importance of a small group of educated workers taking up residence among the poor and working with them to raise the standards of living and inspire "even the lowliest to an effort at self-improvement." He also supported an advocacy role for the settlement residents:

> The poor need leaders to secure and maintain their rights. Civic rules of health and cleanliness that are scrupulously observed in aristocratic neighbourhoods are scandalously abused and ignored in poor districts. With leadership and effort, good lighting may be obtained — more prompt and efficient scavenger service, less crowding and better sanitary conveniences; a limitation of the saloon evil, etc.

The social settlement itself, Kelso suggested, should be a community social centre where the varying social needs of young and old alike would be "catered to in a spirit of comradeship and goodwill, and with an entire absence of the charity or patronizing spirit." Kelso called for "a well-equipped social settlement in every poor district, for no other agency is so well calculated to touch fundamentally and yet acceptably the problems of congestion, poverty and social distress."

Kelso also threw himself into the battle against slums. His first salvo was an effective little pamphlet, *Can Slums Be Abolished or Must We Continue To Pay the Penalty?* which was widely circulated in the winter of 1910. Liberally illustrated with photographs of slum streets and lanes, rear houses, outhouses, unpaved roadways and children playing in the streets, it carried much the same message as that of the student social survey the preceding summer. Kelso personally distributed 250 copies of *Can Slums be Abolished?* to leading officials and citizens in Toronto, among them the recently appointed medical officer of health, Dr. Charles Hastings, who the following year himself issued a carefully researched report on housing conditions in Toronto's poorer districts. Kelso also gave an illustrated address in the spring of 1910 to the Canadian Institute in which he warned of the danger of allowing slums to spread.

This growing awareness of the problems of poverty, slums and immigration in downtown Toronto led to the establishment of four new settlements in the city's poorer districts within the next three years. All of them were located in the area west of Yonge Street and south of College Street where large numbers of immigrants, many from eastern and southern Europe, had been pouring in throughout the first decade of the century. A new multi-cultural experiment had begun, which would have far-reaching repercussions on the future social development of Toronto.

CHAPTER SEVEN

CHURCH INSTITUTES AND MISSIONS

If there is one main distinction between the social settlement movement in Canada and that in the United States, it lies in the preponderant influence of the Protestant churches on the Canadian movement. Evangelism and the social gospel influence shaped the response of the Protestant churches to the problems in the downtown districts of rapidly growing cities. In the nineteenth century and well into the twentieth century, Protestant churches regarded themselves as the protectors of Canadian values — moral, social and religious. In the absence of an existing service network to help foreign immigrants acculturate and overcome hardships, the churches saw a window of opportunity. They were motivated to fill the vacuum in service to immigrants and to dispel criticism inspired by the removal of affluent congregations to the suburbs.

Evangelism had been at the core of Protestantism from the very beginning. It centred on the redemption of the individual soul, on spreading the gospel to others and on the heavenly rewards for the saved in a life after death. However, the new social Christianity held that this was not enough. The church had a responsibility to redeem and reform society, as well as the individual.

The social gospel developed as a moderate, moralistic reform movement combining vigorous attacks on moral evils such as saloons, race-track gambling and white-slave traffic, and a sharp focus on social service matters such as working conditions, housing and sanitation, immigration and health. The development of social services became the major focus of the social reform movement within the churches.

To implement the social gospel, the Protestant denominations set up various temperance, moral and social reform boards. On the national level the Protestant churches formed the Moral and Social Reform Council of Canada, which, for two decades, was one of the most powerful sources in the Canadian social welfare movement. In the early days of the century the Catholic Church did not have any nationwide moral and social reform organizations like those of the Protestant churches. They were roughly guided by the social gospel of Pope Leo XIII's encyclical *Rerum Novarum* of 1891 on the condition of the working classes. By calling attention to the plight of the poor, it encouraged Catholics "to devote themselves to the amelioration of social ills." The result was an increase in social welfare programs in the parishes, as well as the development of citywide Catholic charities in the larger centres.

A TIME FOR DECISION

The Protestant churches found themselves in a quandary as to how best to meet the challenges of poverty in the cities. Broad campaigns of public persuasion were all very well in the battles for sabbath day observance, for temperance or for better working conditions, but to reach the people in the poor downtown areas and to make any real changes in their lives, something else was needed, something practical and personal. There was a need for institutions to be located in the poor neighbourhoods; centres where people could be helped and inspired, where neighbourhood services could be established. What form these neighbourhood institutions should take and to what extent they should be religious, as well as social, became the subject of a number of studies and discussions within church circles.

THE INSTITUTIONAL APPROACH

Protestant denominations saw the establishment of institutional churches in depressed areas as the ideal way to meet a city's problems. The institutional church was a real church with a qualified clergyman and regular religious services, but it also had facilities for all kinds of institutional social programs, usually conducted in a separate location. The first organization like this in Toronto was St. Andrew's Institute. Its success may be attributed to many factors: its educational services programs, a well-equipped building located several blocks from the church, and solid support from its base in the Anglo-Canadian community.

Probably the best known institutional church was the Earlscourt Methodist Church, which was under the leadership of the Rev. Peter Bryce.

Located in a suburban shanty town in the St. Clair-Dufferin area inhabited mainly by recent British immigrants, Bryce's church became the religious, educational and social centre for this poor but culturally homogeneous community. Another important example was the Memorial Institute which was launched as a Baptist institutional church in 1912 in the area south-west of Bathurst and Queen streets.

MEMORIAL INSTITUTE

The Memorial Institute grew out of a mission Sunday school begun in 1873 by the Plymouth Brethren; later it became a Baptist mission, then the Tecumseh Baptist Church. By the 1890s the membership had grown to 240 and the Sunday school had an attendance of 325. In 1897 a new brick building was erected by Mr. and Mrs. William Davies as a memorial to their deceased daughter, and the church was re-named Memorial Baptist Church. The church, located on the corner of Tecumseh and Richmond streets, was in a rapidly changing area. A familiar pattern emerged — as immigrants moved in and poverty increased, the more well-to-do church members moved out. By 1911 the membership was so depleted that the church could not carry on without outside support. In this crisis Walmer Road Baptist Church, located in the middle-class Annex north of Bloor Street and west of Avenue Road, came to the rescue. Under the leadership of Rev. John MacNeill, Walmer Road took the responsibility for work in the downtown locality and for the development of an institutional church that would provide community services "without respect to class, race or religion." Thus the Memorial Institute was born on 14 January 1912.

The work was conducted on evangelical, institutional lines under the direction of a Baptist minister, Rev. Awdrey Brown, B.A., B.Th., who was succeeded by other Baptist ministers. The work was supervised by the Memorial Institute Committee of Walmer Road Baptist Church, which included Dr. Horace L. Brittain, director of the newly formed Bureau of Municipal Research. The district served by Memorial Institute stretched from Bathurst Street on the east to Shaw Street on the west, and south from Arthur Street to the waterfront (usually referred to today as the Niagara Street district). The area contained 2,998 houses and a population of about 25,000 people. These statistics indicate the level of overcrowding in the district. About one-half of the population were of British origin; the remainder were recent immigrants from Europe.

The religious work of Memorial Institute was concentrated in the church. On Sundays there were two English-speaking services (one in the morning and one in the evening), a Sunday school conducted in English for children and young people and a Polish service conducted by a Polish Baptist minister. For its institutional services Memorial acquired a string of residential properties along Tecumseh Street — a two-storey brick house used as a residence for the women workers, and two double-cottages and a duplex which contained the office, clubrooms, a children's library and a domestic science kitchen. One of Memorial Institute's first acts was to open a playground on the church grounds, providing space for swings and baseball games. *The Star Weekly* hailed this as "the only church which provides fun for the children on its grounds."

For many years Nellie McFarland, a warm-hearted trained baby nurse well-known by everybody in the neighbourhood, was in charge of the women's work at Memorial. Through her initiative Memorial become a pioneer in setting up a well-baby clinic and milk station. Club work was a major feature of the program, with clubs for boys and girls, women and men. For the small children four to eight years old, there was a Saturday morning play school. In the summer, a fresh air camp provided holidays for children and families in the country, while in the city the Institute operated a daily vacation Bible school, which included a worship service, handcrafts, plays, games, Bible stories and hymns. Another popular service was a supply depot, mostly stocked by Walmer Road Church, where men, women and children could get clothing and bedding. McFarland supervised distribution and collected a small fee from those she felt could afford it. A girls' worker and a boys' worker were also engaged, but much of the work depended on the help of volunteers.

How well was Memorial Institute able to work with the non-English-speaking immigrants in its neighbourhood? The early available records do not give any indication, but in 1922 when Frances Trotter went there as resident girls' worker, she found that most of the children and families participating in the activities were English, Scottish and Irish. "Memorial Institute," she said, "didn't have many Jews or Catholics because of the church connection — Memorial was definitely a church settlement."

The description of Memorial Institute as a church settlement, as opposed to an institutional church, emerged as the settlement idea grew more popular in Toronto. By 1918, when the Toronto Federation of Settlements was formed, Memorial Institute became one of the four charter members. Unfortunately, Memorial Institute did not survive throughout World War II. In 1943 Walmer Road Baptist Church discontinued its support and the property and work were turned over to the Home Mission Board of the Baptist Convention of Ontario and Quebec. Soon the Institute ceased to function, and the building was later occupied by a Ukrainian Baptist church.

THE CITY MISSION APPROACH

The first response of the Protestant churches in Canada to the influx of immigrants was to extend the existing network of city missions in poor districts. These missions were either general missions for people of all nationalities and faiths or missions for specific ethnic groups. Almost all of the missions introduced strong institutional features such as clubs, classes, clinics and camps to provide for the physical, educational, recreational and social needs of the people. But their religious and spiritual focus remained central; regardless of the framework the mission followed, evangelism and social service went hand in hand.

By 1911 two of the best-known and best-equipped general missions in Canada were the Methodist Fred Victor Mission in Toronto, which served a largely Anglo-Celtic neighbourhood and All People's Mission in Winnipeg in a district which comprised many immigrants. The programs of the two missions, though similar, were adapted to meet the needs of their different neighbourhoods.

Fred Victor Mission, Toronto

The Fred Victor Mission superintendent, Rev. S.W. Dean, claimed that his mission combined all the best features of the institutional church, the gospel mission and the social settlement. He added with conviction that all the institutional services provided by the mission acted as "very good bait for the gospel hook." For all its emphasis on "aggressive evangelism," Fred Victor Mission was also a proponent of social gospel ideals — it had been the sponsor of the students' evangelical campaign in 1911, without changing its main structure, Fred Victor Mission introduced a settlement within the mission. It was a residence for the deaconesses, described as a pleasant home to which the neighbours were invited. Some 150 people enjoyed hospitality there in its opening year and were received "not in a spirit of patronage but as neighbours and friends." Dean described the settlement as "a centre which aims to manifest the spirit of Christ to the community, and the people are coming to it more and more for advice, for help, for comfort and inspiration."

A unique contribution by Fred Victor Mission to expanding the social thought of its student workers was the social studies class organized in 1912 by the students' department under the leadership of its recently appointed secretary, Frank N. Stapleford, who later became one of Toronto's best-known social workers as head of the Neighbourhood Workers' Association. At each weekly session a Methodist minister or professor spoke on the social teachings of the Bible or on the spiritual forces of social reform. This was followed by a social sciences or social work specialist who spoke on society's current problems and on the practical application of social work to these problems.

All People's Mission, Winnipeg

The innovative and progressive development of All People's Mission in Winnipeg from 1907–1913 bore the impression of one man, Rev. James Shaver Woodsworth. As a student at Victoria College in 1898, Woodsworth had been interested in slum conditions in Toronto and admired the work of the Fred Victor Mission. The following year, while studying at Oxford University, he spent a couple of weeks at Mansfield House, an Oxford religious social settlement in the slums of London. There he was particularly impressed by the "pleasant Sunday afternoons" for workingmen, which he described as political and social rather than religious.

After growing discontent with serving as the pastor of an affluent church in Winnipeg, Woodsworth received a welcome appointment in 1907 as superintendent of All People's Mission in Winnipeg's poverty-stricken North End. Here he was in charge of all the Methodist mission work in the area. By 1911 All People's Mission was situated in six main locations and included a variety of buildings — three churches, four institutes and three residences — enabling All People's to provide a wide range of services to different neighbourhoods and to diverse immigrant groups. British immigrants were the chief attendants at the Mission's churches, though services were also held in Polish, German and Bohemian (Czech).

Woodsworth was still troubled by how Protestant Canadians could best help their Catholic and Jewish neighbours. "They have become part of our community — we cannot be indifferent to their welfare." To Woodsworth it seemed that institutional services similar to those in the social settlements would be the most effective answer. He declared, "the effort must be not merely to preach to the people but to educate them and to improve the whole social condition." At Woodsworth's instigation two main institutes were built at All People's Mission to work with immigrants on essentially non-denominational lines. Each institute had a kindergarten (then unknown in the Winnipeg school system), a gymnasium and baths, clubs and classes for boys and girls, men's and women's meetings, a night school and a branch of the Winnipeg Public Library. Although it is virtually impossible to distinguish the type of work done in these institutes from that of the social settlements, All People's Mission was never classified as a social settlement because of its name and strong church connection.

The people's Sunday meetings at the Grand Theatre, inaugurated by Woodsworth in the 1910–1911 season, especially appealed to the men of the community. Crowds of from 300 to 1200 thronged the meetings. Noting that there were large numbers of Jews, Germans, Slavs and "old country workingmen of radical views" in the North End who were not being ministered to by any of the English-speaking churches, Woodsworth was determined to provide "pleasant and profitable" Sunday gatherings for those who had "nowhere to go and nothing to do." The goal of these meetings was decidedly reminiscent of the pleasant Sunday afternoons at Mansfield House, which had so intrigued Woodsworth over a decade before. Woodsworth also saw these meetings as a way to break down the "racial, national, religious, political and social prejudices that divide our heterogeneous population."

The Sunday afternoon meetings, which became known as the people's forum, offered lectures on scientific, economic and social topics followed by free discussion. The Sunday evening meetings were not, in any narrow sense, a religious service, but rather an attempt to create the atmosphere of a "Sunday evening at home" with good music, beautiful pictures and conversational talks. Woodsworth summed up the intangible but valuable results of such meetings: "Jews and Russians, Catholics and Protestants, so-called atheists, Socialists and Christians find they could sit side by side in a common enjoyment of the best things in life and unite in spirit as they considered the things that made for the common welfare."

Beyond providing such programs and services for the people in the North End, Woodsworth saw broader functions for All People's Mission in promoting the development of social services: making investigations of social conditions, training social workers, publicizing conditions in the neighbourhood, providing an experimental station to test various forms of social work which, when the need was demonstrated, could be taken over by more specialized private or public agencies, and cooperating with other agencies — "probably the most important department of our work."

All People's Mission, Winnipeg, had a significance far beyond its own locality, chiefly due to Woodworth's two books, *Strangers Within Our Gates* and *My Neighbour*, which carried the concern for immigrants and the appreciation of the ability of settlement-type services to meet their needs.

MISSIONS FOR SPECIFIC ETHNIC GROUPS

Several Protestant churches dealt with large enclaves of non-English-speaking immigrants by establishing missions directed at specific ethno-religious groups. For example, in Toronto's Ward there was a Methodist mission to the Italians and several Protestant missions to the Jews. These missions were all strongly evangelistic in tone, yet they offered many institutional features. One great drawing-card was that these missions were invariably headed by a missionary of the same origin as the particular group of people to be reached. Usually a convert himself, it was easier for him to influence his compatriots to change their traditional beliefs. However, even though this model was not accepted wholeheartedly within some of the sponsoring churches, the separate missions to specific immigrant groups continued to flourish and achieved a moderate degree of success. They also encountered an apparently unexpected amount of opposition and hostility from many of the very people the missions were so earnestly trying to help and convert.

The Methodist Italian Mission

The Methodist Italian Mission and the embattled response between the Catholics and the Methodists in Toronto for the hearts and souls of the Italian immigrants was an excellent example of this struggle. In 1904 a small group of Italian laymen, who had become interested in evangelical Protestantism through contacts with a mission on LaPlante Street, began to hold services in one another's homes and preach in the streets to their fellow countrymen in the Ward. They approached officials of the Methodist Church for help in starting an Italian mission and received an enthusiastic response, especially from Alexander Mills, a Methodist who had often visited Italy, and from Rev. S.W. Dean, superintendent of Fred Victor Mission. As a result the Italian Mission of the Methodist Church (*Missione Evangelica Italiana*) opened in October 1905 in the Old Agnes Street Methodist Church on the north-east corner of Agnes and Teraulay streets (now Dundas and Bay). Rev. Guiseppe Merlino, a native Italian who had been engaged in Methodist missionary work to Italians in the United States, became the first pastor and Miss A. Marconi, also Italian-born, the first *missionaria* or Bible woman. The work was directed by Fred Victor Mission with financial support from the General Missionary Society of the Methodist Church, the Women's Missionary Society, the Methodist Young Men's Association in Toronto and by the Italian lay people. In 1908 the administration of the Italian mission was transferred to the newly formed Toronto City and Fred Victor Mission Society of the Methodist Church, which had the support of some 24 churches and missions in the city.

The evangelical core of the mission's work centred on the Sunday preaching services and sabbath school, and a prayer meeting and Bible study at midweek. Great pride was expressed when, at the first communion service in 1906, a band of 36 converts became members of the Methodist Church. The number swelled to 65 the next year, and a few years later the mission reported 102 church members. While the numbers of actual converts may seem modest, the mission reached a much greater circle of Italians of all ages through their night schools, kindergartens, clubs and classes. During its first year the mission claimed to have reached over 500 Italian-born people. The most successful activity was the night school where over 200 Italian men took English classes; other early activities included Italian mothers' meetings, classes for Italian girls in domestic science, kitchen gardening and sewing, and a young people's social club. But the mission was still not reaching Italians at their most impressionable age. In 1908 a kindergarten for 40 children proved very successful. Later a primary class was added, as one of the goals of the mission was to get Italian children to enter public schools rather than the Catholic separate schools. In the next few years other activities were added, clubs for boys and girls, athletics and gymnastics, music classes. The mission workers engaged in house-to-house visiting and the distribution of clothing.

In 1908 the original Italian mission moved from the Old Agnes Street Methodist Church to Central Mission on Edward Street in the very heart of Little Italy. In that same year Rev. Merlino withdrew and was succeeded by Rev. Alfredo Taglialatela, M.A., Ph.D., D.D., a leader in Italian Protestantism who had held responsible positions in Milan, Bologna and Rome. He had also just completed a series of evangelical services in Italian missions in the United States. His two years in Toronto were fruitful ones with the building of new mission premises at Elm and Teraulay streets in 1910 at a cost of $28,000, much of which was given by the Massey family. The new building included a residence, a chapel, classrooms, a reading room, office, baths and lavatories. In 1907 a branch of the Italian mission was started in the Clinton-Mansfield area west of Bathurst, and under Taglialatela's dynamic leadership a fine new building was opened on Claremont Street in 1910. There was also an Italian settlement in the Dufferin-Davenport district, and a second branch opened in 1912. However, the Methodist mission encountered difficulties. Its annual report noted that even though the gospel was preached at each mothers' meeting, the women were "very difficult to convert." It also pointed out that mission workers were finding it hard to reach the Italian children because of the "untiring efforts on the part of the priests and nuns to prevent them coming to us."

Catholic Resistance

As the Protestant denominations spread their proselytizing missions across Canada among Catholic immigrants, the Catholic Church countered in 1908 by establishing the Catholic Church Extension Society of Canada, with the principal aim of preserving the Catholic faith among immigrants. This powerful organization promoted the establishment of national Catholic churches, brought in immigrant clergy to minister to various nationalities and opened a seminary to train students in Latin. In 1908, after a request from the Italians of Toronto for an Italian priest to look after their spiritual needs, the apostolic delegate to Canada sent a young Italian priest, Professor Pietro Pisani, to study the situation in Toronto.

At this time St. Patrick's Roman Catholic Church, which was closest to the Ward, was about to open a new church on McCaul Street for its large Irish congregation. It was arranged that the old St. Patrick's Church on William Street (now St. Patrick's Street) become the first Italian parish in the city. Our Lady of Mount Carmel, as the Italian church was renamed, opened in late October with Rev. Carlo Doglia, an Italian priest from Buffalo, as pastor. Mount Carmel offered the Italian community a new sense of identity, with their own religious services and parish social activities. By 1912, as a response to the growing success of the Methodist missions, two more Italian churches were created. In 1915 St. Agnes Italian Church (formerly St. Francis) opened at Grace and Mansfield and St. Clements Italian Church opened on Dufferin.

But churches alone could not stop the threat of the Methodist missions. Catholics soon realized that they must match the educational services offered by the Methodist missions if they were to hold their children and young people. Night schools and kindergartens under Catholic auspices were seen as essential. In 1909 a night school for Italians was opened in a classroom at St. Patrick's School; later another Italian night school opened in St. Patrick's clubhouse next to Our Lady of Mount Carmel Church.

In 1913 the Carmelite Sisters came to Toronto to work with the immigrants, especially the Italians. They founded an orphanage, went on door-to-door visits to Italian homes and taught in a Catholic kindergarten in the Ward to counteract the effects of the Methodist missions. The Catholic Church rented rooms for the kindergarten on Elm Street, strategically located across the road from the mission. By 1917 some 70 Italian children were attending the kindergarten and a sewing class was held for older girls. But the *Catholic Register* warned that "the battle is still going on: the Methodists are still fighting for our little ones."

This very success of the Methodist mission goaded the Catholics into defensive action: to establish national Italian churches in Toronto, to open Catholic night schools for young Italian men and to conduct a Catholic kindergarten for Italian children in the Ward. These counter-activities succeeded in retaining a high proportion of Italian Catholics within the fold; after 1915 the influence of the Methodist missions gradually declined. But the Methodist Italian Mission and its two branches continued their work in Toronto's three main Italian districts until the 1930s when they amalgamated as one church, St. Paul's Italian United Church, which continues on Ossington Avenue to this day.

The Presbyterian Mission to the Jews

The battle between Jewish community leaders and the Presbyterian Mission to the Jews for the allegiance of the newly arrived immigrants was, at its peak, even more intense than the parallel struggle of the Methodist mission and the Catholic Church for the Italian newcomers. Unlike the Italians who had no native Italian Catholic clergy in their early days in Toronto, the Eastern European Jews were always amply supplied with synagogues of their own and with Yiddish-speaking rabbis who gave their congregations a considerable amount of leadership. The Jewish population in Toronto — about 15,000 in 1908 and some 35,000 by 1915 — presented an enormous challenge to the missionary impulse of the Protestant evangelical churches.

The Presbyterians were not alone with their missions to the Jews. An earlier effort, the Toronto Jewish Mission, was established in the Ward in 1894 under interdenominational auspices. The Presbyterian Mission to the Jews opened in 1908 at 156 Teraulay Street near Agnes (Bay at Dundas). In 1912 a third Jewish mission was started in the Ward by the Anglicans. This mission followed the Jewish population westward to a new location on Bellevue Avenue and changed its name to the Nathaniel Institute in 1916. The Presbyterian Mission to the Jews occupied the most dominant position among the missions in the Ward. And while all three missions were bitterly opposed by the Jewish community, the Presbyterian mission seems to have attracted the most violent reaction.

The Presbyterian mission is especially significant because of the influence it exerted, directly and indirectly, on the development and locations of the social settlements organized between 1910 and 1912 to work in the immigrant areas of downtown Toronto. It was also a central component of conflict which developed within the Presbyterian Church in Canada as to the best way to minister to immigrants — whether by separate ethnic missions, all people's missions or social settlements. In 1907 the General Assembly of the Presbyterian Church in Canada authorized the board of foreign missions to commence mission work among Jewish people. As the board of foreign missions had operated a Presbyterian medical mission to the Jews in Palestine in the late nineteenth century, it seemed only natural that the board should be chosen to launch the work in Canada. This work was to begin as a pilot project in Toronto and be extended to other cities as needed and as finances warranted. A special sub-committee on work among the Jews was set up under the chairmanship of Rev. J. McPherson Scott. The opening of the Presbyterian Mission to the Jews in Toronto was followed by a second mission in Winnipeg in 1911 and a third in Montreal in 1915. Their goal was "to Christianize and Canadianize the Jews."

Rohold's Mission

To launch the pilot project, Rev. Sabeti B. Rohold, a Palestinian Jew converted to Christianity, was brought to Toronto from a mission in Glasgow. Rohold was a man of great energy, a persuasive speaker who had a thorough knowledge of Jewish history and religious beliefs. His father had held a high rabbinical position in Jerusalem and he himself had studied in Palestinian rabbinical academies prior to his conversion. Certainly with Rohold at the helm the Presbyterian Mission to the Jews could defend itself against accusations of anti-semitism. Rohold and other members of the mission staff presented to the community at large a very favourable picture of the Jews as devout, hard-working, law-abiding people anxious to give their children a good education. In his speeches and writings Rohold stressed the sufferings the Jewish people had endured, "within the fearful paws of the Russian bear," and used this to explain their apparent aversion to Christianity. "In Russia, Christianity means cruelty," Rohold would say, "here they (the Jews) see that it means love." The entire thrust of the mission was not to disparage the Jews' devotion to the teachings of the Old Testament, but rather to share with them the additional inspiration of the New Testament. It was hard for the workers at the mission to understand the bitter antagonism aroused by their efforts at conversion.

Though the Presbyterian Mission to the Jews, led by Rohold from 1908–1920, always remained aggressively evangelistic, it also provided a balanced program of religious and institutional services. Besides the gospel services on Saturday and Sunday, the sabbath school, and the men's Bible study club known as The Seekers After Truth Society, there were also mothers' meetings, sewing classes for girls, a club for boys, a Boy Scout troop, a summer camp and day outings. The reading room, a popular rendezvous for the men, provided newspapers in English, Hebrew, Yiddish and German as well as other literature. But a Christian Jew, able to speak Yiddish, was always on hand "to point seekers to the cross and explain its message to Israel." The night school attracted hundreds of Jewish men, mostly Russian, who were anxious to learn English; as soon as they were able to read, the Bible was made their textbook, and also each evening a Bible class immediately followed the night school. A night school and reading room exclusively for women was run by lady missionaries. The free dispensary was attended by physicians, a pharmacist, nurses and an interpreter all serving on a voluntary basis. During the first year alone some 2,515 patients were treated, and some 18,000 patients were treated in the first ten years. This golden opportunity was not overlooked. The first annual report noted, "a brief gospel service is held every dispensary day among the patients who are waiting for their turn with the doctor." Mission workers visited homes, shops, hospitals and prisons — some 2,868 such visitations were made in the first year alone. Poor relief, mostly in the form of rent subsidies or coal, was given to several hundred Jewish families each year. Just before World War I a soup kitchen was opened for poor, unemployed Russian Jewish refugees. As the activities grew the original mission on Teraulay Street became overcrowded and, in 1913, an impressive new three-storey building, known as the Hebrew Christian Synagogue, was opened at the corner of Elm and Elizabeth streets.

In spite of Rohold's eloquent preaching, both inside the mission and at outdoor services, the actual number of Jews converted to Christianity remained quite small. In the first year the mission could claim only six converts though ten times that number attended the gospel services. By 1916 the communion roll had reached only 62, though the Bible study club numbered over 200 members. The real success of the Presbyterian mission lay in the practical services it provided to meet the everyday needs of people struggling to make their way in a new country. It was the reading room, the night school and the free dispensary that attracted the greatest number of people; the mission attempted to capitalize on this by linking the proselytizing efforts to these activities.

The Jewish Community Reacts

The opposition of the Jewish community to the Protestant missions was fierce and persistent. The opposition applied indiscriminately to all the missions, but when the Presbyterian mission opened on Teraulay Street in 1908 and hundreds of East European Jews flocked to its doors, rabbis and other Jewish community leaders perceived an especially serious threat.

Rohold's street-corner gospel meetings, which began in 1908, attracted large crowds and inspired the most violent reactions. He frequently preached from a wagon, striking an imposing figure above the crowd, and would bring a portable organ to accompany the singing. Alarmed by the response to these meetings, a committee of Jews distributed a handbill, printed in Yiddish, warning against the missionaries and urging other Jews not to join in the singing or even encourage the missionaries by standing near them. Frequent attempts were made by groups of young Jews to break up Rohold's meetings; one tactic was to organize a rival meeting on the opposite corner. On one such occasion in 1911, a riot broke out between opposing factions and the missionaries were stoned and pelted with tomatoes. The police arrested eight of the Jewish assailants. Subsequently the missionaries enjoyed police protection at all their outdoor meetings, which did nothing to improve their popularity among the Jewish community.

In 1909, the year following the opening of the Presbyterian mission, a Jewish dispensary and a Jewish day nursery were organized as counter-missionary endeavours. A group known as The Alumni, comprising mostly Jewish teenage boys, was formed to intercept Jews at the door of Rohold's mission to tell them of the philanthropic services available in the Jewish community. The same year a Jewish working girls' club, started in the Ward by the Council of Jewish Women at the instigation of Rabbi and Mrs. Jacobs, offered English classes and social evenings to members.

Ida Siegel, a leader in the East European community, was the moving spirit in founding the Jewish Endeavour Sewing School, a Zionist organization for school-age girls, which offered classes in sewing, Judaism, history and Zionism, and provided a library in order to keep young people who wanted to read English away from the missions. Ida Siegel had already been instrumental in launching a mothers' club at Hester How (Elizabeth Street) School, where over 90 per cent of the children were Jewish. The early meetings, conducted in Yiddish and English, brought together the Jewish mothers and the Anglo-Canadian teachers to discuss the welfare of the children; the discussions served as "an instrument of acculturation as well as a vehicle to combat the missionaries."

The concern over the attraction of the missions for Jewish children had been steadily mounting, especially when a committee of Jews visited the Presbyterian mission on Teraulay Street in 1911 and found some 200 Jewish children in attendance; a similar incident occurred when the Christian Synagogue opened in 1913 on Elizabeth Street, across the road from the playground of Hester How School. One immediate result was the rapid expansion of congregational schools for the children in the East European synagogues. Prior to this, Holy Blossom was the only congregation that had an organized sabbath school. Another result was the creation of formal Jewish anti-missionary organizations to discourage Jews of all ages from attending the missions.

The Folks Farein, a Jewish working-class men's organization, with rooms on Elm and Elizabeth streets, began as "a literary and cultural club for immigrants," but when the Christian Synagogue opened on the opposite side of the street the Folks Farein became an anti-missionary organization. Aimed first at simply disrupting Rohold's street meetings, it gradually developed a varied program of practical services to counteract the appeal of similar activities at the mission: these included a soup kitchen, an employment service, English classes, a reading room, visits to the homes of the poor and infirm, and interpreter services. The Anti-Missionary League, formed in 1914, had its headquarters in the same building as the Folks Farein, but it is not clear to what extent they shared activities. The league, with its 600 members, had the backing of both Holy Blossom and the East European Jewish community. With a board which included all the rabbis in the city, it is not surprising that the league adopted a strategy of persuasion to keep the Jews out of the missions, especially Rohold's.

Scott Mission

The influence of Presbyterian and other missions to the Jews gradually waned, no doubt because of the social pressures placed by the Jewish community on their own people and because of the emergence and growth of Jewish organizations to meet the philanthropic, educational and the social needs of Jewish immigrants. However, some of the decrease in the popularity of the missions must be attributed to the appearance in the immigrant communities between 1910 and 1912 of the attractive alternative offered by the social settlements.

After Rohold left the Mission in 1920, the Board of Home Missions and Social Service of the Presbyterian Church decided that a mission exclusively for Jews was unrewarding to say the least. In 1922 the Christian Synagogue was transformed into an all people's mission and renamed the Scott Institute. Following church union, the Scott Institute property was allocated to the Presbyterian Church; the United Church staff and non-Jewish congregation moved out to form the Church of All Nations. For a time Scott Institute reverted to being an exclusively Jewish mission under the direction of Rev. Morris Zeidman, one of Rohold's converts at the Christian Synagogue. Although in 1922 the Scott Institute had become a member of the Toronto Federation of Settlements, along with two secular and two church settlements, the institute resigned from the federation five years later.

During the Great Depression of the 1930s the Scott Institute, led by Zeidman, undertook extensive relief work among the unemployed irrespective of colour, race or creed and won citywide support for its mammoth welfare projects, even from many members of the Jewish faith. In 1941 Zeidman resigned from the Presbyterian Board of Home Missions, as he felt the church was not adequately supporting the institute in the post-depression years. The Scott Institute was closed and Zeidman immediately opened the Scott Mission on Bay Street as an independent, non-denominational, evangelistic and social service organization, with interdenominational support. It transferred its multi-faceted program to Spadina Avenue, for many years under the direction of Rev. Alex Zeidman, D.D., son of the founder.

The Presbyterian mission exclusively for Jews ceased to operate, but its successors, the Scott Institute and the Scott Mission, have continued to provide, with general community support, social service programs to people of all backgrounds for over fifty years.

CHAPTER EIGHT

THE CHURCH SETTLEMENTS

Only the Presbyterian church launched a series of social settlements across Canada on a national basis. The chain of six social settlements established by the Presbyterian church in Canada between 1912 and 1922 was a practical expression of the church's desire to take a more meaningful part in meeting the urgent urban social problems of the day. But it was only one aspect of the social gospel movement within the church that covered a broad program of moral and social reform.

The official channel for the social gospel movement in the Presbyterian church was the board of moral and social reform created in 1907. The board was under the strong leadership of Dr. George J. Pidgeon, a notable Presbyterian minister and religious educator, as convener and of Dr. John G. Shearer, who had just returned from his successes with the Lord's Day Alliance, as full-time, paid general secretary. The new board tackled the moral and social problems with a carefully planned campaign of organization, education and legislation. Directed by Shearer's superb gift for network organizing, the board promoted the establishment of parallel committees on social and moral reform in the synods and presbyteries across the country. The board also cooperated with the committee on the Presbyterian brotherhood in fostering the organization of the men in the individual congregations into brotherhoods, which would, in turn, study and promote the board's reform measures.

The board's initial emphasis on moral issues came to be particularly focused on the commercial exploitation of human weakness, as exemplified by the liquor trade, race-track gambling, the white-slave traffic and immoral literature. Its twofold aims were directed to the study of social and industrial problems and social action.

THE PRESBYTERIAN REFORM LEADERS

The early reform board counted among its members some outstanding clergymen and laymen who were uniquely equipped to give informed direction to the social reform aspects of the work. Among the most active clergymen on the board were Dr. Charles W. Gordon of Winnipeg, Dr. Andrew S. Grant of Toronto and Rev. William J. Knox of Pembroke, Ontario.

Gordon, a pastor in a Winnipeg church, was nationally known for his popular novels written under the pseudonym of Ralph Connor. His book *The Foreigner* (1909) was significant for its vivid portrayal of slum conditions in an immigrant community. During the same period Gordon also acted as chairman of several conciliation boards in labour disputes in Manitoba, British Columbia and Alberta. Dr. Grant, the first ordained Presbyterian minister in the Yukon, came to Toronto in 1908 and took on the presidency of the Moral and Social Reform League of Toronto. He is best known for his work as superintendent of home missions for the Presbyterian church in Canada. Knox was a leader in the Presbyterian brotherhood movement and had made a considerable study of social settlements in Chicago, New York and some British cities. He felt deeply that the church should involve itself in all phases of life — political, municipal, social. He took initiatives to move the board to establish social settlements under church auspices in major cities across Canada.

Four of the laymen appointed to the board were particularly qualified to provide leadership on the social and industrial problems facing Canada in the critical years between 1907 and the beginning of World War I — and the board turned to them for expert guidance. They were: W.L. Mackenzie King, who became minister of labour in the Laurier cabinet during this period; Frederick Urry, a labour leader from Lakehead; O.D. Skelton, then professor of political science at Queen's University; and J.J. Kelso, superintendent of neglected and dependent children for the province of Ontario.

Kelso was invited to speak to the October 1907 meeting of the new body where he stressed the need for better social policies and programs, including the establishment of children's courts, a probation system, better housing for the poor, the abolition of child labour and the establishment of playgrounds for the poor. King, in his new role as minister of labour, addressed the board in 1909 strengthening their interest in industrial problems; this was a natural progression following the creation of a committee on industrial problems the preceding year, with Dr. Shearer as convener and Urry and Kelso as active members. However, the industrial problems mandate appears to have been too narrow and the committee was superseded in 1910 by a new committee on labour, housing, health and relief, under the convenership of Skelton.

Besides Skelton, the board was able to recruit other leaders in education and communications: men such as Principal Robert Magill of the Presbyterian College in Halifax and professor of philosophy at Dalhousie University; Principal William Patrick of Manitoba College (the Presbyterian college in Winnipeg); Thomas B. Kilpatrick, a young Scottish theology professor at Knox College, Toronto; and J.A. Macdonald, editor-in-chief of *The Globe* (Toronto), who had previously founded the two independent Presbyterian journals, *The Westminister* and *The Presbyterian*. The convener of the board, Dr. Pidgeon, was professor of practical theology at Westminster Hall, the new Presbyterian college in Vancouver, for several years during his term of office.

THE EDUCATIONAL APPROACH

These leaders on the board of moral and social reform were thoughtful men, most university-trained, who were trying to bring their church forward with a greater concern for economic and social problems. As Presbyterians they prided themselves on their rationalism as opposed to the camp-meeting emotionalism they associated with Methodism. They approached the church's new involvement in controversial social and economic issues with a deep commitment to academic methods; a broad study of the philosophy and literature of the background disciplines of political science, sociology and economics; and the careful weighing of the pros and cons of issues such as socialism and the relationship of Christianity to social welfare. They valued thoughtful decisions reached after prolonged discussions and efforts to reach consensus.

Above all, they were committed to broadening the understanding and acceptance of the church's need to involve itself more deeply in the social and economic problems of the day. This they proposed to do first by educating themselves, then the students in the theological colleges and the clergy in communities across Canada, and finally their church members and the general public. To meet these goals they published pamphlets on many phases of moral and social reform. They promoted the teaching of sociology in the Presbyterian theological colleges and prepared a reading list on social science. Later they supported the introduction of a training course for social workers at the University of Toronto.

The reading course in social science, proposed to the board in 1908 by Knox and Rev. E.B. Horne, was an ambitious project designed "to present reliable and scientific training on the various aspects of economic, social, moral and industrial problems." Struggling with the input of a large number of experts, the list was eventually published two years later. The list's heavy concentration on economic subjects, industrial problems and the labour movement reflected the board's desire to attune the church to the interests of blue-collar workers, partly to retain and build working-class affiliation with the church and partly to encourage church and labour to work as partners in the campaigns for moral, economic and social reform. This process also helped awaken the consciousness of Presbyterians to the urgency of what came to be called "the problem of the city" and to the need to find innovative solutions.

THE PROBLEM OF THE CITY

On 3 September 1909 Knox wrote a letter to Dr. Shearer urging discussion of "the downtown work in our cities" at the upcoming meeting of the board of moral and social reform. Knox thought the church should address itself to formulating a more positive and practical policy for dealing with the city problem. He suggested, also, that the downtown work should not be left to the individual congregation but that the church as a whole should tackle the problem. Four days later, at the board meeting, the brotherhood committee convened by Knox suggested that the board adopt some policy to be recommended to the church regarding "the problem of the downtown district and the foreign settlements in our great cities." This matter was favourably received and referred to the executive for consideration and action. The executive approached the question with due caution. Before committing the board to any specific course of action, Shearer was asked to arrange a conference on the problem of foreign settlement in Toronto in consultation with the foreign mission committee. Shearer soon reported back to the executive that a conference of representatives from the foreign mission committee, Knox College and the board of moral and social reform had been held and had decided, for the present, simply to recommend "more vigorous prosecution of the excellent work now being done by the foreign mission committee in the interests of the Jews." He also noted that the work being done in the Italian community was under the care of the Methodist church by mutual agreement with the Presbyterian church. In view of this situation it became clear that any social settlement fostered by the board of moral and social reform in Toronto could not be located in the Ward, where it would compete directly with the Presbyterian Mission to the Jews and the Methodist Italian Mission. There were, however, still many other poor districts in Toronto and in other cities across Canada needing attention.

In 1910 the whole question of downtown slum conditions and foreign settlement in Canadian cities was given intensive study by the board. At the March executive meeting, devoted chiefly to these problems, Knox argued that it was the church's work not merely to save the soul at death, but to save the whole man during his lifetime, and "to minister to body and mind, as well as spirit." He reported on his personal study of social settlement work in Chicago and New York, and again urged the church as a whole to adopt some policy on its work in the downtown areas of Canadian cities.

John Paterson, K.C., another member of the board, reported on the recent decision of the University of Toronto YMCA to start, in a small way, settlement work in Toronto during the coming summer. Dr. Grant carried the discussion from the consideration of specific social services to the broader goals of social reform. He declared that the current methods in philanthropy and in reform and rescue work were "seriously lacking in wisdom, inasmuch as they were only in a small way dealing with the product of anti-social influences without endeavouring to get at the economic and other evils recognized by all." He called for the reform work to be carried out on an interdenominational basis, since sooner or later legislation to deal effectively with housing, overcrowding and sanitation would be "imperatively required."

After further discussion the meeting appointed Shearer and Grant to investigate conditions in the cities. Their report on downtown conditions in two American and four Canadian cities was presented to the full meeting of the board in September 1910. A resolution was adopted calling for the church to undertake "some form of work commonly known as social settlement work, adapted to our circumstances, by which we might be able more satisfactorily to touch the total life of the people." A special committee, headed by Rev. Horne, was appointed to work out plans that could be placed before the General Assembly of the Presbyterian church in June 1911.

Church vs. Social Settlements

During 1910 the board of moral and social reform had been amalgamated with the committee on evangelism to form the board of moral and social reform and evangelism. The following year it was renamed the board of social service and evangelism. This change of name and the broadening of the function of the board amounted to an official proclamation that any social service program undertaken by the Presbyterian church in Canada would not pursue a separate course of its own but would go hand in hand with evangelism.

Not surprisingly then, the Interim Report of the Special Committee, presented by Mr. Horne to the executive on 16 November 1910, laid great stress on the importance of a church settlement rather than a social settlement. The argument ran as follows:

> The Social Settlement seeks to harmonize and civilize; this is good, but it is not enough for our purposes. We must seek not merely to harmonize and civilize, but also definitely to Christianize. The Church must tackle this downtown problem as a *Church*. We are going into this work not merely inspired by a thin, sentimental humanism, but because we are Christian people who seek the advancement of Christ's Kingdom and the saving of men's lives. ... What is contemplated, therefore, is a *Church Settlement*, not only to carry on the ordinary activities of a "Settlement," but also a positive, definite, aggressive, evangelistic propaganda ....

REACHING CONSENSUS

Throughout 1911 the problem of the city became an important theme in Presbyterian circles. *The Presbyterian* published a series of articles and editorials dealing with the urban problems associated with immigration and slum housing and the relation of Christianity to these social issues. Early in the year an editorial suggested that the church should reach out for settlement and institutional ideas that had proven of value, "and should wed them to her proclamation of the gospel."

In May a Presbyterian rescue home was opened for "fallen girls and women" in Toronto, the first of a chain of seven such homes located in cities from Sydney, Nova Scotia to Vancouver, British Columbia. This chain of redemptive homes set the pattern, to some extent, for the establishment of the Presbyterian chain of settlements the following year. Also in 1911, O.D. Skelton contributed a section entitled "The Problem of the City" to *Social Service*, a book compiled by W.R. McIntosh and issued by Presbyterian Publications. In this essay Skelton outlined the new problems that had grown out of the Industrial Revolution, the growth of cities and immigration; he stressed the importance of a new realization of neighbourhood responsibilities in dealing with moral and social issues. Skelton recommended that the church "establish social settlements and institutional churches to serve downtown needs and study downtown conditions." Nowhere did he imply, however, that the new insights of the social sciences and social reform should supplant "the traditional evangelical concerns with changed individuals."

By the time the board's report was presented to the 1911 General Assembly, the Presbyterian attitude toward the question had crystallized. "The Problem of the City — Its Solution," appeared in *The Presbyterian* of 8 June 1911 and summed up the prevailing Presbyterian stand: slums must be abolished; the correlates of deprivation in poor areas have to be attacked; immigrants must be taught English and citizenship; everyone must be helped to health, to sanitary housing, to employment; and provision must be made for clean, helpful recreation and an enriched social life.

It was agreed that the church should not confine itself to the provision of mere missions in congested sections, but it should minister to all human needs including physical, intellectual, moral, social and religious. The solution to the problem of the city was seen as an essential combination of "strong, sane, aggressive evangelism with social service including moral and social reform."

THE CHAIN OF SETTLEMENTS

At the 1911 General Assembly, where the report on "The Problem of the City" was presented, the Presbyteries of Montreal, Toronto, Winnipeg and Vancouver requested that the city work of the church be placed under the jurisdiction of the board of social service and evangelism, which undertook the task of grappling with the downtown problem in the large cities. The board moved quickly to develop plans for a chain of evangelical, religious and social settlements in larger cities across Canada, "to reclaim the slum and its dwellers for Christ and good citizenship." It recognized that a trained worker would be needed to survey downtown sections and to launch and coordinate the proposed chain of settlements.

In early 1912 Dr. Shearer persuaded the veteran founder of social settlements, Sara Libby Carson, to leave the neighbourhood work she was then doing in New York and to come back to Canada to supervise the launching of the Presbyterian chain, which she did with her customary vigour. By June, St. Christopher House opened in the Kensington Market area of Toronto. It became not only a local neighbourhood centre but the mother house for the entire Presbyterian chain. Carson made this her headquarters between trips to Montreal, Winnipeg and Vancouver. Here she trained settlement workers to staff succeeding settlements across Canada.

Her activities in those first years were described by Mary Jennison in her "Study of the Canadian Settlement Movement:" "Miss Carson was here, there and everywhere, talking, planning and supervising, injecting a thoroughness and discipline into the work of every centre, persuading interested citizens to take responsibility for buying or renting a house, providing equipment and, as board members, keeping general supervision over the programme."

The general plan for the operation of the Presbyterian chain was for the board of social service and evangelism to establish and oversee the work, for the financing of staff and current operations to come through the board of home missions, and for a group of people to be found in each city who would provide the building and equipment. Carson acted as agent for the board, but because of her recognized expertise in social settlement work she had a high degree of authority to initiate and develop the organization and program of the new settlements. Besides St. Christopher House, the other five settlements in the Presbyterian chain were also located in large urban centres. Chalmers House opened in Montreal in October 1912 and closed soon after Church Union in 1925, apparently starved for financial support. Robertson Memorial House in Winnipeg was organized by Carson in 1913. It was based on a joint institution in existence known as Robertson Church and Burrows Avenue Mission, and Rev. J.R. Mutchmor was put in charge in 1919. She started St. Columba House, Point St. Charles, Montreal in 1917 and put two of her trainees in charge, but after Church Union was established it slipped into the category of an institutional church. Vancouver Community House had a three-year gestation period following a visit to Vancouver by Carson and Ethel Dodds in 1915; it was opened in 1918 as Carson was returning to the United States. In its later years it became an institutional church and closed its doors in the 1930s. The last of the chain was Neighbourhood House, opened in Hamilton in 1922 four years after Carson had left Canada. Encroaching business development and financial problems forced Neighbourhood House to close just before World War II.

The pattern of community work Carson established at Christodora House, New York and at Toronto's Evangelia Settlement spread to the settlements established by the Presbyterian church in Canada. The work of all the settlements centred around neighbourhood services. Each was directed, at least in the early days, by staff trained by Miss Carson in the principles and practice of social settlement work, either at St. Christopher House or at the Department of Social Service at the University of Toronto where Carson gave the course on community work. Stress was put on the residence of staff workers in the settlement houses and on personal contacts with neighbouring families. To meet the needs of people of all ages and backgrounds, programs were developed that included clubs, classes, nursery schools or kindergartens, clinics, gymnasia, recreational activities, social gatherings and personal counselling.

PRESBYTERIAN SETTLEMENTS NOT SPEARHEADS OF REFORM

Although the founding of the Presbyterian settlements had been inspired by the social gospel movement in the church, they were never designed to become spearheads of reform. They were provided by the church as a practical social service in urban slum areas. The provision of such services was in itself a kind of social reform, but the broader aspects of reform — dealing with working conditions, sweatshops, unemployment, poverty and relief, housing and sanitation — were seen as matters for the church itself to tackle, either through the board of moral and social reform and its successors or through interdenominational councils and campaigns. Consequently, St. Christopher House and the other five settlements in the chain concentrated their energies in those early years on neighbourhood services, with little or no involvement in civic action or reform movements such as had distinguished the early social settlements in Great Britain and the United States.

All the Presbyterian social settlements aimed at providing their neighbourhood services in a Christian atmosphere; all offered some kind of religious service, but the type of religious programs provided and the degree of active evangelism differed from settlement to settlement. During this period the Presbyterian church had been placing increasing emphasis on the religious aspects of its social service work. Placing the settlements and the missions under the direct organizational umbrella of the board of home missions and social service in 1915, tended to enhance the religious side of settlement work to such an extent that, in 1918, the management of each house was turned over to the local presbytery. The consequence of this decision was that it led to pressure to change them from settlements to institutional churches.

Over a period of time, enthusiasm and commitment flagged, particulary in hard economic circumstances. Three of the settlement houses eventually succumbed to financial pressures (Chalmers House, Vancouver Community House and Neighbourhood House, Hamilton), while two carried on as institutional churches (Robertson Institute and St. Columba House). Only St. Christopher House, with a strong and flexible board, survived as a true social settlement, expanding and adapting its program to meet the changing needs of its neighbourhood for over three-quarters of a century.

CHAPTER NINE

ST. CHRISTOPHER HOUSE: EVANGELICAL SOCIAL SETTLEMENT

The Presbyterian church in Canada brought the full force of its social gospel to bear on the founding and operation of St. Christopher House as the pilot project and training centre for its national chain of evangelical social settlements. Dr. John G. Shearer, the dynamic general secretary of the board of social service and evangelism, gave his personal attention to the initial organization of the house with the backing of the board of home missions.

By 1920 St. Christopher House had the best plant of any settlement house in the city, thanks to the remarkable personal contribution of James W. Woods (later Sir James). Before a year had passed Sir James engaged the best builder he could find, a man named Walter Davidson, and in only three months the settlement had a new assembly room and an apartment for the caretaker; a library and a men's club were built, and the space between the houses was used for newly constructed bedrooms, a clubroom, and some living quarters; and finally, the playground was enlarged by taking in a laneway. Completion of the project was celebrated at Christmas parties in the auditorium. Two years later Sir James and Lady Woods provided a gymnasium in memory of their son, John R. Woods, who had been killed during World War I. No sooner was that finished than the houses on the east side were rebuilt for the men's and older boy's clubs and the clinics. Woods estimated that his total contribution to the St. Christopher plant was $150,000. The initial strength of St. Christopher House also lay in the expert and dedicated devotion of Sara Libby Carson.

The Goals of St. Christopher House

While the Presbyterian Church had launched its chain of settlements with the avowed purpose "to reclaim the slum and its dwellers for Christ and good citizenship," Carson and Helen Hart, the house's first head worker, shaped the aspirations of St. Christopher House during its first years. They subtly changed the focus of St. Christopher House and subsequent settlements in the chain to two very simple and human goals: friendship and sharing. This may have been the strongest force of all in making St. Christopher House immediately appealing to an immigrant neighbourhood and in forging an enduring link between the needs of the neighbourhood and the ideals of the church-going, well-educated, middle-class people who sought to serve those needs.

At the Social Service Congress of Canada in Ottawa in 1914, Carson gave an address on social settlements. In her effort to convey the very essence of settlement work to her large audience, she defined it as "just being friends to our neighbours."

The Founding

As soon as the 1911 General Assembly of the Presbyterian church gave the green light to the board of social service and evangelism to establish evangelical social settlements in major cities across Canada, Dr. Shearer, its general secretary, began to put the plan into effect. His first step was to persuade Carson to return to Canada from New York to organize and supervise the Presbyterian settlements, beginning with St. Christopher House in Toronto. Carson arrived in Toronto in March 1912 and St. Christopher House opened its doors to its neighbours three months later.

Selecting a site was the next decision to be made. By the spring of 1912 there was not much choice left. Evangelia was well-established as the dominant settlement in the Anglo-Celtic east end of the city, supplemented by Mildmay Institute, the Anglican deaconesses' training school that had added many settlement-type services around 1907 at Pembroke and Gerrard. In the west central area of downtown Toronto, where most of the non-English-speaking immigrants resided, the University Settlement was established in the industrial-residential area near Spadina and Adelaide in 1910, and in 1911 Central Neighbourhood House opened in the Ward. In January 1912 Memorial Institute was established by the Baptists in the region west of Bathurst and south of Queen, a poor area chiefly occupied by British and Polish immigrants. The major remaining immigrant districts in downtown Toronto were the Kensington Market and Alexandra Park areas between Spadina and Bathurst, Queen and College.

James Woods, a Presbyterian businessman with philanthropic interests, undertook the financing of the new settlement with the purchase of a large old house at 67 Bellevue Place (later Wales Avenue) at the foot of Leonard Avenue for $17,000. From the front door, "over one hundred children could be seen playing" in the roadways. This seemed the ideal location for the new settlement. Woods' interests were ideally suited to the new project. As head of Gordon MacKay Co. Ltd., a large wholesale dry goods firm, Woods had made numerous buying trips to Great Britain in the late nineteenth and early twentieth centuries. During these trips he became interested in social movements and spent much of his spare time visiting philanthropic institutions. Woods renovated the original house for an additional cost of over $6,000, and completely equipped the house with furnishings and supplies needed to transform it into a functional settlement. In the Woods' papers is a file of early invoices covering these transactions. The invoice from the T. Eaton Co. Ltd., addressed to Carson, St. Christopher House, but marked "to be collected from Mr. Woods, Gordon MacKay Co.," included large equipment such as beds and bureaux, tables and chairs, down to such minutiae as a box of fly paper and two mouse traps. The personal interest James Woods took in St. Christopher House over the next 29 years was vital to its development.

While Woods was readying the house at 67 Bellevue Place for occupancy as a social settlement, Carson was spending much of her time walking around the neighbourhood talking to the children. She firmly believed that children would spread the word about the new facility better than any printed publicity. When St. Christopher opened its doors in June, children of many nationalities immediately swarmed across the threshold.

During the spring of 1912 Carson engaged Helen L. Hart, B.A., as the first head resident; she was the 21-year-old daughter of Dr. Hastings Hart, a noted penologist and one of the leading pioneers in social service in the United States. Sara Libby Carson was a personal friend of the Hart family and had known Helen since she was a child. In Helen's last two summers at college she had worked as a counsellor at Friendship Farm near Bethel, Connecticut, where Carson ran a summer camp for the New York settlement she then headed. Carson was well aware of the skilful way Hart handled the recreational activities of both boys and girls in such informal surroundings. With the opening of St. Christopher House, Carson and Hart had quickly established effective community service work. By 1913 Hart was able to inform friends at Mount Holyoke College, her Alma Mater, of the impending expansion of St. Christopher House and her busy daily schedule working with clubs, giving Sunday sermons and organizing dramatics for the girls.

THE ATMOSPHERE AT ST. CHRISTOPHER HOUSE

The staff of St. Chris attempted to create an atmosphere of warmth and beauty modelled on a cultured, middle-class Toronto home. There were filmy, bright-coloured curtains at the windows and the walls were painted in pastel shades. Bowls of flowers decorated the tables in summer and fires glowed in the grates in winter. There were framed pictures on the walls, and comfortable chairs and cushions gave a cozy touch to the clubrooms. Every effort was geared to creating an inviting atmosphere.

In its early years St. Christopher House was very much a women's settlement, and the congenial atmosphere resembled a women's college dormitory. In residence at the original house were Hart, the head resident, Carson (when she was not out of town on speaking or organizing trips) and two or three workers-in-training. The only man who lived in the building was the caretaker; he later married the cook. As more buildings were added, increasing the number of bedrooms, more and more student trainees from Toronto University's Department of Social Service were included among the residents, and the staff was also enlarged.

The leadership of Carson and Hart was largely responsible for the women's college atmosphere at St. Christopher House. Both were the product of leading women's colleges in the eastern United States. These institutions supported the relatively new concept of women being able to manage large undertakings themselves and, with their well-trained minds, analyze situations and to conceptualize goals. Jean Whitelaw, one of the workers in the 1920s, said in an interview in 1984, "that was the happiest time in my life." Barbara Finlayson, a worker in the same period, said in her *Recollections* for the fiftieth anniversary of the settlement: "Most of all it was the people of St. Christopher House who made it what it was — its neighbours, board members and staff."

The attitude of the workers was invariably warm and welcoming, never patronizing. When Carson was asked to speak about settlement work, she was always accompanied by a child from the house, whom she would place "in the front seat to be a constant reminder that nothing must be said that could offend any settlement member." A major concern of the staff in those early days was the logistics of space management and crowd control. Even though the house, with 12 rooms, was relatively large, Carson and Hart were well aware that they could only achieve their remarkable results by using the available space over and over in a single day. A particularly helpful group of volunteers was known as the floaters. They performed a variety of useful duties, such as moving kindergarten chairs out and larger chairs in when an older age club replaced the play school; they also saw that gavels and minute books, scissors and thread, kitchen and cooking utensils, games and craft materials were set out for the various clubs and classes, and that one group was ushered out of a room before the next was allowed in.

At first Hart took all the groups herself. The play school for children too young for the big school started off the agenda from 8:45 A.M. to noon every school day. From noon to 1:00 P.M., Hart attended to office work, and from 2:00 P.M. to 3:30 P.M. to calls and errands. After school came the junior children's clubs, a different one every day, with their business meetings conducted according to parliamentary procedure, followed by folk games, discussion and athletics "according to which club we are." At 7:30 P.M., clubs and classes for the older boys and girls began, mostly athletics for boys and dramatics for the girls. Then, on Sunday, came religious programs, chiefly song services and Bible stories.

NEIGHBOURHOOD SERVICES

The doorbell at St. Christopher House rang day and night with dozens of anxious appeals for help. Of course not all were matters of life or death, but many concerned very troubling problems — locating a missing daughter or going to the juvenile court to speak for a youthful offender. Some problems were relatively minor — a cut finger, explaining the contents of a bureaucratic letter, the use of the telephone in a neighbourhood that boasted few telephones.

"My baby would have died if it hadn't been for the woman at the settlement house," cried an appreciative, rather rough-hewn woman; she had never been to St. Christopher House until a major crisis drove her in desperation to its door. Her husband had taken ill, her baby was sick, and she was unable to take care of them. The women at the house did take care of the baby and Nurse Young went to visit the sick husband while others prepared food for the family. Carson gave this account in her first annual report to the board of social service and evangelism, and in turn the board included it in reporting to its own annual meeting in 1913. In this way, the urgent needs the new Presbyterian settlements were meeting became known to clergy and laymen alike across the breadth of Canada.

The personal development that took place at the settlement spilled over to the school where teachers could identify pupils who participated in the settlement programs by their better performance. Word about the good work quickly spread in the neighbourhood. Because of its success in its first year the settlement had to face the need for expansion; the house's success in Sunday gospel service ensured the continuing support of the Presbyterian church. St. Christopher House engaged its own nurse who ran a milk station to distribute milk products prepared at Sick Children's Hospital. The station was used by as many as 30 neighbourhood women who picked up their pasteurized milk and baby formulas at the settlement. The following year Nurse Patterson, one of the new public health nurses installed by Dr. Charles Hastings in the city's department of health, was sent to St. Christopher; among her many accomplishments was the establishment of a flourishing well-baby clinic. Often the nurse, sometimes accompanied by a settlement worker, would visit the homes of babies and children brought to the clinics.

SETTLEMENT ACTIVITIES

A rich array of clubs was formed once the settlement opened, and the number of clubs, classes and play periods rapidly expanded to 28. Within six months, the daily attendance at St. Christopher House was more than 150 and climbing steadily. Age-related clubs soon came; the youngest joined Happy Hearts, followed in order of seniority by the Marigolds, the Merrie Maidens (girls 10-11 years), the Queen Marys, and finally the Campfire Girls. By 1921 a newspaper story reported total attendance for February of 6369 individuals counting all the various events, daytime and evening. "No Charity in It" reported the Toronto Star (19 April 1919), for there were membership fees: one cent a week for babies and five cents for older children; mothers paid ten cents a month. These were small fees, but enough, the settlement believed, to encourage a feeling of independence.

A play school, which offered activities five mornings a week for two to five year olds, was started by Mina Barnes who began working there in 1926. She eventually brought the play school up to university nursery school standards, a remarkable achievement in service. For neighbourhood mothers who were at home with an infant and doing the daily wash for a large family, it gave welcome relief. The play school, rather like head start programs in much later years, provided activities for 30 or 40 children with milk or juice between the games and singing. The mothers knew their children were safe and, in addition, the school supervised the children's development in a way that was impossible for mothers during the busy mornings at home. Sundays were also important for the area's children. Five story-telling hours on Sunday attracted up to 150 children. The settlement also ran a library stocked with donated books. The library was taken over in 1921 by the boys and girls division of the Toronto Public Library, which provided a librarian at the settlement. The full-fledged children's branch continued in operation at the settlement for nearly 40 years.

The mothers who first met at the well-baby clinic came together in 1914 and formed the White Shield Club, with the membership drawn largely from British immigrants. In a few months, with more than 100 members, the club had to be divided into two groups. Then the young girls at the settlement decided to form a volunteer cradle club to babysit for the mothers.

In early 1921 the board had an earnest discussion about whether modern dancing should be allowed. The settlement found that its Saturday evening square and folk dancing class for older boys and girls was experiencing falling attendance, while there were increasing requests for modern dancing. Within a few weeks, boys and girls separately were having "lessons in desirable positions and customs connected with dancing." The boys and girls eager to maintain decorum when dancing the waltz, two-step and three-step, appointed conduct committees to take care of the slightest misdemeanour.

With the settlement intentionally located in a high delinquency area, boys' work was a high priority. The first boys' worker, J.M. Wyatt, arrived in 1914. Although he left the next year to become the first juvenile court probation officer in Toronto, this was regarded as an opportunity to establish a continuing connection with a key resource for the neighbourhood. Wyatt maintained that the area, once the worst in the city for organized criminal gangs of boys, now could proudly boast of their disappearance — no doubt thanks in part to the settlement's wholesome boys' program.

The work soon expanded beyond the neighbourhood when the Presbyterian church purchased property on Lake Simcoe. Called St. Christopher Farm, the summer camp offered respite to hundreds of weary mothers and children each summer. Reached by the Canadian Pacific Railroad from a country stop appropriately named the St. Christopher Station, excited groups of summer campers would arrive with their luggage at two-week intervals throughout the summer.

Extreme urgency was expressed in developing programs for immigrants since the board of social service and evangelism took it on itself to contribute to the nationalization and Christianization of people from abroad. Teaching materials prepared by the International YMCA and adapted for Canadian readers were used, and a component about Canadian citizenship was intentionally included. The board hoped that these services would lead immigrants to accept the gospel of salvation.

The University Connection

St. Christopher House, carrying on its wider role as the training centre for settlement workers throughout Canada, forged a link with the Department of Social Service at the University of Toronto, which first opened for the academic year 1914–1915. In its founding year the department had four of its thirteen full-time students living in the settlement while doing their field placements. Ethel Dodds, who went on to become the head worker at St. Christopher House, was among the group. St. Christopher House continues as a field placement for the Faculty of Social Work to the present day. Another connection in those early years involved the household science staff at the University who made housekeeping and cooking classes available in the neighbourhood.

STAFF LEADERSHIP

At the end of 1917 Ethel Dodds, who had spent a year as head resident at the University Settlement, replaced Helen Hart. Ethel was the daughter of parents who were missionaries in Saskatchewan and northern Ontario. She became head resident at an important formative period of the settlement. She was outstanding in the field, both as a staff member and in subsequent years as a board and committee volunteer in social welfare councils locally, provincially, and nationally. Her contact with the settlement movement was lifelong.

Marion Yeigh succeeded Dodds as head worker. Born into a Congregationalist family in Brantford in 1882, she came by her interest in community service rather naturally, having a father employed by the YMCA in Toronto. For many years he managed the Y camp at Geneva Park on Lake Couchiching, where Marion gained considerable camp experience. She recalled that she lived for many of her early years as a semi-invalid because of a heart condition, until she became "sick and tired of being a half-invalid." In 1918, when she was 36 years of age, she was taken by a family friend to work as a volunteer at St. Christopher House. Following completion of the one-year social work program, which included field work at St. Christopher House, she succeeded Ethel Dodds as head worker in 1921 and remained in that position for five years.

KEEPING THE SETTLEMENT AFLOAT

In her last year at St. Christopher House, Ethel Dodds had eight staff members and six students running the programs. The budget provided by the church amounted to $14,915 and, in addition, there were substantial donations from board members. This was the financial highpoint for some years. When Marion Yeigh was head worker, there were severe budgetary cutbacks with the recession in 1922 and 1923: the budget was first cut to $13,556 and the loss of one worker in 1922, and then to $12,534 and the loss of a second worker in 1923. With the budget slashed again in 1924, down to $10,535, only five full-time workers and one part-time worker could be paid. The situation slowly turned around, however, so that by 1926 the church budget was increased to $12,865, and donations amounted to $3,000. Yeigh was followed by Gwen Goldie, and then in the summer of 1928 Lally Fleming was appointed head worker — a position which she held for five years. The effect of the 1929 stockmarket crash on the budget was a replay of the situation in the early 1920s. As the need increased with the deepening depression, the staff was reduced and the budget was steadily slashed with serious consequences for the program.

Chapter Ten

University Settlement

The impetus for a university-sponsored settlement originated with the students in the University of Toronto Young Men's Christian Association who were spurred on by the social gospel to a greater involvement in social service work in the city's poor neighbourhoods. The aims of the University Settlement, as set out in its first leaflet in 1911, were "to bring the university students into direct contact with those living amidst the unfortunate conditions of our modern cities and thus broaden the one and elevate the other" and also to carry out "all sorts of social work and investigation."

For several years the city mission committee of the University YMCA had been sending a corps of students to assist in the work of the Toronto Mission Union on Hayter Street in the Ward where they organized boys' clubs, conducted gospel meetings and provided medical help in the dispensary. The students' first impulse was to carry on "the note of active evangelism" that had always been maintained under the University YMCA. But by the time the settlement was actively launched in the summer of 1910, it had become a university settlement, rather than a YMCA settlement, with its own independent board. This put the University Settlement on a secular basis from the outset; it was the only way to include the students, staff and graduates from all the university's colleges, special schools and faculties, whether religious or secular. Its secular nature also made it easier for the settlement to work with the large number of Jewish, Roman Catholic and Greek Orthodox immigrants in its neighbourhood.

That final decision to launch University Settlement was made at the University YMCA annual meeting in May 1910. On June 21 a meeting was held in the office of University of Toronto President Robert Falconer when an independent committee, composed of university faculty members, representatives of the University YMCA and several business and professional men was chosen as a temporary board of directors. The committee had authority "to expend on the security of the University YMCA, $3,500 in the inauguration and conducting of the work for a year." Members of this organizing committee included Falconer (chairman); Prof. R.W. Angus, Department of Mechanical Engineering; Prof. E.F. Burton, Department of Physics; Dr. W.B. Hendry, Faculty of Medicine; Prof. G.I.H. Lloyd, Department of Political Economy; Prof. Malcolm W. Wallace, Department of English, University College; G.A. Warburton, member of University YMCA executive; J.J. Kelso, Superintendent of Neglected and Dependent Children for Ontario; R.J. Clark of the Toronto Street Railway Company; Harry McGee of the T. Eaton Company; and J.S. McLean of the Harris Abattoir Company (later Canada Packers).

THE NEW SETTLEMENT

On 1 July 1910 the lease for the new University Settlement at 467 Adelaide Street West, west of Spadina, was signed for $50 a month. The building, a store with living quarters upstairs, was situated on a busy thoroughfare in a manufacturing and residential area where about 70 per cent of the population were non-English-speaking immigrants. Over that summer the building was remodelled — the ground floor was divided into four fairly large rooms to accommodate a free dispensary, a games and reading room, and space for boys' athletic clubs and various classes. Early in the summer two students had been chosen to live in the settlement during the coming year: W.A. Scott, a medical student, and E. Murray Thomson of University College. Along with J.M. Shaver they spent part of the summer getting the settlement ready for its opening in September and studying conditions in the neighbourhood. By the time University Settlement opened in the autumn there were four residents. Shaver had married in June and brought his bride with him to the settlement, where she kept house for the three men, receiving room and board and a monthly stipend of $25 per month.

When a constitution was drafted in the autumn a formal board of directors was named to provide overall direction. A single students' work committee including the resident secretary, the secretary of the University of Toronto YMCA, the resident students of the settlement, the leader of any settlement club or class, and a representative from each of eleven student organizations was established to supervise the program.

In its first year University Settlement was essentially a man's settlement, run by men for men and boys. The program included recreational and educational work with some 90 boys, a free dispensary every weekday evening at which, it was reported, 100 different patients received over 250 treatments, English and citizenship classes for 82 foreigners, and a library of over 400 books. Activities began by organizing the older boys into the Young Varsity Athletic Club, which entered a team in the junior rugby football league of the city. The younger boys were enrolled in gymnasium classes, "which afforded an excellent opportunity for coming into close touch with the real boy life of our city." Shaver also stressed the important influence that a "leader in good clean sport," like campus rugbystar Thomson, had on the "moral upbuilding of these boys' lives." These were the days when the University YMCA took a good deal of pride in its members' "muscular Christianity."

In the winter, the city flooded a rink in St. Andrew's playground for neighbourhood use and placed its supervision in charge of the settlement. Hockey and skating became part of the settlement's athletic program. There was also a games and reading room in the settlement itself where 50 or 60 boys would gather in the evenings.

The second resident student, W.A. Scott, was in charge of the preparations for opening the free dispensary where a doctor, assisted by a medical student, was on duty for an hour each evening; this was later increased to two hours. The work of the dispensary was supervised by Dr. W.B. Hendry of the Faculty of Medicine. Some of the other well-known doctors who shared in the work at the settlement in the early years were Dr. Ramsey Graham, Dr. Cooper Cole, Dr. Kendal Bates and Dr. Gordon Bates. A dental chair was added to the equipment of the dispensary and a final-year dental student was in attendance each evening.

The educational program at the settlement included tutoring by university students, a carpentry class, and English classes. Boys flocked to the library to obtain books from the student librarian on duty every night. The major donors were Dr. George Locke, head of the Toronto Public Library; Dr. Charles Hastings, Toronto's medical officer of health; and the boys of the University of Toronto Schools (U.T.S.) who contributed "a most appropriate collection of boys' books."

In the first year of operations, Shaver saw proof of "the latent possibilities of our university life which may be turned to the community's good and, at the same time, prove a source of education to the students themselves." By the spring of 1911, however, Shaver was sent by the Methodist church to Fort William to head Wesley Institute, a mission for immigrants in the coal docks area, where he conducted work along settlement lines. Shaver's later years were spent as head of All People's Mission in Winnipeg.

A MAN FROM HULL HOUSE

The first experimental year of University Settlement had been an undoubted success, but it was obvious that the work needed to be expanded and working relations with other social agencies developed. With Shaver's departure the settlement faced a critical period, which was made more urgent by the advent of a second settlement in the immigrant areas of downtown Toronto. Central Neighbourhood House had been founded by a group of concerned citizens meeting at city hall on 1 May 1911 to provide a secular neighbourhood centre for the mixed population of the Ward with trained social workers to launch its program. If University Settlement wished to retain its initial leadership role, it needed to clarify its secular stand and to secure a trained social worker as head. Since there was no school for the training of social workers in Canada, the University Settlement board turned to the United States. The board chose Milton B. Hunt, then working at Hull House, as University Settlement's second resident director. Hunt possessed a Master's degree in economic and social science from Brown University, a year of experience at the Chicago School of Civics and Philanthropy, and two years' experience in Chicago settlements, one year being at Hull House.

To establish its secular nature more clearly, in its second year the University Settlement separated its work more definitely from the University YMCA. The forthcoming campaign for funds was to be separate from the University YMCA, although the Y would continue to give the settlement the use of its office and staff. The campaign would now be directed to the female as well as the male students and graduates of the university.

With Hunt at the helm, the Hull House model was increasingly reflected in the University Settlement's aims, programs and relationships with the community. "The Settlement draws no distinction as to creed, race, colour" became a basic credo. To the settlement's original goals was added a new aim: "To establish in the community a permanent socializing agency for bringing about civic betterment."

Work with women and girls and health services for babies were the main new features of the settlement's second year. Two sewing classes were started, one for young working women and one for school-age girls who were taught by students from the school of household science. A woman's club was organized among working mothers who left their babies and young children at the West End Crèche during the day.

Earlier in the year a group of faculty wives from the university organized a woman's committee. Their aim was to help the settlement in any way they could, but especially in the work with women and girls. Their first project was organizing the woman's club, which met one evening a week at the settlement where talks, sewing and social events provided a pleasant diversion from the monotonous existence many of the women led.

The services for babies began in the spring of 1912 when the settlement decided to make some attempt to reduce the district's high infant mortality rate due to impure foods and to ignorance regarding the proper care of infants. As a first step the settlement opened a milk depot where mothers could obtain pure certified milk at a reasonable cost. A trained nurse was engaged to supervise the distribution of the milk and to visit the homes. The next step was to open a weekly clinic where mothers could bring both well and sick babies. The settlement initially provided its own nurse, but the work was such a success that by the winter of 1912 the department of public health was providing, from its child welfare division, a nurse to assist in the clinic and visit homes. This was the beginning of well-baby clinics, supervised by public health nurses, which were soon established in all the social settlements in the city. Because fresh air was considered an essential factor in the babies' health, especially for those who came from overcrowded and poorly ventilated homes, a babies' rest station opened during the summer in a tent in a neighbouring park..

In the autumn, Mabel Newton, who had had experience in both nursing and social work in England, was engaged as the first paid woman worker at the settlement. She was placed in charge of organizing and supervising the work with women and girls with the assistance of the woman's committee. She was paid an annual salary of $800; she remained with the settlement until 1915.

Work with boys continued to expand so much during Hunt's tenure that it became necessary to employ a boys' worker to supervise the various clubs. The enrolment almost doubled between April 1912 and the following winter. University Settlement and Central Neighbourhood House developed a new method of organizing the boys' work to include training in citizenship as well as sports. A 1913 settlement booklet, *Some Facts — University Settlement* states:

> The whole work is organized as a University Settlement Province of the Toronto Boys' Dominion. The latter is a self-governing boys' club in the downtown district. The settlement boys, as citizens of the Dominion, have privileges in both places. As they are a self-governing boys' club, lessons in

civics, such as the holding of elections, the making of laws, administrative work, procedure in court, etc., are taught. In the settlement a provincial government was formed with the boys serving as members of the cabinet. A novel feature was the appointment of a minister of athletics, who directed the various athletic teams of the settlement.

Other activities included a Boy Scout troop, an electrical class and a summer camp at Lake Simcoe where the boys enjoyed swimming, boating, fishing, games and contests over a two-week period at a nominal cost of $2.50 per week. This was the first of a long line of summer camps in various locations, which proved to be one of the settlement's most popular attractions for about half a century. The English classes for immigrants continued to be popular, but they were almost exclusively patronized by Jewish young people. In 1912 some fifty young Jewish men and women were enrolled in six classes — two for beginners, two for more advanced students and two for those matriculating. The teachers were encouraged to hold classes in their own homes, which made it possible to accommodate more students than in the limited quarters at the settlement.

COOPERATION WITH OTHER COMMUNITY ORGANIZATIONS

Hunt's most important contribution to the development of University Settlement may well have been his emphasis on cooperation with other organizations. The dispensary cooperated with the social work department of the Toronto General Hospital and with the city's department of public health. The latter provided the assistance of tuberculosis nurses in the settlement's weekly tuberculosis clinic, which began in 1911, as well as that of child welfare nurses in the well-baby clinic after the autumn of 1912. The settlement also cooperated with Associated Charities by visiting relief cases in the neighbourhood and with the parks department in playground activities nearby.

Another significant contribution orchestrated by Hunt was the formation of the first case conference in the city at the settlement in September 1911. The conference met twice a month to discuss particular cases involving difficult problems of relief and implemented "a concerted plan of relief." One of the dynamic figures at the early meetings was Eunice Dyke, who had recently been appointed by the medical officer of health, Dr. Charles Hastings, to head the public health nursing staff. A month after the first conference at University Settlement, a second case conference opened at Evangelia Settlement, and in January 1913 a central district conference was organized at the Fred Victor Mission. A fourth case conference opened in east Toronto in 1913. These early case conferences led to the formation of the Neighbourhood Workers' Association (now the Family Service Association) in 1914.

LEADERSHIP

As the search began for a third resident director the board decided to try to find a Canadian who had trained in the United States: a man with dynamic leadership qualities who could make University Settlement a force, not only in its own community, but in the social welfare of the city as a whole. The field soon narrowed down to two Canadians who were then studying in the United States. One was Arthur H. Burnett, former leader of the Victoria College student social survey and founder of Central Neighbourhood House. He was spending the year on scholarship at the New York School of Philanthropy and living at Greenwich House, a cooperative social settlement directed by Mary Kingsbury Simkhovitch, an acknowledged leader in American social work. The other was Norman J. Ware, who was about to receive his Ph.D. in sociology at the University of Chicago. Ware had graduated from McMaster University, then in Toronto, and went on to Chicago for his postgraduate work. He became a fellow in the Department of Sociology but also worked for a year as director of the boys' club at Hull House.

In the final decision Burnett lost to Ware, but in the autumn, when Ware was launching a new epoch at the University Settlement, Burnett was starting equally important work as a special social service assistant at Toronto's department of public health.

Falconer offered Ware the secretaryship of the settlement, "for a year on trial," at a salary of $1,200. In choosing Ware, Falconer had to weigh his obvious qualifications for the job against his equally obvious predilection for academic work in the social service field. In preliminary correspondence with Falconer and Kelso, Ware suggested that he might give "a course or so in the university in connection with the work of the settlement."

Kelso's reply was sympathetic, as this was something Kelso himself had long advocated and hoped to see established. Kelso said that he had talked to Professor Lloyd who thought it could be managed to have a few lectures in connection with one of the other departments. Lloyd replied, "once the work is started it would be sure to grow and I will certainly do my best to have the matter arranged as you suggest."

Falconer was only mildly encouraging. In a letter to Ware on 25 June he set forth quite clearly the priorities for the settlement position:

We do not wish to appoint anyone as secretary whose interests
are mainly academic and theoretical ... this settlement is not a
part of the teaching side of the university nor is the university
officially responsible for it, though the man who proves his
worth in the organization and direction of social work would,
I believe, in the future find some moderate scope in academic
work proper.

A NEW EPOCH

When Ware took up his post at the University Settlement in September
1913, he envisioned the settlement as entering a "new epoch" in its history.
In *The Futurist Number, University Settlement Review* that autumn, Ware set
forth the new goals as follows:

The function is threefold: to organize the social workers of the
city around the University Settlement as a centre; to carry on
the more scientific work of investigation and study of social
problems; and to experiment and initiate in new lines of
settlement activity. We admit that this is some job, and we
don't expect to get it finished tomorrow, but that is our plan of
action.

Ware stressed that the settlement was entirely undenominational and
rarely gave material assistance. "The University Settlement aims to help
these people to help themselves," he declared.

One of the innovations Ware introduced immediately was a greater
emphasis on clubs rather than classes for people over the age of 18. The one
exception was the English classes for newcomers. The reason for the change
was Ware's perception of the club as "a training in democracy." Ware wrote
in *The Futurist Number*: "The club may do exactly what the class does, but it
does more. It is a self-officered, self-governing and self-supporting body."
By way of elaboration, he expounded what was a rather new concept of
leadership: "It has a leader from the outside, but the leader is not the
autocrat of the classroom, but a very human leader who allows himself or
herself to be led as much as to lead."

The new clubs included the glee club, the dramatic club and a social club
for young people of both sexes, which actually included dancing in its
program. These were followed by two men's clubs, Pioneer and Acme, and a
social-political club for young people. The earlier boys' sports clubs and the
woman's club, together with the English classes and sewing classes, continued.

THE HOUSE ON PETER STREET

University Settlement's move to a large, semi-detached, three-storey house at 95 Peter Street, on the southeast corner of Peter and Adelaide streets, did indeed usher in a new era in the scope of the work the settlement undertook. Peter Street had once been in a good residential district and boasted a number of large houses that had originally been the homes of well-to-do families; now most were dilapidated and overcrowded. When renovated and fitted up for settlement purposes, the house at 95 Peter Street provided three times the space than the settlement's former cramped quarters at 467 Adelaide Street West. There were four large rooms, used for a gymnasium, an auditorium, the dispensary and clinics, while eight smaller rooms accommodated clubs and classes. On the upper floors was a residence for social workers with eight bedrooms, dining-room, kitchen and library.

As University Settlement's new home was just a few blocks east of the settlement's original site, the community served was virtually the same: a number of factories, printing and publishing establishments, and boarding houses along the main streets with much overcrowding in the homes in the residential areas and many rear houses along the lanes and alleyways. The southern part of the district was largely populated by English, Irish and Scottish immigrants; the northern section by Jews who were beginning to move north, gradually being replaced by Finnish, Polish, Russian and other European immigrants. With its enlarged facilities the settlement found it possible to open a lunch and rest room for girls working in the vicinity. Coffee and tea were provided at low cost, and the girls who brought their own lunches with them were glad to have a pleasant place to eat and relax.

The district case conference continued to hold its weekly meetings at University Settlement; several other outside organizations, such as the Social Democratic Society and the Junior Suffrage Society, were also allowed to hold their meetings there. In 1914 the city's public health nurses, who were in charge of the downtown district between Sherbourne and Shaw streets, made their headquarters in the settlement. This move reinforced the settlement's image as a centre for social work since the city nurses were serving all the downtown settlements and many other agencies, not just University Settlement. What had been a pilot project both for the settlement and the city nurses two years earlier was now a citywide system organized by districts.

THE LARGER SOCIAL ISSUES

One of Ware's main concerns was the plight of the working man in an industrial society; this carried over into a concern about labour problems.

Scarcely had he arrived at the settlement, when he began to take an advocacy role for workers who felt themselves unjustly treated. An exchange of letters with Albert Matthews, head of a nearby packing plant, attests to this. Ware wrote Matthews informing him that an employee of his plant, who had been injured after working there only two weeks, found himself without any money after having an operation. Matthews wrote back promptly, saying that he had no personal knowledge of the case but would investigate immediately, "we would be the last to cause any of our people to suffer through lack of thoughtfulness on our part." He said they had insurance to cover such an incident and asked Ware to have the man call at his office.

In order to launch the investigative work of University Settlement, Ware carried out a study during the autumn and winter months on the commercial employment agencies of Toronto to find out "just how successful and unsuccessful [they] are." In conjunction with this study Ware planned to run a small employment agency at the settlement as a model, but available records suggest that this did not get beyond a few personal placements before other events made a labour bureau at the settlement unnecessary.

In the winter of 1914 the Neighbourhood Workers' Association (NWA) was born as a central, coordinating body for social services in the city. The four district case conferences, which had already been formed, called a mass meeting in city hall on 22 January 1914, at which a committee was appointed to draw up a constitution that was adopted at a second mass meeting in February. The constitution provided for the division of the city into nine districts and for a central council composed of representatives of the district associations and citywide organizations.

Dr. Ware was active in organizing the fledgling NWA, serving on the constitution committee and later on the central council. Commissioner E.W. Boyd, first judge of the juvenile court, became the first president, and Arthur Burnett became the first secretary. While the central council of NWA coordinated the activities and methods of the district associations, which were really "clearing houses for the relief being given by various institutions," it also provided a channel for united action on problems related to poverty.

By the summer the central council had turned its attention to "the present acute employment situation," and in August presented a list of urgent recommendations to the city of Toronto's board of control through the social service commission. The recommendations included a call for better distribution of outdoor relief during the winter months, a variety of public works to be undertaken to provide employment, and the immediate opening of a civic labour bureau by the city of Toronto.

By the spring of 1914 Ware was being drawn more and more into activities outside of the settlement. Not only was he involved in the launching of the NWA but also in the preparations for the forthcoming meeting of the Canadian Conference on Charities and Corrections, and in planning the new department of social service to open in the fall.

The documentation for these latter developments is scanty — just two letters in working papers on the history of Canadian settlements' in the Baldwin Room of the Metropolitan Toronto Library. The first is a letter to Ware from Jane Addams, dated 8 May 1914, declining his invitation to address the Canadian Conference of Charities and Corrections in September. The second letter was from E.A. Bott, secretary of the committee of university extension, dated 2 April 1914, informing him that he was a member of the committee to consider the steps necessary in establishing courses for the training of social workers, and that the committee was to meet on 4 April at University Settlement.

When the department of social service opened at the university that autumn, Dr. Norman Ware was on its teaching staff, fulfilling his dream of combining academic work with his settlement responsibilities. Professors from the social science departments of the university lectured in such basic subjects as social economics, social psychology, and social ethics; special lecturers from the social work field, most of them with experience in the settlements, were brought in to provide the more applied courses. Ware gave the courses on the urban community, which dealt with industrial, social and administrative elements in the structure of the modern city (this was probably the first Canadian course in urban studies). He also led a discussion on probation, covering the development of the juvenile court, probation systems and movements on behalf of children.

In the spring of 1915 Dr. Ware resigned from his position as head of University Settlement and returned to the United States for an academic career. After his return to the United States he was for many years a professor at the State University in Louisville, Kentucky, where he contributed editorial articles on economic and sociological subjects to the *Louisville Courier*. During his summer vacations he frequently revisited the Toronto settlements, especially University Settlement and Central Neighbourhood House.

The opening year of the new department of social service clearly marked a trend in the new profession of social work in Canada that would last for many years. Social work turned out to be a profession primarily of women. The fledgling department was overwhelmed with women students — of the 293 students registered, 274 were women. Many were nurses and deaconesses taking a few specialized social work courses to help them in their regular professions. All of the 11 students taking the full course leading to a certificate in social service were women — a man would only occasionally take the full course, a practice that would endure for many years.

There were several reasons for the female domination of this new profession: there were a growing number of university-trained women searching for an outlet for their energies; the outbreak of war quickly drew large numbers of young men into the armed services; and there was a prevailing impression that social work was a woman's job, that men could not make a living at it. Kelso, who had worked so long to bring about professional training for social workers, was deeply disappointed, feeling that social service was "undoubtedly a work and career worthy of the finest men in the university." Much as he had encouraged women to get out of the stores and offices and into some form of social work, he still felt that "the key positions should be held by men."

REORGANIZATION OF UNIVERSITY SETTLEMENT

Falconer may have shared Kelso's feelings, but he was a realistic man who now faced a University Settlement suffering from financial, perhaps even organizational weaknesses, and a fledgling university department filled, for the foreseeable future, with women. Falconer turned for help to his friend Dr. Shearer of the Presbyterian board of social service and evangelism. He arranged to borrow Sara Libby Carson for a year on a part-time basis to organize and supervise University Settlement.

In the autumn of 1915 Carson came to University Settlement as a recognized expert on social settlement organizations and management. Besides founding Christodora House in New York and Evangelia Settlement in Toronto, in the past three years she had organized three settlements for the Presbyterian Church — in Toronto, Manitoba and Winnipeg — and all of them were running effectively. Carson had also been teaching settlement work.

With her usual energy and confidence she set about re-organizing University Settlement along the lines of St. Christopher House and her other settlements, as she described "the community welfare plan." The central emphasis of this plan was neighbourhood work. She visited many of the homes in the vicinity of the settlement, getting to know the families personally and seeing the conditions under which they lived. Although all Carson's previous experience had been with settlements in which there was a strong religious element, she accepted the idea that University Settlement must be conducted on secular lines in order to appeal to members of all the various colleges and faculties, "the entire university public."

Carson's major innovation was to make self-governing clubs for people of all ages the central focus of the settlement. Of course there had been self-governing clubs before — the boys' parliament for senior boys and the clubs for those 18 years of age and over. Within a couple of months she had set up a whole new network of self-governing clubs for boys and girls of all ages, for young men and women, and for mothers. Most of the settlement's established services, such as the free dispensary, well-baby clinic, library and English classes for immigrants were retained. Except for the English classes, there were no programs for men at this time. With some 75 per cent of the men connected with settlement families having enlisted for overseas service, the men's clubs seemed to have withered away. Each of the clubs had its own distinctive name: the Jolly Chums, the Merry Maidens, the Young Citizens, the Loyal Young Canadians and the White Shield Club (formed exclusively of English-speaking mothers). Each of the young people's clubs had its own club song, club cheer and club yell. As "schools of citizenship," the clubs all opened with a salute to the flag and conducted their business according to parliamentary procedure. "I wish," Carson said to a *Varsity* report, "that you had been in our Marigold Club to-day ... you should have seen that nine-year-old chairman control the meeting." But, of course, the clubs were not all "business." Carson and her workers always tried to infuse a sense of joy into the lives of those the settlement touched. So the clubs had plenty of activities including games and songs, social activities, folk dances and festive parties for special days. No one had to come to the settlement clubs; they came because they wanted to.

Carson's skills in building an effective staff and training student workers were particularly useful at a time when the management of the settlement was being transferred to women workers. When she arrived she brought with her two graduates of the previous year's course at the department of social service and two graduates of the Sergeant School of Physical Training, affiliated with Harvard University. She also brought into residence three or four students from the current social work course. Professor E.F. Burton wrote enthusiastically in the *University Monthly* that the settlement was now "an up-to-date social service laboratory" — but it was a laboratory to train social workers rather than to seek ways to change the environment.

By March 1916 Carson had sufficiently reorganized and staffed the settlement to be ready to install the first woman head resident Ethel Dodds (later Mrs. G. Cameron Parker), a graduate of the first year's course in social service at the University of Toronto who had been working for several months at Chalmers House in Montreal and had lived in St. Christopher House as a student-in-training.

One of the Sergeant School graduates Carson brought was Anne F. Hodgkins, a vibrant personality who provided leadership for the athletic and playground activities of University Settlement, including those at Ogden School in cooperation with the Toronto Playgrounds Association. In the summers of 1915–1917 she also ran a joint playground project at Orde Street School in which three downtown settlements — St. Christopher House, Central Neighbourhood House and University Settlement — participated. One of the students-in-training from the social service course at the university was Hannah Matheson, who succeeded Dodds at the settlement when the latter left in 1917 to become head worker at St. Christopher House. Miss Matheson, in later years, became director of the division of family welfare for the city of Toronto.

During Dodds's tenure the social service commission, which was the city's welfare and relief agency at the time, had its district office in the settlement building. Mary Shenstone (the late Mrs. Donald T. Fraser), who was in charge of the office, remembered having her lunches with Dodds and the settlement staff. The proximity of the two institutions kept alive University Settlement's earlier image as a centre of social work for the area. When Carson and Dodds finished reorganizing University Settlement in 1917, the general pattern of its program was set for decades to come. This was hardly surprising when two of the key figures, Hannah Matheson and Marjory W. Gregg, were Carson-trained workers.

Although the traditions established were to continue, two major changes in the funding and cooperative arrangements of the settlement occurred. In 1918 the Federation of Community Services (forerunner of the United Way) was formed to centralize and unify voluntary contributions to the city's welfare institutions. As a direct result University Settlement, as one of the first agency members in the federation, began to receive stable funding. Also in 1918, the Toronto Federation of Settlements was created at a meeting held at University Settlement. This development brought two religious and two secular settlements together to exchange ideas at monthly meetings and take joint action when needed.

Several important new activities were introduced by the Carson-trained staff during the early 1920s when the settlement was still on Peter Street. The music school was started in 1921 with just two pupils, and the childrens' lending library became a branch of the Toronto Public Library. The same year saw the opening of the first summer camp on Lake Simcoe near Jackson's Point; in 1924, another camp opened at Copper Beach on the shores of Lake Ontario at Newcastle. The camp on Jackson's Point, accommodated mothers with small children. Older children would have required more supervision than the limited number of summer staff would comfortably allow. Some concessions were made, however, since they took on a group of boy campers from 10 to 16 years of age, and one of girls.

In 1923 Myrtle Pascoe described a culturally mixed group of older boys at camp representing different faiths, all of them acquainted through settlement clubs and none with more luggage than would fit in a Laura Secord chocolate box. She portrayed them helping with the chores and the joys of roast beef dinners, baseball, swimming, boat trips and marshmallow roasts culminating in a two-day hike for which they had to pack their own blankets and food supplies. Another group comprised 47 mothers, children and babies who enjoyed old country songs and games as well as swimming, boat trips and picnics. The rest of the 216 campers that summer were young girls. Private donations and a grant from the Daily Star Fresh Air Fund for food and transportation kept the camp going. Those who attended were expected to pay if they could: $10 for 12 days for a mother with children, $5 for a boy or girl and those who could not pay were fully subsidized.

The second camp situated at Copper Beach was named after an old and beautiful tree that shaded an ancient house that had been built before 1800. The main building housed the dining room, living room and workers' bedrooms; the campers slept in three wooden shacks with colourful names — The Better Ole, The Ritz Hotel and Casa Loma. In 1930 the University Settlement rented Camp Boulderwood on Gull Lake near Gravenhurst, which belonged to the Protestant Orphans Home.

The settlement was beginning to burst at the seams at its location on the corner of Adelaide and Peter streets. An illustrated article pointed out that University Settlement had earned a well-deserved place "in the affections of the community which it serves, in the respect of the social workers of the city, and in the hearts of the students and graduates of the university." It was, the journalist wrote, definitely not a centre for the distribution of charity, but a "community centre of recreation in its widest sense." By this time there were five paid workers in residence, most of them college graduates, a few students and some young women in the employ of civic social organizations who worked as volunteers.

A distinctive feature at University Settlement was the social service committee, which worked with all faculties of the university and recruited student volunteers for the settlement — some to teach English, dramatics and sports and others to work in the clubs and the library. In total about 175 students participated in the 1922–23 program in which about 3000 children and youths passed through the door every month. Some of the clubs had never lost a member in years, and all had waiting lists.

The University YMCA continued to have a pervasive and important influence on the settlement. Sometimes Y men would take settlement boys on hikes to roam the woods in search of new flowers, weeds, leaves, ferns and grasses. Then there would be woodcraft, and after, wieners, rolls and coffee, with singing around the campfire, "echoing far beyond the Humber Valley." Every Thursday night Y representatives conducted group games for teenage boys or organized instruction and entertainment. On Friday afternoons a Y representative would be meeting with nine- to twelve-year-old boys who had their own Wolf Cub Pack. On Saturday mornings a coach often gave pointers on rugby; later in the season three men would coach teams from the three settlements in the inter-settlement league. To bring the week to a close the Y gave nine- to twelve-year-old boys a social evening, with a mixture of boxing, group games, dancing and singing.

THE WEEK OF CHRISTMAS

Christmas celebrations were a memorable experience that became an established tradition for University Settlement and the other settlements in the city. The Christmas week schedule must have been a daunting one for the staff. Grace Campbell described the daily events of Christmas week 1922 in the *University Monthly*.

> On Monday evening a dance for the Young Varsity Club, but only for those over age 17! Boys and girls over age 14 in the Royal Young Canadians and the Polly Annas had their party however. Tuesday evening, Lady Falconer spoke at a party for the Mothers' Club, followed by carolling and, by the smaller children, a now-forgotten cantata, *Red Pepper*. Every mother went home with a basket, each containing a cup and saucer. The youngest came later in the week, with a party for the Happy Hearts and the Marigolds on Wednesday afternoon; from the Christmas Tree a doll for each little girl. The Little Lads and the Jolly Chans came the next day for their party with Santa and gifts. And so it went through the week until the Edith Cavell Club's dinner on Friday evening.

Some five years later, from their new home on Grange Road, new ideas included the boys and girls hanging holly wreaths woven by each settlement family in the front windows, and in each window of the settlement a candle burned as a symbol of good fellowship. The men and boys were invited to a Christmas party at Hart House, a real Christmas treat at this all-male club and athletic facility on the university campus built in memory of Hart Massey.

A MOVE TO THE GRANGE PARK

In 1925, faced with the remarkable increase in attendance at 95 Peter Street, the board of directors put together a hastily conceived plan to take over 93 Peter Street. Very quickly though the two houses on Peter Street were found to be inadequate for the demands being made on the program. More than that, the old district was being invaded by factories and the residents were moving to the north. The board started to search for a more suitable location. Spadina Lodge, a double house, came on the market at the right time at the reasonable price of $15,500. The location was made especially fortuitous with a beautiful park, called the Grange, in front of the house. In the neighbourhood were the Art Gallery of Ontario, the Ontario College of Art, and not far away was the University of Toronto and the Conservatory of Music.

CHAPTER ELEVEN

CENTRAL NEIGHBOURHOOD HOUSE

Like University Settlement the founding of the Central Neighbourhood House was a direct result of the student social surveys of slum conditions in downtown Toronto conducted in the summers of 1909 and 1910. Two of the surveys' participants, Arthur H. Burnett and George P. Bryce, were so struck with the bad conditions they had found that they consulted the veteran social crusader, J.J. Kelso, as to how best they might undertake some social welfare work. Kelso recommended that they start a social settlement in the Ward, the central area officially bounded by Queen Street on the south, College on the north, Yonge on the east and University Avenue on the west. The Ward had the greatest population density in the city, the highest proportion of immigrants and some of the worst slum conditions. Bryce and Burnett began work by starting a Boy Scout troop at the McCaul Street School in the winter of 1911. By spring they were ready to take the initiative and launch a settlement for the central district of downtown Toronto. Kelso helped the efforts of these two enthusiastic young men by lending his personal prestige and chairing the organization meetings and providing secretarial services from his office in the parliament buildings.

The preliminary meeting was held on 13 April 1911 in the opposition lobby of the parliament buildings. A small committee composed of Kelso, Bryce, Burnett, Dr. MacMurchy and G. Frank Beer, a leader in the campaign for better housing and town planning, was appointed to arrange the next meeting at which they would draw up a statement of aims and objects for the proposed settlement. At the formal organization meeting in city hall Kelso read the statement of aims and methods for a neighbourhood house for central Toronto. When suitable quarters were secured the settlement would serve as a democratic meeting place where people of all races, creeds and stages of culture could get together and come to a better understanding of each other; a social centre for the neighbourhood where persons of all ages would have opportunity for development; a headquarters for sane and sympathetic observation of the conditions and needs of life in the nearby overcrowded district, and a clearing house for social information of all kinds; a centre where various methods of social service could be tested and developed; a kind of powerhouse where data properly interpreted and methods sufficiently tested could be used for promoting definite movements of social reform. The meeting passed a resolution heartily endorsing a settlement in central Toronto and appointed a committee to carry out its organization. To emphasize the secular nature of the new settlement, the organization committee included a rabbi, a Catholic priest and a Unitarian minister, as well as laymen from most of the Protestant denominations.

SETTING UP THE SETTLEMENT

The first steps of the organization committee were to choose a name for the new settlement, locate a suitable and affordable site and select a head worker with the peculiar abilities needed for successful work among the immigrants of the Ward. The name Central Neighbourhood House was chosen and during the summer, Kelso, Bryce and Burnett examined house after house in the Ward until 84 Gerrard Street West, at the corner of Laplante Street, was finally selected. It was a narrow, three-storey brick building with nine small rooms and rented for $31.00 a month. The third and the most important choice was that of a head worker, Elizabeth B. Neufeld, a young settlement worker from Baltimore. The choice of this dynamic woman to head the settlement in its first years ensured that Central Neighbourhood House would not only have a well-organized program of typical settlement activities, such as clubs, classes, and clinics, but it would also play a civic activist role unlike anything undertaken by the other early Toronto settlements.

Although born in the United States of Russian parents, she was sent back to Russia for her education and was attending Warsaw University at the time of the riots of 1905 when, according to her own account, "so many students for both sides and all creeds suffered and died in the cause of liberty." After her return to the United States she studied at the New York School of Philanthrophy and had four years' experience in settlement work in Baltimore. She was fluently multi-lingual, speaking Yiddish, Russian,

Polish, German and English, enabling her to communicate easily with the large Jewish population and the small Slavic and German groups in the Ward.

Initially, Neufeld was the only paid worker, and she accepted the position as head worker knowing that her salary was not guaranteed beyond an understanding with the committee that it would be adequate if the funds permitted. For the first few months, her salary was $50.00 a month, but this was later raised to $100.00 a month, retroactive to the time of her appointment. Her colleagues, George Bryce and Arthur Burnett, were the first residents of the house, and they took any odd jobs they could find to keep solvent while working without pay at the settlement in their spare time. Neufeld and several women volunteer workers lived in a women's residence on McCaul Street, largely at their own expense. The work was only made possible by the help of scores of volunteers, many of them university students.

SEEKING FINANCIAL SUPPORT

Soon the chief preoccupation of the organization committee became financial — how to raise money to pay the rent and Elizabeth Neufeld's salary. In a letter to Mrs. H.D. Warren on 29 September 1911, Kelso set forth the problem succinctly: "The chief and practically the only discouragement just now is the lack of money .... At the present time there is not more than twenty-five dollars in sight for running expenses." He also sent a more general letter to a select list of leading citizens asking for their financial support. He wrote in part:

> This is not a mission nor a charity but the planting of a friendly group of trained workers in a district where example and influence may lead to higher civic and national ideals. It is a movement that commends itself to all lovers of humanity, for it emphasizes the spirit of universal brotherhood and goodwill, avoiding religious controversy, racial prejudice and caste distinctions. For its support it must necessarily depend on well-to-do citizens of public spirit.

This campaign for funds was relatively successful. By the end of the first year the list of subscribers included well-to-do individuals, business firms and organizations such as the Toronto Local Council of Women, the Council of Jewish Women, the Social Study Club, the Toronto Suffrage Association and the City of Toronto Parks Department. But the need for larger quarters and more paid staff was also growing.

TACKLING THE WARD

Central Neighbourhood House was strategically located in the northern section of the Ward, a few blocks from the Elizabeth Street playground and the new Hester How School in one direction, and from the Hospital for Sick Children and the new location of the Toronto General Hospital in the other. The house at 84 Gerrard Street West, though its lot was narrow and its rooms small, was a well-built structure erected in the mid nineteenth century by a builder for his own use. The roadway was narrower in 1911 than it is today, and the settlement house had a tiny yard and trees in front of it.

On 18 September 1911, Central Neighbourhood House opened its doors and within six weeks there were some thirty-four educational and recreational activities in operation — a veritable cafeteria of clubs, classes and other programs. There were play hours for the little children two to six years of age; self-governing clubs for boys, girls and young people eight to eighteen years old; English classes for men and women; and a library stocked with some 800 books. Classes for the children and young people included sewing, cooking, arts and crafts, folk-dancing, physical training, geometry and electricity. Athletic clubs were popular with the boys and eventually included rugby, hockey and baseball teams. Later in the year a Province of the Boys' Dominion was organized in the house. A few lessons in piano and violin were offered to gifted children. Central Neighbourhood House's unique contribution to the cultural enjoyment of the entire community was a series of monthly concerts, from October to May, performed by artists from the various Toronto conservatories. A highlight was the first spring festival in May when the final and most successful concert of the year was given and the settlement's first publicly performed play was put on by a girls' dramatic club. A feature of the festival was the distribution of 250 geranium plants to the children and older people by the Toronto Parks Department; these plants were to be brought back in the autumn for judging and awarding of prizes. The regular activities closed down for the summer but sand pits in the small back yard delighted many of the younger children, and picnics to the Island or High Park were arranged with financial help from the Star Fresh Air Fund for about 350 children and 50 mothers. Games and dances were regular features of these outings.

By the beginning of its second year there was a solid core of about 200 immigrant children and young people enrolled in the clubs and classes at Neighbourhood House, and the attendance figures were running at roughly 500 people a week. The tiny space at 84 Gerrard Street West was taxed beyond capacity.

ADAPTING TO JEWISH TRADITIONS

With Jews comprising some 80 per cent of immigrant families in the Ward, it was vital for Central Neighbourhood House to keep in mind at all times their religious beliefs, traditions and taboos. The appointment of a Jewish head worker was the first important step in gaining the confidence of the Jewish community; but the fears of proselytizing aroused by the Christian missions, which were still active in the area, were not easily dispelled. Neufeld, though herself Jewish, had to devote a great deal of thought and effort to reassuring the Jews as to Neighbourhood House's good faith. One of the early decisions of the house was not to have any Christmas celebrations that first year, but instead to arrange a series of parties in late January, which would give the children and young people happy social times without any religious connotations. In the cooking classes only meatless meals were served, so that children of each faith could prepare the same food without embarrassment. For the day outings in the summer, Central Neighbourhood House workers prepared hundreds of salmon sandwiches, which all the children and mothers could eat.

REACHING THE ADULTS

There was never any doubt of the children's attachment to Central Neighbourhood House nor of their deep devotion to Elizabeth Neufeld. But at the end of her first year she deplored the fact that the settlement had only two major programs to appeal to adults: the English classes for men and women and the monthly concerts. Gradually, a few older people began to consult Central Neighbourhood House staff on personal matters; and the house referred some of the needy people to the appropriate charitable agencies for food and coal, and provided some legal aid and medical attention. Some of those who were part of the T. Eaton strike in the winter of 1912 turned to the settlement for advice — "a very hopeful sign," according to Neufeld who wrote, "there seemed to be a feeling that the settlement was vitally interested in the welfare of the working people."

The summer brought new avenues of contact as the staff had more time to visit homes in the neighbourhood and more and more people began to consult them when in trouble. The inclusion of a number of mothers in the summer outings brought further contacts and led to the formation of a small mothers' club, but the immigrant men never took the active role in Central Neighbourhood House's affairs that working men had played in most of the early British and American settlement houses.

EDUCATING FOR CITIZENSHIP

One of the most interesting experiments in education for citizenship carried out at Central Neighbourhood House was the boys' parliament. During the winter of 1912 the boys' work at the house was reorganized as a Province of the Boys' Dominion, a downtown boys club developed by C.J. Atkinson. The settlement's province was headed by the lieutenant-governor, a role assumed by Neufeld. The neighbourhood was divided into constituencies, a parliament elected, a court of justice established and a criminal code enacted. The crimes outlined in the code included creating a disturbance at any meeting of parliament or a club, wilfully damaging or stealing any property of the province, smoking tobacco, using bad language, or giving false witness at any trial or judicial proceedings of the province. Penalties for infractions included fines of five to twenty-five cents and suspension from club activities from a few days to one month. A citizen charged with an offense had the right to choose whether to be tried by judge or jury. Balancing the budget was an important fiscal lesson to be learned by the make-believe members of parliament. A national debt was incurred by borrowing money from the settlement management at five per cent per annum, and then the boys taxed themselves in order "to pay back the loan and secure necessary baseball outfits."

The prevailing interest in woman's suffrage had a rather amusing but significant impact on the boys' parliament. Neufeld, herself an ardent suffragette, reported as follows:

> The boys of the federal party wanted to eliminate the girls from the evening activities. The unionist party, however, firmly believed in a softening influence of the girls as one of the necessities. The girls organized and took an active part in compaigning. The evening of the election they addressed a meeting of voters on the outside of the house and also electioneered twenty yards from the poll. Needless to say, the unionist party was elected by an overwhelming majority. They have pledged themselves to bring in a bill giving the franchise to the girls.

CIVIC ACTION

The interest of Neufeld and her volunteer colleagues reached out to embrace the whole neighbourhood. They advocated better housing, garbage collection, mail delivery and lighting of streets and playgrounds. They made contacts with public officials, gave interviews to the press and numerous talks to organizations on conditions in the neighbourhood and wrote magazine articles. Within a few months of taking up her duties at Central Neighbourhood House, Neufeld was commissioned by a privately financed venture to visit large eastern American cities and study low-income housing projects. She visited New York, Philadelphia, Baltimore and Washington, D.C., and on her return recommended starting a company to build inexpensive two-storey houses on the plan adopted in Philadelphia.

Central Neighbourhood House, along with the other Toronto settlement houses, played a prominent role in the formation of a social workers' club. Twenty-one charter members, chiefly social workers at the settlements and in the various health services, met at Evangelia Settlement to set up an organization where they could consult and plan with one another. Three of the four officers elected were workers from the settlements: Edith Elwood of Evangelia Settlement, president; Milton B. Hunt of University Settlement, secretary-treasurer, and George Bryce of Central Neighbourhood House, corresponding secretary. Louise Brent, superintendent of the Hospital for Sick Children, was elected vice-president. Neufeld served on the membership committee along with Lina L. Rogers, superintendent of school nurses, and Eunice Dyke of the medical health office at city hall, who was soon to become head of the distinguished division of public health nurses.

THE BATTLE OF THE PLAYGROUNDS

In 1912 Central Neighbourhood House fostered plans for training playground supervisors and assumed "a conspicuous part in accelerating the School Social Centre movement." After the Hester How School was built on the northwest corner of Elizabeth and Elm streets, Central Neighbourhood House offered to provide settlement services in the old Elizabeth Street schoolhouse if the city would move it to the centre of the playground and renovate it for use as a community social centre at an estimated cost of $15,000. Kelso presented the proposal at a conference of public school teachers, chaired by James L. Hughes, chief inspector of schools for Toronto, and the idea met with general approval. However, unforeseen controversy arose when the formal request from Central Neighbourhood House to the board of education finally reached city hall. The parks committee referred the matter to a special sub-committee. In a short time the two Jewish missions in the Ward submitted their own counter proposals. Henry Singer, head of the interdenominational Toronto Jewish Mission, sent a letter stating that his mission was "entitled to a substantial grant, if the Neighbourhood House receives its $15,000." Rev. S.B. Rohold, head of the Presbyterian Mission to the Jews, which was about to erect a new building on the northeast corner of Elizabeth and Elm, directly across from Hester How School, requested a city grant of $25,000 to outfit its new building.

A report from the special sub-committee chair stated that there were already ten organizations in the Ward doing work similar to that of Central Neighbourhood House, and that to accept its request would create a troublesome precedent. Despite all arguments by Central Neighbourhood House and indignant protests from the press and Parks Commissioner Chambers, the city turned down the Central Neighbourhood House request.

This rejection by the city of the settlement's plan was a bitter blow at the time. The settlement acquired the house next door, 82 Gerrard Street West, had a door cut between the two buildings and used the enlarged quarters for a residence and club activities. But even with this expansion, the two houses combined could only accommodate an enlarged residence and the relatively small clubs and classes.

PIONEERING ROLE IN USE OF SCHOOLS AND PLAYGROUNDS

Over the next few years Central Neighbourhood House continued to play a pioneering role in the movement for the use of Toronto's schools as social centres and the provision of better equipped and supervised playgrounds. The first step occurred in 1912-1913 when, by arrangement with the board of education, the night school classes in English at the new Hester How School were conducted under the auspices of Central Neighbourhood House. The board provided the salary of George Bryce as principal, but all the teaching was done by volunteers, mostly university students recruited by Bryce. The experiment was a great success, with peak attendance of about 300 adult immigrants organized in small classes of 10 pupils each that were carefully graded according to the language facility of the participants. A series of lectures on various aspects of Canadian citizenship and some concerts were also arranged as part of the night school program. An illustrated lecture on "Pure Milk and Water," given by Dr. W.S. McCullough, medical officer for Ontario, attracted over 500 people. A lecture by James Simpson, a labour leader and future mayor of Toronto, "How to Become a Canadian Citizen and Why," drew an audience of 300.

The following year, when Bryce left Central Neighbourhood House to pursue a calling as a missionary in India, the night school classes reverted to the board of education, but Hester How School continued to be available to

Central Neighbourhood House for citizenship lectures, concerts and entertainments.

The settlement's 1913 spring festival was held at the Elizabeth Street playground, complete with troups of folk dancers in colourful costumes and the distribution of geranium plants to the children by the parks department. In the autumn, Neufeld suggested that the basement of Hester How School be fitted up with showerbaths, a gymnasium and apparatus, which could be used by school children during the day and older working people in the evening. The idea met with initial approval, and plans were made for the board of education to supply rooms and equipment for adult gymnasium classes while the city's recreation department would supply the paid instructors.

However, by early winter a new and more elaborate plan had emerged. Elizabeth Neufeld learned through the commissioner of parks that the city had been asked to give $20,000 to build a shelter house including baths and gymnasium on the Elizabeth Street playground, which now served the children of both Hester How and McCaul Street schools. The recreation department of the city would be in charge of the work. Although Central Neighbourhood House would have no direct involvement in managing the revised project, Neufeld viewed it as a "neighbourhood improvement," which the settlement should do all in its power to promote. She organized the community to take an active role in securing this new project. She lead a deputation of 200 children to march on city hall to present their case to the mayor and board of control and arranged a mass meeting of voters to send a resolution to the mayor and aldermen representing wards 3 and 4 asking for the shelter house.

THE CHILDREN STORM CITY HALL

The children's march on city hall attracted a great deal of attention from the Toronto newspapers. When the 200 girls and boys reached city hall, they found their entrance blocked by three burly policemen. Pushing past the men in blue, Neufeld rushed up the stairs to the mayor's office, only to learn that the board of control meeting had been cancelled for lack of a quorum. The mayor had his hat on ready to depart for another engagement and Controller Simpson had been deputized to see the children. Neufeld appealed to Mayor Hocken; he succumbed and repaired again to the board room where he was joined by several other controllers. The children were shepherded up the two flights of stairs by the very policemen who had previously barred their entrance.

"Well, what can we do for you?" the mayor asked. Johnny Senson, aged ten, the spokesman for the group, stepped forward and delivered his speech, brief and to the point:

> Mr. Mayor and members of the Board of Control. We the children of the Ward are asking for a playhouse on the Elizabeth Street playground. We need a place where we can have baths, gymnasium and entertainments. Mr. Chambers [the parks commissioner] said we might have it, so we thought we had better come and ask you to give it to us.

By May the city council had finally passed the appropriation necessary to build the recreation house on the Elizabeth Street playground, with the city recreation department in charge of the work. The settlement planned to turn over a good deal of its inside work to them. This would seem to be a stirring climax to the campaign Central Neighbourhood House had been waging for the past two years to induce the municipality to take responsibility for much of the city's community recreation program. However, the settlement's archives contain no further mention of this plan, which seems to have been replaced within the month by a rather exciting new venture in the use of schools as community social centres.

NEW SERVICES

The milk depot and the well-baby clinic established in the summer of 1913 in cooperation with the Hospital for Sick Children and the welfare nurses of the city health department were the most important of the new neighbourhood services. These services for babies opened channels for contacts with the neighbourhood families. For Central Neighbourhood House these links were especially valuable when the public health nursing division employed an Italian nurse. The welfare nurses visited each family in its home, explaining to the mother how to dress and feed and care for the baby. Social workers from the settlement frequently accompanied the nurses on these home visits, which introduced them to many family problems not directly related to the baby's health. This practice led the settlement to provide legal aid on occasion, hunt for positions for unemployed neighbours, act as interpreter, and cooperate with relief-giving agencies to provide material aid.

Central Neighbourhood House launched several innovative programs in those early years: a newsboys' club, which enjoyed the privileges of the house during noon hours and early afternoons when the boys were not at work; a model flat equipped by the settlement in three of its rooms and rented to the board of education to conduct housekeeping classes for which the board supplied the teachers and running expenses; and a public dance hall organized and financed by a special committee of the settlement to provide an alternative to some of the rather unsavory commercial dance halls in the area. Two well-to-do members of the board, Walter Laidlaw and Howard Douglas, members of the dance hall committee, undertook to meet any deficits that might occur. Neufeld personally supervised the weekly dances, which were held in a hall at the corner of Teraulay and Elm streets. The dances were well-attended and the young people behaved well, but with the low entrance fees (members of the house, five cents for girls, ten cents for boys; non-members, girls ten cents and boys fifteen cents), only about one-half the expenses for the dances were recovered. When the McCaul Street School became available for social evenings for boys and girls the following year, it took the place of the public dance hall.

Despite the success of the day outings in the first few summers, Neufeld felt strongly that the ideal was to have "a country home where whole families can be taken for a few weeks of rest." The first camp experiment took place that summer when Mary Millman, then a young student volunteer, took a group of girls between 15 and 19 years of age for two weeks to the farm of Mrs. L.A. Hamilton at Lorne Park. The girls, who had never been camping before, were given the use of cabins which had been used earlier in the year for berry pickers. They paid $2.50 a week each for their food, and Millman acted as cook.

The summer of 1914 saw Neufeld's dream of a summer home in the country for mothers and babies, boys and girls finally realized. It was estimated that $2,000 would be needed to operate a camp for eight weeks in July and August to accommodate 25 people a week. The Star Fresh Air Fund promised $500; Neufeld raised the rest. This first real camp was located on the shores of Lake Simcoe, near Jackson's Point, in buildings formerly used by Evangelia Settlement for a summer home. The first two weeks were "an unqualified success," Neufeld reported happily. The mothers in the party had a "beautiful rest" and the children all put on weight "and their cheeks painted to a coffee colour."

THE WIDER COMMUNITY

Neufeld showed a remarkable ability to move forward on many social welfare fronts at once. During her first three years she lead the civic campaign to obtain better playgrounds and to use schools as community social centres in the immediate vicinity of Neighbourhood House, and she also became personally involved in a number of group efforts to study and improve conditions in the city. She was instrumental in getting the Toronto Local Council of Women started on an investigation of women in industry, and while visiting Chicago as the council's delegate to a city planning conference she obtained the trained workers to make the survey. She was also active on the minimum wage committee.

Neufeld played a not inconsiderable role in the move to get the city to appoint a social survey commission (commonly referred to as the vice commission) to study the white slave traffic, moral conditions in general and the problems of social disease in Toronto. During the winter of 1913 she had worked with a group of four university students to investigate houses of ill-fame in the district. She was also a member of the delegation from the local council of women, which asked the board of control to appoint a vice commission, and was one of the three women members of the resulting social survey commission.

The report of the commission, presented to city council 14 October 1915, contained a broad study of the contributing factors in the problem of social morality, such as poverty as a cause of prostitution, overcrowded housing, inadequate recreation facilities and services to immigrants. Among the recommendations of the report for improving conditions were a minimum wage law, a reception home for immigrant women arriving alone in the city, a fuller provision of wholesome recreation facilities, including more playgrounds, more sports and school social centres, and sex education as part of the regular system of public education.

THE NEIGHBOURHOOD WORKERS ASSOCIATION

Elizabeth Neufeld and Central Neighbourhood House played a significant part in the development of district case conferences and the formation of the Neighbourhood Workers Association. In January 1913, with the cooperation of Neighbourhood House, the headquarters of the new central conference was located at Fred Victor Mission, but Neufeld held a key post as secretary. By Christmas 1913 Neufeld had become secretary of a joint executive of the four case conferences and organized a confidential Christmas exchange. Forty organizations cooperated in the exchange, with the work of filing some 9000 names for them being done at Central Neighbourhood House.

When Arthur Burnett returned to Toronto after his year of study at the New York School of Philanthropy, he rejoined the board of Central Neighbourhood House as secretary and was engaged by the department of public health as social worker in the division of public health nurses. Later, Burnett's title was upgraded to director of social work. His primary responsibility was to train the public health nurses in the social welfare aspects of their work. Representatives of the four district case conferences met at city hall on 22 January 1914, to form a central organization for united action, and in February a second meeting adopted the constitution. Burnett and Neufeld and Dr. Ware from University Settlement all took a prominent part in these meetings. The central council of the Neighbourhood Workers Association held its first meeting in April and elected officers at its June meeting. In its early days the central council not only coordinated the nine districts established in the city, but it united the social agencies in promoting progressive action in the welfare field, a function similar to that later assumed by the Toronto Welfare Council.

THE NATIONAL WELFARE SCENE

In 1913 the Canadian Conference of Charities and Corrections invited Neufeld to read a paper, entitled "The Education of the Immigrant," at its fourteenth meeting in Winnipeg. The board agreed to send her with all expenses paid. As the financial state of Central Neighbourhood House earlier in the year had been such that Neufeld had found it necessary to pay for household expenses out of her own pocket, this was quite a gesture for the board to make. The Winnipeg meeting was an especially significant one in the annals of Canadian social work. From 1898, when the conference had been founded in Toronto to provide efficiency and economy in welfare administration, until 1911 it had always met in Ontario and had been essentially an Ontario conference. Then, in a vigorous effort to extend its national scope, the conference held its annual meeting in Montreal in 1912 and in Winnipeg in 1913. This first conference in western Canada was a crest for the secular social welfare movement in Canada. At last, it seemed, the reform goals of men like Kelso in the east and Woodsworth in the west were about to meet on a truly national scale. During the Winnipeg conference the Canadian Welfare League was formed to take scientific social work out of the control of the churches, to foster social research and to promote Canadian training schools for social workers throughout the dominion. J.S. Woodsworth, who had just resigned as superintendent of All People's Mission in Winnipeg, became the league's dynamic and indefatigable secretary; J.J. Kelso, who had long been promoting professional training for social work, was elected to the executive.

The conference provided a broad forum for the discussion of major Canadian welfare problems of the day such as the minimum wage, unemployment, immigration and development of the social life of a community. In the session on immigration Neufeld recommended that all immigrants be required to learn to read and write English, to know something also of the history of Canada and its laws before being granted the privileges of citizenship. "If the privilege of citizenship is such a difficult one that women are not fit to vote," declared Neufeld, herself a dedicated suffragette, "surely it is too good a thing to give men who do not know how to vote."

But Neufeld also pointed out that immigrants from Europe brought their own culture and ideals to Canada, their love of art, music and noble deeds, and that Canadians should accept these gifts "graciously, and make [them] a part of our own life." At the conclusion of her address, wisely or unwisely, she protested strongly against the proselytizing that was going on across Canada in the Protestant churches and missions. "It is better," she said, "to have a good Jew than a poor Protestant, and a good Catholic than a poor Protestant."

In Winnipeg she not only spoke at the conference but was a guest of the Women's Press Club and addressed the Women's Canadian Club. On her way back she spent three days in Fort William where she addressed the Women's Canadian Club and presented the evening sermon at the Wesley Methodist Church. The aftermath of the 1913 Winnipeg Conference was not quite the happy outcome for the secular social settlements that she had originally imagined.

According to Richard Allen in *The Social Passion*, the Social Service Congress of Canada was "hastily called" by the Protestant churches in Ottawa in the spring of 1914. No reason is given for the haste, but it seems reasonable to suggest that it was due to some or all of the following developments: the growing national scope of the secular Canadian Conference of Charities and Corrections; the founding of the Canadian welfare leagues led by J.S. Woodsworth, who aimed to take social work out of the control of the churches; the attacks on proselytizing by churches, missions and evangelical settlements; and the growing radicalism of Woodsworth himself who was beginning to proclaim the likely need for "public ownership," a position that may have raised concern even among many of the progressive social gospellers in the churches. There was no open breach between the Social Service Council, with its religious centrality, the Canadian Conference of Charities and Corrections and the newly formed Canadian Welfare League, with their secular orientation. Many social reformers associated with the latter two bodies were also included on the list of speakers at the congress. But when it came to debate the controversial social settlements, it was Sara Libby Carson, veteran founder of Christian and Christianizing settlements in the United States and Canada, who was chosen as speaker.

In her address at the 1914 conference Carson gave a glowing account of the neighbourly services provided by the Evangelia and St. Christopher House settlements she herself had founded. She pointed with pride to the Sunday religious services attended by "Jew and Gentile and Greek" alike. Some settlements, she noted, were doing "strong, helpful work" by bringing problems such as housing or industrial difficulties to the attention of civic bodies, or by linking themselves to educational, recreational and social service agencies. None of the secular settlements, such as University Settlement and Central Neighbourhood House, which were in the forefront of such efforts, were mentioned by name.

Indeed, discreet as Carson may have been in her public references to the work of the secular settlements, it was no secret to the young women staff and students who worked with her at St. Christopher House that she thoroughly disapproved of Central Neighbourhood House in particular. One of the early staff members commented: "Oh, she thought it was a heathen place!" The prevalent view around St. Christopher House was that Central Neighbourhood House had "rather a Greenwich Village atmosphere" and was "not quite Christian." This general atmosphere of gentle ostracism and veiled reproach of settlements taking the non-religious approach to neighbourhood work finally drove Kelso to make a vigorous defense of the spiritual foundations of Central Neighbourhood House:

> We do not profess to be an evanglistic organization or mission, and religious doctrines are not taught. Workers connected with the house are, however, actuated by deep religious conviction, and are believers in creeds broad enough to include Protestant and Catholic, Jew and Gentile. Surely we can all unite on the commandment, "Thou shalt love thy neighbour as thyself." The Neighbourhood House believes in cultivating and exercising a friendly, kindly feeling for all humankind, giving to the neighbourhood of our best and gaining in return a richer experience of friendship, and goodwill. It is a co-partnership, a peaceable, righteous and loving living and working together for the improvement of social relations and the upbuilding of our civic life.

Although Central Neighbourhood House may have been out of favour with some of the religious forces in Canada, it began to receive recognition in the more secular American social welfare circles. The American National Conference of Charities and Corrections invited Neufeld to address its meeting in Memphis, Tennessee in May 1914, and again the board paid her expenses for the trip.

THE BLEAK BLASTS OF WAR

The outbreak of World War I on 4 August 1914, had a devastating effect on Central Neighbourhood House. The first casualty was the closing of the summer camp two weeks early because of the difficulty in raising funds in the face of competing war needs. Soon it was obvious that the whole budget for the ensuing year would have to be cut back. However, in this bleak period, the good news was the launching of an experiment in a community social centre at the McCaul Street School financed by the Toronto Playgrounds Association. The operation of the McCaul Street School Social Centre by Central Neighbourhood House provided an opportunity for an extension of programs requiring larger space such as plays and folk dancing. The funding provided by the playgrounds association in essence meant an extension of the settlement's staff budget. The new department of social service at the university engaged the Central Neighbourhood House director to lecture on the topic of recreation, and founder and board member Arthur Burnett taught the course on the family and the community.

When Neufeld resigned in late 1915 to marry, the settlement board hired Mary Joplin Clarke, the assistant head worker during the previous year. Clarke had actually been running the settlement for some time during Neufeld's recent illness. The board decided that such a young and inexperienced head worker needed more assistance to carry out the job, so they appointed four other paid workers. The board also took greater personal responsibility for raising money to support the settlement. Helen Austin succeeded Mary Joplin Clarke as head worker in 1918, a position which she held until her death in 1942.

THE PROGRAM

The program at the settlement was greatly enriched by its connection with the community social centre at Orde Street Public School. The enlarged and creative program included gymnastics, games, dancing, plays, concerts and lectures; drama received special attention. The energetic Mary Millman, one of the new workers, was put in charge of the centre and organized a play there each week. A highlight of the 1915-16 program was the performance of *The Bluebird* in January under the direction of Dora Mavor, a sorority sister of Millman, who had just returned from drama studies in New York. She was the daughter of Professor James Mavor, a man who was involved in social causes, and she later gained fame in the Canadian theatre as Dora Mavor Moore. Good promotion of *The Bluebird* attracted 900 people for the two shows.

Although lessons in the violin and piano were given as early as 1912, in 1913 Neufeld suggested a full-fledged music school in conjunction with the settlement as she had seen done in New York. Vera Parsons started the music school in 1915. This particular school was the first organized music school in the major Toronto settlements, and it continued until 1948. Vera Parsons, who spoke Italian, started a highly successful Italian women's club in the autumn of 1915. Evidently, it touched something deep among the Italian women for 20 and 30 years later, when the settlement had long since left the Ward, former members would trudge across the city from beyond Bathurst to Sherbourne Street to attend the meetings, at which they still danced the tarantella to the jingle of their tambourines.

A small Jewish women's club, started by Neufeld, already existed at the settlement. In 1915 clubs for Slavic and British women were organized; later, Mary Millman organized a club for a small group of Chinese women. Five girls' clubs were formed according to ethnic background, four for Jewish girls and one for English girls; a group for Italian girls was also being planned. In her September 1915 report Mary Clarke wrote that a Jewish men's civic club was being organized, although it was never mentioned again in the records. However, men's clubs were an important part of the program; for example, it was reported to the annual meeting the next year that the Jewish Workman's Society, "has identified itself with the centre [the settlement's community centre at Orde Street School], by using it for classes in public speaking."

Much of the work with ethnic groups involved English language instruction, such as the attempt to help unemployed Italian men find work on Ontario farms where there was a serious shortage of labour. Unfortunately, this particular program ended when it was found difficult to place the workers. However, Central Neighbourhood House's Miss Simoni, an Italian-speaking nurse in the department of health, started a successful mothercraft class for Italian women.

By 1918 Central Neighbourhood House was able to open its third camp at The Gables on Kempenfeldt Bay, Lake Simcoe. This camp, owned by Sir William Osler, had been used by Evangelia Settlement, but Evangelia had closed its doors by this time. In the mid-1920s Walter Laidlaw purchased The Gables from the estate of Sir William Osler for his summer home. While keeping a few rooms for his own use, Laidlaw made the rest of the main house and the camp available as the settlement's summer home. The contribution of wealthy businessman Walter C. Laidlaw to the life of the settlement and its members was always important, although he was a retiring man of influence and political standing who avoided recognition. For the extraordinary period of 50 years, from 1912 until his death, he served on the board in various capacities as member, treasurer, vice-president, president and honourary chairman. He helped Helen Austin with the financial accounts, and assisted Vera Parson's studies at Osgoode Hall.

CONTINUED PARTICIPATION IN NATIONAL WELFARE

Central Neighbourhood House maintained its tradition of providing important linkages with various aspects of social welfare in the country. Arthur Burnett continued to act as secretary of the Canadian conference. Although a conference was not held in 1914 and 1915, the 1916 conference was held in Toronto. The following year Mary Clarke was convener of a new national committee of the conference on neighbourhood work, with Helen Hart of St. Christopher House a member. Clarke's report to the 1917 conference in Ottawa was a remarkable document, which contained a thoughtful picture and analysis of neighbourhood work across Canada.

PORTRAYING THE WARD

Soon after its founding on 1 March 1914, the Bureau of Municipal Research agreed to a joint request from the public service division of the department of health and Central Neighbourhood House to collaborate on a survey of the Ward. The survey not only contained a devastating description of the physical environment and its effects, it also contained twenty-one family case studies contributed by Central Neighbourhood House, which graphically portrayed the destitution experienced by people in the area. The majority were immigrants with large families sporadically employed at menial, low-paid jobs; many had physical or mental handicaps. For these people there were few support services besides temporary relief or handouts, referrals to hospital clinics, or, in the case of family violence or desertion, the police. It fell to Central Neighbourhood House to struggle to improve the lot of the children and counsel the mothers. Some of the ideas captured in the report were already being promoted by Central Neighbourhood House even while the survey was taking place. In 1918 a rather remarkable, one-time publication, *Ward Graphic: Happenings in the Heart of Toronto*, contained informative short articles written by the staff and members of settlement programs. In her article, "Sunday in the Ward," Mary Joplin Clarke called for a new kind of Sunday in which the public school would become the neighbourhood club-house, an appropriate suggestion because the city board of education had refused to renew permits that had given the school space for recreational programs since 1915.

THE HOUSE ON ELM STREET

In 1918 Central Neighbourhood House moved below Gerrard Street and for the next ten years occupied two semi-detached houses at 25 and 27 Elm Street; number 27 became a workers' residence, and number 25, taken over later that year for a rental of $50, became a clubhouse. A gymnasium was established in a factory building, and a better playground was built for small children, complete with sandpile and swings. A nursery school, modelled after Dr. Blatz's Institute for Child Study, and a dance program, under Evelyn Beahan, were added. The move to Elm Street necessitated the hiring of other new staff: Mary Shenstone Fraser, Elsie Wishart Bethune, Marjorie Twitchell, Drs. Ruth and William Frank, Carol Stanton. Vera Parsons still lived in the house and continued to work with the Italian-speaking neighbours. Mary Millman returned as chaperone, and Helen Austin was engaged as head worker in October 1918 at an annual salary of $1200. Lawrence Tew was appointed to the important position of boys' worker in January 1919, also at a salary of $1200. Yet, while there were new and more extensive programs, 1917 marked the end of an era with the departure of Kelso and Burnett from the board. Helen Austin and Walter Laidlaw were left to run the settlement virtually alone.

Hockey teams developed throughout the 1920s, and at the end of each season a hockey banquet took place in the largest rooms at 25 Elm Street. Staff and volunteers covered trestle-tables with large sheets of shelf paper, and the boy's committee made the decorations. A typical banquet began with a song, followed by the meal and the presentation of badges and crests to the young players. Helen Austin always came on their big day to admire the decorations and congratulate the boys. About the banquet she recorded: "In deference to these Jewish boys present, because of their food rules, `milk first, then meat,' we had the ice cream first then the hot dogs with Kosher wieners, followed by the cake and pop."

The main activities at Elm Street included a nursery school, established in 1924; clubs for children and adults; a variety of classes in sewing, dance, dramatics, music, art; and a kindergarten program. A children's branch of the Toronto Public Library was situated there for a time but was moved to Scott Institute when the latter became an All People's Mission. Orde Street kindergarten collaborated in an after-school program and folk dancing. There were concerts and sports of various kinds, day outings for mothers and camping in the summer. In addition to all these activities, extensive neighbourhood work was maintained — there were up to 3000 home visits a year, and from 1500 to 5000 office interviews. During these times of heavy unemployment, Central Neighbourhood House also dispensed emergency assistance. As the 1920s progressed, Central Neighbourhood House became a veritable beehive of activity — in 1923 the total attendance at the settlement was more than 27,000 persons. In 1924 the Department of Social Service at the University of Toronto approached the settlement to find placements for student social workers, eleven were placed in the 1926-27 academic year. The Ward was in transition. The Toronto General Hospital and Sick Children's Hospital were enlarged, the central Greyhound bus terminal was built, and other businesses were established. Meanwhile, immigrants were moving away, into the area served by St. Christopher House and University Settlement, and to the more distant suburbs.

Another reason for the settlement's move was the need for a new settlement in the east end of the city since the area between Church Street and the Don River was not well-served by recreational or cultural programs after Evangelia closed in 1918. Mildmay Institute existed at Pembroke and Gerrard streets, but it seems to have been a small operation. In 1929, after a year at a Pembroke Street site, Central Neighbourhood House moved to 349 Sherbourne Street, where it remained until 1970.

PART 2

FIFTY YEARS OF CHANGE, 1930-1980

Allan Irving

CHAPTER TWELVE

THE SETTLEMENTS IN THE GREAT DEPRESSION

Toronto did not escape the Great Depression. By January 1933, 30 per cent of Torontonians were out of work; by early 1935, 25 per cent of the population was receiving relief. Since the nineteenth century Toronto, like other municipalities, provided relief through a tattered net of public and private measures. A civic unemployment relief committee was established in 1930 by the city council to compile a list of jobs that might be available; the city also created a civic employment office and a central bureau for unemployment. By 1932 a new public welfare department became part of the city administration. Throughout the 1930s Toronto experimented with various combinations of public work projects (sewers, water mains), in-kind relief (food, clothing, fuel), direct relief (the dole) and work for relief (breaking up rocks for road construction). The federal government contributed a percentage of the costs, as did the provincial government. By 1939 Toronto had spent a total of $61.3 million on direct relief. In line with the 1834 principle of less eligibility, relief rates were dismally low, contributing, as the Toronto medical officer of health and the Child Welfare Council of Toronto noted, to malnutrition in families of relief recipients.

THE APPROACH OF THE SETTLEMENTS

The approach of the Toronto settlements reflected the many contradictory and conflicting attitudes prevalent in Canadian society at the time about unemployment and relief. The settlements tended to dispense relief in-kind such as bedding, clothing and food hampers rather than cash relief. There was a gradual drift during the 1930s on the part of relief-giving agencies toward cash relief. By 1934 the Canadian Council on Child and Family Welfare outlined a restructured system of relief-giving, in which cash would be given only if there had been sufficient social work investigation to prove conclusively that monetary assistance would be helpful.

Workers at all three settlements included home visits in their daily schedule, and the staff often arranged referrals to relief agencies, interceded with unsympathetic landlords and scanned the city for whatever work might be available. They constantly offered what encouragement they could to people caught up in the panic of depression hopelessness. St. Christopher House, in conjunction with University Settlement, held an open house for unemployed men on Saturday evenings which included games, concerts and refreshments; various churches in the neighbourhoods provided food. Considerable debate occurred in settlement board meetings about the respective merits of providing services to single, unemployed, often transient men, or to married, unemployed men with families. By 1937 the Saturday night open houses at University Settlement, which included unemployed men and women and boasted an average attendance of 250, were a swirl of card games, checkers tournaments and square dances.

SOCIAL ACTION AND POLITICS

During the 1930s the Toronto settlements, particularly Central Neighbourhood House which had a tradition of social reform, did not initiate or participate in much political action directed at changing the inadequate relief structure. Still there were a few attempts in this direction. In 1934 members of University Settlement worked closely with Harry Cassidy of the University of Toronto's Department of Social Science to gather data on slum housing conditions in Toronto. In March, Cassidy had been appointed secretary to the lieutenant-governor's committee on housing conditions in Toronto, and he ultimately carried out a good deal of the committee's research and the final writing of its report. Throughout the 1930s there were a number of attempts to encourage settlement members to take a more active interest in civic affairs; efforts were also made to whip up support among the women at the settlement to speak out collectively against the prohibitive cost of such basics as milk and butter and to openly challenge the consumers' gas company for its high prices.

The settlements themselves may not have been directly involved in political action, but individual workers often took an intense interest in political ideas and movements. Olive Ziegler, who was head worker at

University Settlement from 1928-1933, first heard and met CCF leader J.S. Woodsworth at a meeting at the settlement. She had reluctantly agreed to let CCF leaders speak about social problems if they agreed "to keep it from being too political." Ziegler was so tremendously impressed by Woodsworth and his obvious concern for social and economic injustice that she subsequently joined the party and played an active role. She was pressed to run for office on the CCF ticket, but after much soul-searching decided against such a course. She did, however, approach Woodsworth with the idea of writing a short piece on his life, and after repeated requests he relented and made available to her two large diaries containing a great deal of information about his political career. During her subsequent work on Woodsworth in Ottawa, on what was turning into a full-length biography, CCF MP Agnes MacPhail made her office in the parliament buildings available to Ziegler. The result of these labours was *Woodsworth: Social Pioneer* published in 1934.

University Settlement was in an area of the city that became a hotbed of communism. Inevitably, the communist influence spread to some degree to University Settlement. Frances Crowther, head worker from 1935-46, recalled that during her time there were two young communist women on staff, many communist volunteers and a debating club that often featured communist speakers and ideas. Most of the time no one seemed particularly concerned about these firebrands at the settlement; it seemed nothing more than yet another example of the deep bewildering changes that were underway in Canadian society.

THE CHANGING POPULATION OF THE NEIGHBOURHOODS

St. Christopher House underwent quite a remarkable transformation from 1930-1960. There was also a dramatic alteration in the membership of the house. In 1931 membership was 41 per cent Jewish and 8 per cent Catholic; by 1956 this had reversed and membership was 19 per cent Jewish and 40 per cent Catholic as waves of Italian, Polish and Portuguese immigrants flooded into the area. While St. Christopher House, as did the other settlements, viewed itself as a place of tolerance for different races and cultures, the reality was sometimes unfortunately quite different. Mina Barnes distinctly remembers an attempt to keep down the number of blacks involved in individual clubs at St. Christopher House: "if we got over a certain number [...] in the clubs, we had trouble."

In the early 1930s the composition of the Grange neighbourhood surrounding University Settlement underwent significant changes. Germans, Slavs, Hungarians, Finns, Latvians and Estonians were arriving in their new city with little or no knowledge of English. Some members of the board, such as Professor Vincent Bladen of the University of Toronto's Department of Political Economy, expressed mild concern about the possible social implications of such changes in ethnicity and raised the possibility of social conflict in the neighbourhood. Before 1930 the settlement had served a population that was 75 per cent Jewish, but by 1934 the settlement's population was 33 per cent Jewish, 25 per cent British, 10 per cent Finnish and 32 per cent other groups. When Frances Crowther was appointed head worker in 1935 it was with the understanding that University Settlement was now responsible for the integration of 32 nationalities.

PROGRAMS AT ST. CHRISTOPHER HOUSE

Throughout the 1930s the settlements continued to offer an array of programs for all ages. St. Christopher House made the point in its 1931 annual report that "the whole family from baby to grandmother can, and does, find interest and opportunity for development at St. Christopher House." In 1931 St. Christopher House had a total attendance of 106,308, making for a weekly rate of approximately 2000. The house, in cooperation with the city's department of public health, held two well-baby clinics a week and children from three to five years old could attend a play school each morning for supervised free play and simple games and songs. Overall there were 21 self-governing clubs at St. Christopher House during the 1930s. Boys, described by one worker as "irrepressible embodiments of perpetual motion and mischief," could immerse themselves in a woodworking class, a stamp club or mouth organ band. Each settlement had a drama club, and in 1935 an ambitious group of teenagers at St. Christopher House put on a performance of Shakespeare's *Midsummer Night's Dream*. St. Christopher House had a thriving library too, with a total circulation of 44,000 volumes in 1935. Always aware of its religious affiliations, the 1935 annual report boasted that, among children's libraries in the city, St. Christopher's held second place in the circulation of Bible stories.

Many of the clubs at St. Christopher House would, from time to time, become involved in helping to improve the physical condition of the house or in trying to raise money for specific programs. For example, in 1934 the Sir James Woods Men's Club organized a cleaning crusade in which they washed and decorated the walls, ceiling and woodwork of their club room; at the same time the women had a bee to strip the wallpaper in the girls' club rooms, wash curtains and raise money for house funds. Not to be outdone, the boys' and girls' clubs helped out by washing their part of the house. In the summers St. Christopher House continued to operate its camp on the shores of Lake Scugog about seventy miles northeast of Toronto; each year about 500 boys, girls, mothers and little children were able to take advantage of this welcome escape from the city's heat.

One of the most popular and important programs at St. Christopher House was the music school, which was organized in 1930 by Helen Larkin. Six, and occasionally more, piano teachers from the Toronto conservatory would come twice a week to give lessons at a fee of ten cents each for beginners; more advanced pupils paid slightly more. The house owned six pianos and each year there were about sixty students in all. Larkin's view of the program was that it was intended to give individuals a chance to enjoy music, rather than turn out musical geniuses. This fitted with St. Christopher's goal of attempting to "bring about a richer fuller life for all, realization of individual, family and district possibilities ... greater sympathies, a spirit of mutual helpfulness, a wider horizon and a more abundant life for all."

CHURCH INCREASES INFLUENCE OVER ST. CHRISTOPHER HOUSE

St. Christopher House continued to derive financial support for its many activities and programs from the United Church's board of home missions. This monetary arrangement made for a great deal of tension throughout the 1930s between representatives of the church and the house, which can best be illustrated by a stiff exchange of letters between Sir James Woods and Reverend D.R.B. Cochrane, the United Church's general secretary of the board of home missions. Woods made it clear to the general secretary that "our expenditures always exceed the mission committee's allowance, the difference being provided by members of our board and their friends." Furthermore, Woods pointed out that the year before he had personally donated over $2000 toward the costs of running the house. In his sympathetic but firm response Cochrane acknowledged the needs of the house and at the same time outlined the broader financial problems of the church: "If there is to be another deficit in our church finances, it will be particularly unfortunate for those of us in the department of home missions because the newer parts of the west are pressing for extensions ... and the problems of new and growing cities are always with us." This, in turn, drew a spirited response from Woods who now made no bones about the personal investments —

over $150,000 — he had made over the years to meet the expenses of the house. Wood's fulminations concluded by asserting that the church ought to loosen its reins on St. Christopher House and allow the house to join the Toronto Federation of Community Services, which had been assisting other community centres finance their operations; as it turned out, St. Christopher House did not become a member of the federation until 1939.

Squabbling over finances continued throughout the 1930s with the board of home missions reducing its grants to the house. These simmering discontents over funding between the United Church and St. Christopher House were part of a larger battle emanating from the church's efforts to increase its influence over the house. Since Church Union in 1925 there had been increased pressure on the house to demonstrate that it was doing God's work. Head worker Mina Barnes recalled going to a presbytery meeting when church funds were being allocated and having a fiery, red-headed minister from northern Ontario shouting at her, "And how many souls have you saved?"

By 1933 a forced merger of St. Christopher House and the Social Services Department of College Street United Church had been completed. The house now was to be managed by a special committee of the Home Missions Committee of the Toronto Centre Presbytery and was to be chaired by the minister of College Street United Church. This merger nudged Sir James Woods out of any position of influence over the continuing affairs of St. Christopher House. Initially, Woods tried to put a brave face on these events, telling his son, "we must not show a single sign of resentment or annoyance, let us just accept the situation with a smile." He was, however, unable to conceal his bitter disappointment for long. He wrote to his son: "I think that Sir James Woods Men's Club should change its name and my photograph disappear. Under the new church plan, I can see nothing but gradual disintegration and we must get out of the connection now that an excuse has been thrust upon us." With these pessimistic sentiments Woods' long and crucial connection to St. Christopher House effectively came to an end.

St. Christopher House did not disintegrate following the merger, and in 1939 joined the Toronto Federation of Community Services, an act which signalled its transition from a religious to a secular institution. When the house joined, Federation chairman H.W. Crossin remarked, "it is non-denominational as is evidenced by the fact that it is a member of the federation for community services, which contributed to its support." The 1939 annual report for the house stressed that "it does not try to convert people to any creed, although it humbly strives to work out in practical ways the commandment, 'love thy neighbour as thy self.'" In the same report Mina

Barnes put forward her vision of the house as a place where character could be developed, deep friendships formed and a "level bridge between different people or classes, a common meeting ground, created."

PROGRAMS AT CENTRAL NEIGHBOURHOOD HOUSE

Although Central Neighbourhood House had originally defined itself as a powerhouse of social reform, by the 1930s its main thrust was inward. There was an apparent unwillingness to venture far into the fields of social action and social reform. By the Great Depression, Toronto had had 40 years' experience with a children's aid society that administered the 1893 path-breaking provincial child welfare legislation. Attitudes toward children, as Neil Sutherland tells us in *Children in English-Canadian Society: Framing the Twentieth Century Consensus*(1976), had changed dramatically. Children were no longer seen as sinful miniature adults to be moulded by harsh discipline, they were now viewed as tender shoots to be nourished and encouraged in their growth and development.

Throughout the 1930s Central Neighbourhood House continued to be concerned with the welfare of the area's children. A well-baby clinic, supervised by the city's department of public health, provided young children with such basics as vitamin D, milk and eggs. A doctor was also in regular attendance to administer diphtheria shots and offer advice on the raising of healthy children. In 1931 one of the house's workers, Marjorie Twitchell, proudly reported, "in spite of the prevalent unemployment among these families, the babies have been thriving splendidly as the doctor is able to get extra milk for those who need it and cod-liver oil in sample bottles is supplied by some of the wholesale drug companies."

In 1932, under the direction of a faculty member from the University of Toronto's Department of Psychology, a parent education group met every second week to discuss the most up-to-date research and views on the best methods of raising children. Central Neighbourhood House was pleased to announce that by the end of 1934 there were no longer any cases of malnutrition among the children visiting the agency. However, the settlement's most persistent efforts in child and family work were unable to come to grips with one of the depression's most intractable problems — lack of adequate housing. Families, some of them quite large, often found themselves huddled in one or two cramped rooms with more bodies than beds.

The music school at Central Neighbourhood House, in existence since 1915, offered older children a temporary release from life's daily difficulties and an opportunity for creative expression. By the end of the 1930s there were 10 teachers of violin and piano and 75 pupils, many of whom made creditable showings at the Royal Conservatory of Music examinations every year.

The summer camp at The Gables continued to be operated by Central Neighbourhood House, funded in part by the *Toronto Star* Fresh Air Fund. Most years, over 400 children and parents (usually mothers) attended The Gables and enjoyed a few weeks' welcome respite from their inner city surroundings.

PROGRAMS AT UNIVERSITY SETTLEMENT

University Settlement offered an even wider range of programs than the other two settlements during the depression. As well as the usual recreational programs and club activities, there was a vigorous flowering of culture at University Settlement. The founding of the Children's Little Theatre in the fall of 1929 had been hailed as "one of the most interesting dramatic experiments in Canada." A new auditorium, which also housed the nursery school, made children's dramatic activities a reality. Two of the settlement's most energetic workers, Muriel Boyle and Eugenia Berlin, directed the house's children in various performances. The young people's theatre quickly established connections with Hart House Theatre at the University of Toronto, the Toronto Conservatory of Music and the Ontario College of Art, which assisted in the dramatic presentations.

Important connections were also established with The Toronto Art Gallery. Group of Seven painter Arthur Lismer had suggested in 1930 that the settlement send art groups to the Grange just across from the settlement. He proposed that the groups come three days a week for instruction, with the art gallery providing all the necessary materials. These art classes quickly became popular and by the mid-1930s about fifty eager students were attending on a regular basis. The settlement also offered classes in various handicrafts including pottery making.

For years University Settlement had had a tradition of holding an outdoor celebration at Christmas for the local community. A large brightly decorated Christmas tree would be placed on a platform on the settlement grounds. By the 1930s, in recognition of the large Jewish population served by the settlement, a Chanukkah party was also held. These December celebrations were like a tonic to those in the neighbourhood struggling to cope with the gloom of the depression and of course were a perennial favourite with children. After a few especially cold years when the grip of winter dampened enthusiasm for the Christmas/Chanukkah party, it came to be held in the settlement's auditorium. When the weather would be more welcoming, a spring festival was held outside in Grange Park. All the children who could play instruments would go through the streets of the neighbourhood inviting people to the festival. Singing and dancing in the park marked the rites of spring for the settlement's community.

University Settlement also offered the usual array of services; a well-baby clinic was constantly expanding its services, and the nursery school had a long waiting list of over 60 children and had to adopt a policy of only accepting those children recommended by nurses or social agencies. A summer camp, Boulderwood, on Gull Lake near Gravenhurst, was rented and later bought from the Protestant Children's Home. The Night Hawks was a senior boys club that taught social dancing and the importance of dress and comportment for social occasions. When dances were held at the settlement, the staff would put on their finest to set a proper example for the teenagers and to stress the importance of social graces. Nonetheless, many of the boys associated with this group found themselves caught up in the legal system for such infractions as pilfering equipment from a sporting goods store or stealing cars. Settlement workers often intervened in such cases. Muriel Hyland recalled once persuading officials at Toronto's Don Jail to release a boy into her custody. She then took the boy to her summer cottage and put him to work looking after boats and guests. "He never got in trouble again," she boasted to friends.

In 1929, under the determined leadership of Muriel Boyle, University Settlement launched what it described as "a real adventure in international friendship." At the meetings of the new international club it was not unusual to have over 18 nationalities represented. The usual procedure was for the men to play billiards downstairs in the early evening, while the women remained upstairs to sing folk songs. To prepare for these occasions, Muriel Boyle scuttled about collecting folk songs in all languages and spent many long hours translating them. At 9:00 P.M. tea would be served after which there was folk dancing. The founding of the international club was an important step in the multi-cultural approach of the Toronto settlements to the many ethnic groups in their neighbourhoods. Previously the many adult groups and clubs at the settlements had been of a single nationality. At Central Neighbourhood House, for instance, there had been an Italian women's club, a Chinese women's club, a Slavic women's club, a Jewish women's club and a British women's club. But there was no club that attempted to bring women of all nationalities together. The international club was also the first to break down gender barriers by including both men and women.

University Settlement's music school flourished in the 1930s. Established in 1920, by the end of that decade it had more than one hundred pupils enrolled in piano and violin lessons and an orchestra had been assembled. But when Olive Ziegler arrived as head resident in 1928 she found the teaching at the music school to be quite inadequate with the children tediously playing "the same little pieces over and over again." With her customary determination Ziegler set about reorganizing the music program. She approached the Royal Conservatory of Music where she managed to interest Norman Wilks, head of the conservatory, in the problems of providing satisfactory musical training for the hundreds of children in the neighbourhood who were enthusiastic about music lessons. Wilks proved to be an ardent supporter of the settlement's musical endeavours and arranged for advanced students at the conservatory to teach classes at the settlement. Boris Berlin, one of the conservatory teachers who became actively involved with the settlement, helped design a planned music curriculum. In addition, a special music advisory committee comprising prominent musicians such as Healy Willan was formed to oversee the work and continued development of the school. Many of the children at the settlement had never heard a concert; to remedy this situation, monthly concerts featuring prominent musicians were arranged and were eagerly attended. Like other aspects of the settlement's programs, the music school was constantly beset by insufficient financial resources. On one occasion Boris Berlin informed Olive Ziegler that the settlement desperately needed a new piano, particularly if they were to continue to invite well-qualified people to give concerts. Ziegler was unremitting in her attempts to raise the necessary $700. She met with the president of the Pan-Hellenic Association (an umbrella organization for ten university sororities) and was successful in asking if she could speak at their upcoming annual dinner on the topic of music in the settlement. When Ziegler appeared at the dinner and she saw all these privileged girls and thought of the children at the settlement, she was compelled to give a very emotional speech. She suggested that if each member would give 10 cents at each association meeting, they soon could raise the money for the piano. Moved by Ziegler's fervour they took on the project and in less than two years had bought and paid for the piano.

The social philosopher E.J. Urwick, head of both the University of Toronto's Department of Political Economy and Department of Social Science (social work) from 1927-37, was greatly involved in the activities of University Settlement in the 1930s. He wrote, "the soul of the young must be steeped in beauty and attuned to beauty in every form if it is to be firmly set in the first principles of goodness. That is the essential first step in the formation of character." This inspirational reflection, so typical of Urwick, was often cited as the embodiment of the spirit that lay behind the University Settlement's music school.

STRAINED RELATIONS AT UNIVERSITY SETTLEMENT

The birth control clinic at University Settlement, which operated from 1938-1946, was the most controversial development at any of the settlements in the 1930s and 1940s. Attempts were first made in 1935 to establish a clinic at the settlement, but ultimately it was vetoed for three reasons: the legal position was not clear, Toronto hospitals were the logical place for a birth control clinic and there already was a clinic in Toronto where referrals could be made. While these discussions were taking place, head worker Frances Crowther had written to A.R. Kaufman at the parents' information bureau in Kitchener seeking his support. Kaufman, a pioneer in the Canadian birth control movement, was head of a company in Kitchener that manufactured contraceptives. Kaufman's response was enthusiastic in the extreme and he offered to make available to University Settlement birth control devices such as condoms at much lower than wholesale prices.

Three years later Crowther again contacted Kaufman indicating that the board now seemed ready to put earlier objections aside and proceed with a clinic. "We feel that a settlement is a logical place for such a clinic," Crowther reported, "because from the broad social point of view all our work is preventative rather than remedial, and of course the whole birth control programme is to forestall future suffering and inadequacy." She went on to explain that several hundred women in the district were regular participants in settlement clubs and most had close relationships with settlement staff. Women who otherwise might be reluctant to attend a birth control clinic would probably feel more comfortable seeking out such a service in a familiar environment. The board agreed to the birth control clinic, but laid down some strict guidelines: women would be accepted at the clinic only if they had been referred by a social service agency, doctor or nurse; they had to be married or a common-law wife living with her husband whose written consent she needed before counselling would be given; and service would not be extended to those who were not members of the settlement. The clinic was to be supervised by a small committee of gynecologists and lay members. Kaufman, always eager to promote birth control, offered to supply free contraceptives and to loan the required equipment to launch the clinic. Controversy over the issue signalled the resignations of a number of board members. The chairman of the board, "the courtly and somewhat prudish Professor Urwick, was a little shocked," Crowther recalls, "at a lady bringing up such a topic."

After the first three months of operation the results were disappointing. Contrary to what had been anticipated, women were not flocking to the clinic. A number who came for an initial visit did not return, confiding in the staff that their husbands did not approve; others were struck with nagging doubts about the wisdom of proceeding. Many who would have benefited from the service were turned away because they did not meet one of the requirements. Kaufman himself, after two years of the clinic being in operation, commented to Crowther about the small number of clients: "I am surprised and disappointed to learn that you do not have a great many patients; in view of the vast need you apparently are contacting a very small fraction of it." He asked for his sterilizer back: "In view of the limited use, it will not be much inconvenience for you to do the sterilizing in a pan on the stove." Although somewhat jolted by Kaufman's loss of confidence in the clinic she wrote a reasoned and considered response:

> Aside from the value of the very limited service of our clinic to the mothers at the settlement, I think there is great importance in running a clinic in Toronto at all, especially as a demonstration that such clinics can be sponsored by a semi-public agency without raising too much public antagonism. As you know Toronto is exceedingly conservative and it takes a long time to convince them that there is nothing inherently vicious or dangerous in birth control.

The birth control clinic finally closed its doors in December 1946 when the board decided that the services offered in local hospitals by then were quite satisfactory.

THE FEDERATION AGENDA: PRESENT AND FUTURE

Since its founding in 1918 the Toronto Federation of Settlements had been promoting the interchange of ideas about settlement work. As a collective voice representing the various Toronto settlements, the federation attemped to speak out on matters of social concern. One issue which was particularly troubling in the early 1930s was the question of movies and children. What worried the federation members was that many movies purportedly intended for children were, in their opinion, not at all suitable for young and impressionable minds. One suggestion put forward to counteract the baleful influence of children's movies was for the settlements to run Saturday programs that would take the place of movies; however, it was quickly realized that most children would go to the movies anyway. Another approach was to speak to the operators of movie theatres in the city to see if better quality films could be obtained. This too proved to be a dead end since movie theatres were given little choice in what was offered for showing by distributors.

The question of unemployment naturally occupied space on the agenda of most federation meetings in the 1930s. Many suggestions were put forward about how the settlements could best help people weather this prolonged crisis. One idea that worked for a time provided work for unemployed women in poor homes where there was sickness. The women were paid from a special settlement fund collected for the purpose. Freida Held of the Neighbourhood Workers Association addressed the federation in October 1931 on the unemployed situation and its devastating effects. She portrayed, in vivid language, how social agencies in the city were simply ill-equipped to deal with the rising number of relief cases. She stressed the need for recreational diversions to relieve the constant strain under which people were living and proposed that the settlements open reading rooms, provide special classes, teach different languages, organize debating societies and offer free concerts and dramatic performances.

At most federation meetings in the 1930s a highlight of the evening would be a featured speaker. In March of 1932 Helen Hart, the first head worker at St. Christopher House, outlined the experimental work that Kingsly Settlement House in Pittsburgh had started. According to Hart there was a body of opinion in the United States that settlements had outlived their usefulness and had largely been replaced by the programs of family welfare agencies. Hart brushed aside this view and argued that settlements had an important role to play in group development. She maintained that dealing with the whole family and its social context gave the settlements a considerable advantage in group work over all other agencies. Hart set great store in the need for settlements to develop a "group work technique — to let people work at their own problems." To develop character in a child, she told her depression-weary audience, you must do it in a group — personality could be developed only through human relations. She concluded her remarks by saying that "there is the great function of helping people to live together happily and harmoniously. That, it seems to me, is the place where the settlement fits in." At the time her call for a group work approach had little impact, but by the 1940s it rapidly became the accepted method of settlement work.

Harriet Parsons, 1950

Roof garden of Central Neighbourhood House,
349 Sherbourne Street, 1944.

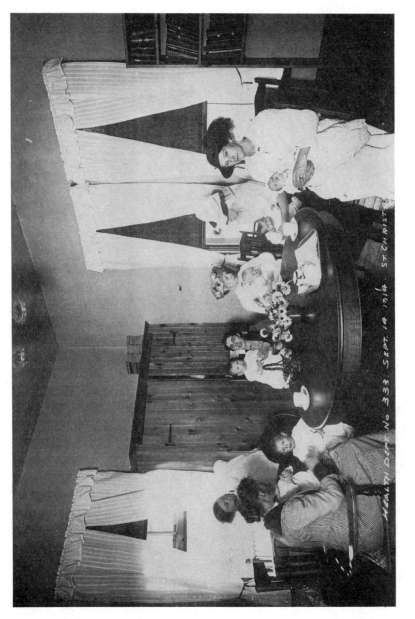

Early health care at St. Christopher House, 1914.

Photograph reproduced courtesy of the City of Toronto Archives. (RG8 32–333)

University Settlement House, 1945.

Photograph reproduced courtesy of the City of Toronto Archives. (SC 24–52)

Spring festival at Grange Park, 1935.
Photograph reproduced courtesy of the City of Toronto Archives. (SC 24-218)

Vera Parsons, Helen Austin, Lawrence Tew, Helda Keene,
Millie Tew and Mary Millman, circa 1917, Central Neighbourhood House.
Photograph reproduced courtesy of the City of Toronto Archives. (SC 5–13)

St. Christopher House, 67 Bellevue Place (later Wales Avenue) circa 1912.

Lawrence and Millie Tew and the Central Neighbourhood House boys' baseball team. Photograph reproduced courtesy of the City of Toronto Archives. (SC 5–14)

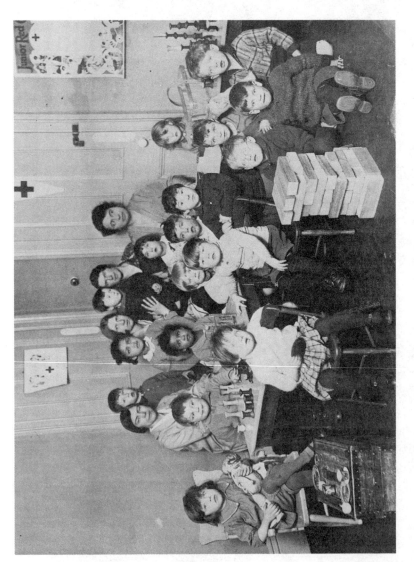

Playschool children at Central Neighbourhood House, circa 1929.
Photograph reproduced courtesy of the City of Toronto Archives. (SC 5–61)

University Settlement hockey team, circa 1954.

University Settlement girls' club, a picnic at High Park.
Photograph reproduced courtesy of the City of Toronto Archives. (SC 24–51)

Chapter Thirteen

War and Peace:
The Settlements, 1940-1960

The War Years

The Toronto settlements grappled with the problem of how to meet the challenges of World War II on the home front. Honorah Lucas, head worker at Central Neighbourhood House from 1945-49, remarked that the combination of absentee fathers and working mothers "had a drastic and somewhat bitter effect upon the families concerned ... adding considerably to feelings of unrest and instability."

At St. Christopher House in the early 1940s the need for male volunteers and staff members was a recurrent theme. No sooner had a man been taken on as a volunteer when he would be called away to enlist in the armed forces or be required to work overtime to meet wartime production demands. George Wiggins, boys' worker at St. Christopher House, bemoaned the difficulties in recruiting volunteers, lamenting that they "were almost impossible to secure at the present time." It proved equally difficult to hire qualified staff. By 1944 St. Christopher House was forced to curtail some programs owing to staff shortages, and head worker Beatrice Wilson commented that "we need an additional trained social service worker, but apparently due to war conditions, we have been unable to locate anyone considered suitable for the position." In fact, the rate of staff turnover was substantial; at University Settlement from 1939-45, 41 individuals joined and left the staff.

For many settlements the war was not a distant battle but an almost daily concern. Some settlement members had relatives in Britain or Europe who were subjected to the horror of bombing raids. At least one settlement felt compelled to pay attention to the logistics of accommodating warring factions under one roof. Central Neighbourhood House's board of directors suggested in 1940 that, in order to avoid any potential conflict, the Italian women's club meet at a time when the British members of the house were not present. This sense of ongoing unease did not exist to the same degree at all the settlements. At University Settlement head worker Frances Crowther was quick to make the point that "the manner in which we can all play and work together happily in spite of events in the old country, is one of the finest proofs that an active spirit of friendliness can break down any barrier, including the nationalistic one." Workers at Central Neighbourhood House were startled when Crowther informed them that there was one adult club operating at University Settlement that served to unite Finnish, Russian, Polish, German and Austrian; all danced together without bitter remarks about the war and all accepted the fact that they were now Canadian.

Attendance at settlement clubs and programs fell off dramatically during the war. During the peak years of the Great Depression, Central Neighbourhood House drew between 55,000-60,000 visits annually. By 1942 this figure was cut in half with no more than 30,000 participating each year. At University Settlement numbers also dropped, by the early 1940s, 1000 fewer persons a month were entering its programs. Many of the young people and children who used to participate were now required to work after school delivering newspapers or in movie theatres.

The Toronto settlements struggled to respond to the many family and personal problems accentuated by the war. Mina Barnes, head worker at St. Christopher House, reflected, "war is now felt in the smallest community, materially, emotionally and spiritually." Despite the fact that the heated-up war economy put many back to work, unemployment continued to be a problem. St. Christopher House workers found that many of the unemployed were labourers and had no training for the types of jobs available; in addition, middle-aged men who had been unemployed for some time continued to be without work. More adults and young people were afflicted with emotional problems, and many of these difficulties were directly related to the strain and uncertainty in families whose men were overseas and in new Canadians whose countries were being destroyed by the war. The settlement's role was to offer reassurance to those in distress and provide a stabilizing influence in the community for adults and children by stimulating interest in club activities, providing recreational outlets and offering group involvement.

Now that many women were working in war-related industries, how could the settlements assist the many school-age children who had traditionally gone home at lunch-time for a warm meal? St. Christopher House tackled the problem with its usual pragmatic determination by making an arrangement with the principal of Ryerson Public School. From January 1944, St. Christopher House provided hot meals for up to 35 children whose mothers were absent from home during the day; in turn, the school board paid for the cook, supervisors and some minor renovations to the settlement. The various clubs at the settlements immersed themselves in the war effort. The women's club of St. Christopher House raised money by knitting sweaters, socks and mittens, while the mother's club came up with over $1000 one year through various fundraising activities. A large proportion of the funds were used to send goods overseas to men who were associated with the settlement. The Sir James Woods Men's Club regularly sent cigarettes overseas; the club also busied itself with raising $550 through a bazaar.

In the early war years the Toronto settlements quickly came to the conclusion that they ought to provide social and recreational activities for armed forces personnel stationed in the area. At St. Christopher House a young women's club, optimistically named the Cheerios, organized regular dances for servicemen, while every Sunday night the house held a hospitality evening for servicemen. In order to make these evenings as pleasant as possible the house relaxed its strict no smoking policy when servicemen were in attendance. Thirty-five young women associated with the junior international club at University Settlement financed and organized Saturday evening dances for servicemen stationed in Toronto. In the fall of 1944, University Settlement organized a veteran's group which met on Wednesday evenings for socializing, dancing and playing cards. These activities aided in the rehabilitation of those who returned from overseas service with their emotional and physical lives shaken and assisted in reintegrating demobilized troops back into Canadian society.

For children a wartime day nursery was located in Boulton House at 15 Grange Road, which had been recently donated to University Settlement. Infants were brought to the settlement's child health centre where they were weighed, had their diets regulated and were inoculated against disease. By the age of two, children could participate in the nursery school, which, by 1940, had already been in operation for fifteen years. Music schools continued to play a central role in the settlements. St. Christopher's music school celebrated its fourteenth anniversary in 1944 with 157 pupils taking lessons in piano, violin, singing and theory. The school continued to expand its educational philosophy as one where "each child, regardless of talent, should have an opportunity for a musical education." Examinations were held twice a year under the direction of musicians from the Toronto conservatory and, from time to time, a scholarship was awarded by the conservatory to a particularly deserving student.

The stress and strain of wartime domestic life led to an increase in juvenile delinquency in the areas served by the Toronto settlements. In trying to gain control over the problem, the Toronto Welfare Council recognized that the sheer number of absent fathers and working mothers was creating a whole host of problems for children and young adults. The council asked all relevant social agencies, including the settlements, to set up additional programs to help counteract delinquency. Central Neighbourhood House's annual report for 1945 reflected that the settlement was only too well-acquainted with the problem of delinquency:

> A trained worker comes to Central Neighbourhood House one afternoon a week to counsel boys whose families or themselves have requested these services; some of these boys have juvenile court records; many are borderline cases whose families are having difficulty in directing them away from the glamour of minor and sometimes major offences against society. A number of these offences have been committed right at Central Neighbourhood House and we have handled it at home with advice from Dr. Rogers and the approval of the juvenile court. By handling it in this fashion we have avoided laying a charge against our own members, thereby strengthening, rather than weakening our contact with them.

Since police department records indicated that early evening was the peak time for juvenile acts of theft and vandalism, Central Neighbourhood House took the initiative and ran classes between 7:00 P.M. and 9:00 P.M. in woodworking, clay modelling, airplane building and leather work. Afternoon programming for boys was increased, and at the summer camp more attention was focused on the problem of juvenile delinquency. A special staff member was provided by the federation for community services to work with the boys at camp to reduce the simmering tensions that often exploded in acts of vandalism. Since resources were limited, as always in social agencies, all the attention directed to the problem of delinquency drained services away from other aspects of the house's work and meant a considerable readjustment in the agency's programs.

NEW INTEREST IN SOCIAL ACTIVISM

The increase in juvenile delinquency sparked a renewed interest in social activism on the part of both board and staff at University Settlement. The issue that sparked the anger of those associated with the settlement was drastic cuts in the city's funding for playgrounds. There appeared to be a direct relationship between the reduction of playground funding and the increase of juvenile delinquency in Toronto in the early 1940s. In February 1942 a city of Toronto controller spoke to a meeting of the inter-settlement federation held at University Settlement on the issue of playground funding. Feelings ran high over a recently announced $60,000 cut, and the action proposed was to have a delegation of neighbourhood mothers converge on city hall to protest the spending reductions. The leaders of this protest action voiced the argument that "it is the duty of the city as a part of the war situation to see that children are adequately supervised." The protest proved successful and sufficient funding was restored to ensure that playgrounds would be adequately supervised during the critical summer months. Buoyed by the success of the playground protest University Settlement staff pushed for social action on several other fronts as well. There was a meeting to discuss the inadequacy of mothers' allowance payments, and the board and staff criticized the Hospital for Sick Children for the hospital's reprehensible and negative attitudes toward the poor. The board, with the full urging of the staff, wrote to the prime minister asking that the government take a more lenient attitude towards Japanese Canadians. University Settlement organized and conducted discussion groups that attempted to take stock of the major competing ideologies of the war years: communism, fascism and democracy. Round table sessions on trade unionism were also set up with the specific purpose of preparing young people for leadership roles in the union movement.

In line with these more political thrusts, the staff of University Settlement focused their attention on the quality of life of factory workers. By 1942, 20 young men from a factory on McCaul Street were coming to the settlement to eat their lunches and to use the recreational facilities; notices announcing English classes were posted in nearby factories. The summer of 1943 saw up to 3000 people, many of them industrial workers from the area, attending Sunday evening entertainments put on by University Settlement in Grange Park.

FUNDING DIFFICULTIES

As always, funding for settlement activities in the 1940s was unsatisfactory. St. Christopher House, however, received a considerable boost as the Toronto Federation for Community Service began to substantially increase its support of the house; simultaneously, the board of home missions gradually reduced its share of funding. By 1945 the federation was the major funder of the house providing $12,000 out of a total budget of $17,000; in that year membership fees were raised from 15 to 25 cents.

During the years of growth and change at St. Christopher House, Sir James Woods had been a constant presence. With his death in 1941, this long connection came to an end. Over the years, Woods had personally contributed more than $150,000 toward the running of the house. Woods was a key figure in Toronto's business community and the Presbyterian and United churches. During World War I he served as head of the buying department of the British War Mission in New York and was honoured with a knighthood for his work. At a board meeting following his death the house paid a glowing tribute to his benevolence:

> ... from his youth until the end of his days, he gave freely of his time and means to the improvement of life about him and the enhancement of Christian ideals. His help was most notable for its consistently practical and beneficial form, his efforts were also directed toward promoting the means by which people were able to help themselves .... There was probably no work dearer to him than the work carried on in St. Christopher House, much of it made possible by his generous donations.

JAPANESE CANADIANS AND UNIVERSITY SETTLEMENT

University Settlement was one of the few organizations in Canada that responded to the desperate situation of Japanese Canadians in the early war years. By 1941 there were close to 22,000 Japanese Canadians in British Columbia, mostly along the coast and the Fraser River Valley. Following Pearl Harbor in December 1941 all persons of Japanese birth or descent were evacuated from the B.C. coast, an operation carried out by the B.C. Security Commission and the Royal Canadian Mounted Police. As Ken Adachi recounts in *The Enemy That Never Was* (1976), all their property and belongings were vested in the custodian of alien property for protection and management. Many were placed in internment camps in the B.C. interior; some went to work in sugar-beet fields in Alberta or Manitoba; others were employed in road camps in B.C. and Ontario. A number of Japanese families began to drift into cities like Toronto where the girls were encouraged to take domestic jobs. The Toronto city council was less than welcoming and passed a number of resolutions, which conveyed the blunt message that the Japanese were not wanted.

Kay Kato, born in Kingcome Inlet, a well known Indian settlement on the B.C. coast, was to play an instrumental role in University Settlement's work with these Japanese Canadians. Her early years were spent growing up in a longhouse, a communal arrangement where six families lived together. Showing early promise as a student, she won a scholarship to the University of British Columbia and graduated in 1941 at the age of 21. That fall she planned to enter the University of British Columbia's School of Social Work, but was turned down on the grounds that it would be too difficult to find the required field work placement in a social agency. Also, as a Japanese Canadian, there was no assurance of a permanent job in social work after graduation. Temporarily discouraged by this rejection Kato's spirits were lifted and her resolve to get a social work education renewed by a chance meeting with J.S. Woodsworth in Vancouver. Inspired by his words of encouragement she lined up her own field placement at the YWCA. She also obtained assurances from Kunio Shimizu (who later became her husband), executive secretary of the Vancouver Japanese Welfare Federation, that she could work there after she graduated. A few short months after entering the UBC School of Social Work in the fall of 1941 her situation changed abruptly, as it did for all Japanese Canadians on the west coast.

At the end of March 1942 all Japanese students were required to leave the university. However, Kay Kato was the one Japanese student allowed to remain on campus for, as she described it years later, "the B.C. Security Commission needed me so badly." To assist in the evacuation of the Japanese from the coast, welfare services were in the process of being established and Amy Lee, a social worker with the provincial government, was put in charge of these services. Lee came to the university seeking a Japanese-speaking social work student to assist the Security Commission. Kay Kato was the natural and only choice, and arrangements were made for her to complete her field work requirement with the commission.

After graduation she continued to work with the commission as it carried out its mandate "to get rid of the Japanese problem." Naturally, she became increasingly unhappy with her role as an agent of the state in carrying out its repressive measures against the Japanese. She resigned her position, joined the trek eastward and ended up in Toronto where she obtained employment as a kitchen assistant scrubbing floors and cleaning toilets and later worked at the Vineland Experimental Farm in the Niagara Peninsula. It was here, at the end of August 1943, that she encountered, in another one of those chance meetings, Mary Jeffary whose husband taught at the University of Toronto School of Social Work and was on the board of University Settlement. Kay soon received an invitation from the settlement's head resident, Frances Crowther, to join the staff and work with teenagers. In 1943 staff members still lived in residence at the settlement, and once she was offered the job Kay Kato wasted no time in moving into one of the settlement's rooms. When she joined the staff she was the only member with formal training from a school of social work. Kato recalled that Frances Crowther was "very austere, not too easy to talk to, but she had a very delightful smile, it just lit up her face. She was a very intellectual person. Her concept of what a settlement house could be in a community was not haphazard, it was well thought out." Kato vividly recalled that Crowther always insisted on having fresh flowers in the front hall at University Settlement and made a point of going to the market to get them. Dinner at the settlement continued to be served in a very formal manner, and afterwards the staff would retire to the upstair's living room for tea and coffee.

After coming to University Settlement in 1943, Kato's first task was to identify the Japanese families in the neighbourhood; however, she met with little success involving Japanese families in the adult activities of the settlement. Basketball was the initial link for male Japanese teenagers. She did manage to start a Japanese teenage club at the settlement and broadened her work to include other teenage groups. One was Club Hutton, a large, mixed club for boys and girls that met every Thursday evening, mostly for dances. She began to work with a sub-teen group of boys and girls which met as a dance club, with the Amicis, primarily a Jewish club, and with an all-black group of teenage girls who were interested in sewing and liked to sing together. In 1947, after four years at the settlement, Kay Kato, now married, left to take up a new position in Ottawa.

Another community that found solace at University Settlement during the war years was a small group of Viennese Jews who came to Toronto around 1944 and formed a club that met at University Settlement. Before and during World War II Canada took in a relatively small number of refugee Jews from Germany and German-dominated countries, although as we know now from Irving Abella and Harold Troper's book *None is Too Many* (1982), Canadian policy toward not admitting large numbers of Jews fleeing Hitler was driven by strong anti-Semitic attitudes.

CENTRAL NEIGHBOURHOOD HOUSE — POST-WAR DEVELOPMENTS

Like all the other settlements in the 1940s, Central Neighbourhood House underwent a change in leadership. Helen Austin, who had been head worker since 1917, died in 1942. For the next two years Elsie Bethune, who for many years had been Austin's assistant, was acting head worker. From 1944-45 Mary Blakeslee, also a trained social worker, served as head worker and then resigned apparently for health reasons. Following Blakeslee's departure in 1945, Honorah Lucas was appointed head worker at Central Neighbourhood House where she remained until 1949. Lucas was introduced to settlement work in the late 1930s while she was a piano student at Toronto's Royal Conservatory of Music. University Settlement employed her part-time as a music teacher and she quickly became intrigued with her pupils, their home lives and their problems. In fact she began to spend so much time at the settlement that her teachers at the conservatory complained about her lack of attention to her piano studies. Laying aside any lingering doubts she may have had about her future, Lucas accepted a position at Central Neighbourhood House. In 1944 Lucas left the settlement to work for wartime housing in Hamilton and returned the following year as head worker.

One of the reasons Lucas was eager to return to the settlement as head worker was to be in a position to make changes in a number of areas that she had found deeply troubling. She was bothered by the fact that "only the nice people came to Central Neighbourhood House with its plush drapes, beautifully polished floors and oriental rugs scattered here and there." A longtime advocate of increased neighbourhood involvement, Lucas held the firm conviction that the settlement should do more to reach out to people in the neighbourhood who really were in need of help. During her tenure as head worker she devoted considerable energy to redirecting the settlement's program along these lines.

Almost as soon as she took over in 1945, Lucas strenuously objected to the way the nursery school was run. Privately she was irritated by the fact that most of the workers were "Margaret Eaton girls, not trained in child psychology." Children who said bad words would have their mouths washed out with soap; children who misbehaved were put on chairs on top of a table as a form of punishment. These and other practices were quickly done away with by Lucas. Shortly after taking over Lucas realized that she faced an uphill battle, for when she brought her plans before the board her concerns fell largely on deaf ears.

In the late 1940s Lucas recommended to the board that they develop employment contracts with the staff that would outline the conditions of employment, wages, hours and holidays. This was prompted by a number of the new staff who had recently joined a C.I.O.-affiliated union headquartered in the United States, and by a recent study that suggested minimum social work salaries be in the range of $1800-$2000 annually. Although the board's response to Lucas was less than enthusiastic, they did instruct her to prepare a draft contract for consideration. However, with her resignation in May 1949 to get married, the issues of unionism and salary standards were quietly dropped and not taken up again for a number of years.

When she assumed the position of head worker in 1945, Lucas was acutely conscious of her lack of formal training in social work. To rectify this deficiency she began to take courses at the University of Toronto's School of Social Work, and by 1947 was in the process of putting her own stamp on the agency by hiring a number of staff who enthusiastically embraced, what seemed to many, the new, radical social group work theories. In her first annual report Lucas put forward the idea of greater cooperation with other agencies as one way to meet the needs of the community at large:

> It is our aim that in the year 1946, through cooperative planning with other agencies, public and private, churches, schools and all organizations doing a group work or recreational job, we in Moss Park can build a programme suitable for all ages and requirements. A small beginning in this direction has been realized by some joint planning with one church and the Moss Park community council.

A year after she wrote this Lucas advanced the idea of community representation on the board; however, the board, which consisted mainly of affluent businessmen from outside the area, was far from ready for such a radical notion. Ever determined to broaden the base of decision making at the settlement, Lucas organized a house council with representatives from all groups who used the settlement. Lucas, taking direction from this council, attempted to act as the council's and the community's link to the board.

By 1946 Lucas, with her characteristic zeal, had redefined the nature of the work at Central Neighbourhood House. Her refashioning was based on her definition of the new philosophy of social group work: to work in small groups with children who may be emotionally and economically deprived and to use the group as a medium through which to work with the individual.

By 1948, Central Neighbourhood House seemed to be returning to something resembling its original mandate of community outreach and social action. Despite these high-minded sentiments community work and social action never amounted to much in the early post-war years. Instead, with its primary emphasis on direct service through a group work approach, Central Neighbourhood House unwittingly maintained its focus on changing the individual rather than the community at large. Nevertheless, the founders and followers of social group work here and at the other settlements had no doubt that their approach was pivotal in bringing about constructive changes.

Social group work as a social work method can be traced back to the 1920s when the School of Applied Social Sciences at Western Reserve University in Cleveland made a place in its curriculum for what was called group service work. In 1930 the first key text, Grace L. Coyle's *Social Process in Organized Groups*, appeared; it was an impressive array of material from a wide range of disciplines including the sociology of Charles H. Cooley and the philosophical pragmatism of John Dewey. For Coyle and other adherents of this approach, groups were an essential ingredient in a democratic society. At the end of the 1930s Coyle wrote: "one of our purposes is to contribute to the creation of a socially awakened and socially intelligent body of citizens. Such a result can only be obtained by an educational method that starts within the actual experience of the group and encourages the growth of a sense of social responsibility to the larger whole." By the 1940s the social group work method had clearly taken hold. The best definition of what group work was becoming was provided in the opening pages of Harleigh B. Trecker's *Social Group Work: Principles and Practice* (1948):

> Social group work was seen as a process and method through which individuals in groups in social agency settings are helped by a worker to relate themselves to other people and to experience growth opportunities in accordance with their needs and capacities. In social group work, the group itself is utilized by the individual with the help of the worker, as a primary means of personality growth, change and development. The worker is interested in helping to bring about individual growth and social development for the group as a whole as a result of guided group interaction.

It was obvious that social group work as a method was ideally suited to settlement house work, and it is not surprising that the Toronto settlements in the 1940s turned to this method. At the University of Toronto School of Social Work, Alan Klein taught group work in the late 1940s and early 1950s, and in 1953 he published a leading work in the field, *Society, Democracy, and the Group.*

At the YMHA on Brunswick Avenue, some staff were, "the prophets and messiahs of group work — the great new thing." This was recalled by Jean Palmer, a student social worker at Central Neighbourhood House in 1948, and later executive director of St. Christopher House. She remembered that social work students were being taught to be permissive with their clients and instructed to perform the somewhat delicate role of directing the group process and letting the group determine its own programs. This certainly could describe the staff that Lucas hired at Central Neighbourhood House. Cuthbert Gifford, hired in 1947 as the settlement's boys' worker and program director, had originally trained as a minister and later became director of the University of Manitoba School of Social Work. He had attended the School of Social Work at the University of Pittsburgh, which was considered, in the mid-1940s, to be the Mecca for group work training. Gifford made no effort to conceal his strong socialist bent and did not seem to particularly mind that some viewed him as an outright communist. Gifford was joined by other radical staff: Helena Rosenthal, Eileen Coates, Barbara Greene and a number of students from the University of Toronto School of Social Work including the outspoken Reg Bundy. They were unrestrained in their enthusiasm for leftwing points of view. Things quickly got out of hand for Lucas, and the extreme permissiveness of the staff, combined with the new type of young people at Central Neighbourhood House, led to a great deal of trouble at the settlement.

On one particularly harrowing occasion teenage gangs managed to ruin five pianos, set two fires and break a number of windows with billiard balls. In a separate incident, word leaked out that two rival teenage gangs planned to stage a massacre at the house. Lucas, in consultation with her staff, decided to alert the police to the possibility of trouble but agreed they would be called in only if things got completely out of hand. Unfortunately, they did. In the evening the gangs stalked in with steel rods concealed up their sleeves and, at the signal of a broken pop bottle, a vicious fight began. The police arrived to find quite a bit of damage, but mercifully for Lucas no one was seriously injured.

After Lucas left in 1949, all the radical staff were let go. Reg Bundy, whom Lucas had recommended as her successor, was not hired. Even those social work students who had been at the settlement since its earliest days were now considered by the board to be too disruptive an influence. They would not be allowed to return until the 1960s. Instead of Reg Bundy, Helen Sutcliffe, an army nurse, was appointed head resident and served in that capacity until 1970.

Helen Sutcliffe's first winter at Central Neighbourhood House proved to be especially difficult. A group known as the Cabbagetown Gang comprising over 100 members, many of whom were constantly in and out of jail for thefts and other misdemeanours, decided to make the settlement their headquarters. The board, determined to rid the house of this undesirable element, instructed Sutcliffe to toss them out. Reluctant to do this without first trying to bring about some positive changes in their behaviour, Sutcliffe continued to work with a number of the gang's members with some apparent success. Years later Sutcliffe boasted that "almost all did extremely well — one became a doctor, one a plumber and one won five scholarships at the university." When Sutcliffe took the position as head worker she had done so on the condition that she do the job for six months while a permanent replacement for Lucas was found. Her unqualified success in handling the Cabbagetown miscreants was undoubtedly a factor in Sutcliffe remaining at Central Neighbourhood House for 21 years.

During her first decade of service, Sutcliffe resided at 1 Homewood Avenue, near the corner of Sherbourne and Carleton streets, just minutes from the settlement. Immersing herself fully in the community, Sutcliffe became intimately acquainted with many of the neighbourhood's families and ultimately became godmother to a number of the area's children. Shortly after taking over it became apparent that Sutcliffe seemed blessed with an ability to make newcomers to the community feel that Central Neighbourhood House was also their family. By the mid-1950s Sutcliffe had set the tone for work in three basic principles of policy, which were in a sense old ideas recycled: to work with people in learning how to live together and to achieve individual growth and good human relations; to recognize the needs of the community as a major factor in securing better living conditions, strengthening family life, good health, education, seeking employment, the development of a feeling of neighbourliness and responsibility for local conditions; and to relate the concerns of local neighbourhoods to the whole community.

The dramatic increases in Toronto's population — in the 1940s the population increased by 23 per cent and in the 1950s it doubled — began to significantly alter the complexion of the city. Many new immigrants settling in the area of Central Neighbourhood House created the need for a new level of services. Poor housing continued to be one of the most serious social problems confronting settlement workers. Many families had no choice but to live in one or two rooms in houses that were in such a poor state of repair that they were often reported to the city's public health department. Most spent their time dreaming of moving out of the area. As a 1954 study of the settlement reported, "a few of our younger families that are mature in their outlook are planning to buy their homes in districts that are cleaner, safer and less crowded for their children. To this end, many of their husbands are taking evening courses to qualify themselves for better and more secure positions in their work." By the winter of 1954 rising rates of unemployment created further hardships for many of the district's families who were already discouraged by not being able to participate in the pleasures of the post-war consumer society.

The large rented house at 349 Sherbourne Street, which had been Central Neighbourhood House's location since 1929, continued to serve the agency well throughout the 1950s. On the first floor were three large rooms used for clubs and programs, a staff dining room, kitchen and several washrooms; a gymnasium and members' kitchen had been added to the rear of the house. The second floor consisted of three offices, a staff lounge and another larger all-purpose room; on the roof of the gymnasium at the back was a garden with a sand pile and wading pool used by the nursery school in the summer. Several rooms used for woodworking and other arts and crafts were located in the basement. In 1956 attendance at the various clubs, classes, interest groups and the nursery school numbered well over 72,000. Over 300 home visits by agency workers and over 4400 babies and pre-school children were examined in the house's health centre, which was staffed by two doctors, four nurses and two volunteers. However, even as Central Neighbourhood House expanded its community involvements during the 1950s its board was reluctant to comment on larger social issues confronting Canadian society. For now the emphasis shifted to the individual and the family. By the end of her first decade of service, Sutcliffe had created a climate where the human potential of the neighbourhood residents, so often choked by disadvantage, was given an opportunity to emerge within an environment that promoted warmth, understanding and gaiety.

ST. CHRISTOPHER HOUSE — POST-WAR DEVELOPMENTS

Throughout the early post-war years and into the 1950s the hub of community and social life for residents in the overcrowded area bordered by College, Queen, Spadina and Markham streets continued to be St. Christopher House, which had been situated at 67 Wales Avenue since 1912. The years from 1945-60 saw a steady improvement in staff qualifications at St. Christopher House and a greater reliance on social work methods such as group work. In 1943 Mina Barnes stepped down as head worker having received an offer to become the director of Alexandra Neighbourhood House in Vancouver. Replacing her was Beatrice Wilson (1943-53) who brought a considerable background in YWCA work, school teaching and United Church work. Those who encountered Wilson were immediately struck by her intelligence, warmth and lively sense of humour, as well as her single-minded determination to get things done. After taking over, Wilson lost little time in setting out three major tasks: review the qualifications of the various staff; re-establish connections with the school of social work at the University of Toronto; and strengthen connections with the United Church.

Wilson inherited a staff from a variety of backgrounds, although none had a degree in social work. Wilson was of the view that staff qualifications generally were not up to the mark. In the 1940s Betty Quiggan and Evan Bross, both graduates of the University of Toronto School of Social Work, were brought on board. Wilson also took it upon herself to upgrade the calibre of the house's volunteers. She instituted a system whereby volunteers were required to write weekly reports and meet with a supervisor to discuss their work. Closely associated with this thrust to raise staff qualifications was a wish to improve relations with the University of Toronto School of Social Work. A number of years earlier the university had lost interest in placing social work students at the house for part of their training because there was no one there who could provide adequate supervision. Determined to rectify this long-standing problem, Wilson agreed to pay part of the salary of a faculty member of the school of social work who would in turn provide student supervision. This relatively simple solution did the trick, and University of Toronto social work students have been placed at St. Christopher House ever since.

With the return of social work students, group work as a method took hold firmly at St. Christopher House. Psychology students placed at the house in 1949 were required to observe groups of children under 12 years of age, while the four social work students at the settlement that year were each responsible for leading two groups. According to the 1949 annual report, groups for children were seen as critical "in light of Toronto's concern with teenage and juvenile delinquency." In fact there seemed to be no end to the number of groups formed. In May 1947 a group of nursery school mothers was established; presentations were made on food, diet and the physical and mental growth of the pre-school child. Throughout the 1950s other new groups came into existence: one for problem girls, one for parents of six- and seven-year-olds, one for immigrant Italian girls who needed special help in English and adjusting to Canadian ways, and one for girls with special behavioural problems. Group activities ranged from skating and cooking to group discussions. Other activities continued to flourish at the house during this period. Enough interested students were found to fill four ballet classes, while a group for intermediate girls busied itself with such activities as a production of *Cinderella* and raising money for the March of Dimes. The nursery school was expanded to include 20 additional students, and the music school was accepted into the national council of music schools in 1957. A few years earlier the music school had moved into permanent quarters, using two studios at the east side of the building.

One of the first students to be placed at the house in the 1940s, under the new arrangement with the University of Toronto, was Louis Zimmerman. Although Zimmerman spent the early years of his life living on Wales Avenue, very near the settlement, his parents prohibited him from going to St. Christopher House fearing that the settlement had a missionary purpose and would try to fill his mind with Christian dogma. Some thirty years later, however, in the fall of 1946 he found himself at the settlement for the field work component of his MSW training. Zimmerman wasted no time in immersing himself in the Japanese-Canadian boys' club, a mixed ethnic group of 13-year-old boys, and the organization of a neighbourhood council. It was this latter task that was most to his liking and occupied the bulk of his time. Zimmerman called together representatives of organizations in the neighbourhood — social agencies, schools, churches, trade unions — to form a neighbourhood council, which was known as the Ward 4 South Community Council. The central question occupying the council's attention was: Can we improve the neighbourhood? Safety was identified as a pressing issue with one example being a particularly bad street crossing at the corner of Beverly and Dundas. A brief was prepared and presented to Toronto City Council with the result that a traffic light was installed. With the establishment of the neighbourhood council, community development work as a social work approach was established in Toronto by St. Christopher House.

By the end of the 1940s Wilson had succeeded in improving the qualifications of the staff and re-establishing ties with the school of social work. But strengthening connections with the United Church was not so readily accomplished. The bonds had loosened in 1940 when the house was forced to turn to the Toronto Community Chest for financial support. This clearly marked the beginning of the house's transition from a church-based settlement to a secular agency.

By the 1950s settlements throughout North America were increasingly subjected to the criticism that they had too much of a building-centred approach to their work, people came to the settlement for services and activities, and had been neglecting their traditional neighbourhood/ community work function. After considerable internal soul searching from

1954-55, the staff and board at St. Christopher House decided to expand the community work focus as much as possible while maintaining solidly entrenched programs.. The next several years saw increasing community involvement by the settlement's staff and volunteers as they struggled to fulfil their new-found commitment to client community work.

It was estimated that at least 12,000 people of a wide variety of ethnic backgrounds were crammed into the district in 1950. Streetscapes were characterized by old, tumble-down housing, mostly semi-detached buildings with little play space for children. It was a highly transient neighbourhood with one-third of families moving away each year. After 1945 the area harboured many people displaced by World War II. They had known a better way of life in their countries of origin and were anxious to improve their living conditions as soon as possible. At the first opportunity they moved out of the district

Unemployment was an underlying structural problem throughout the St. Christopher House community of the 1950s; dry-cleaning establishments, small grocery stores, clothing, fur and tailoring businesses were the only sources of work for many. Black people were forced to find work outside the area, often as porters with the railways. Almost every nationality represented in the area had a public hall where recreational programming and education, often language classes, were carried on and where cultural connections were strengthened. In many respects the area was a self-contained district with shops, shows, synagogues, churches, schools, public health nurses and other social services forming the contours of a unique community. New Canadians suffered many hardships. House workers were deeply touched by the home visits they made and they often responded by accompanying new Canadians to social welfare offices, the immigration department and on shopping trips to buy furniture. Others came directly to the house seeking advice about court cases, divorce proceedings, other legal matters and family problems. From 1953 the house employed at least one worker to deal specifically with new Canadians. These workers were multi-lingual and able to communicate with many ethnic groups in their native tongues. Offering English classes was another means adopted by the house to assist newcomers. In November 1957, 250 inhabitants of the district were attending 23 separate classes. Reaching out to isolated immigrant women whose husbands prohibited them from attending English classes at the house, the teachers and staff began to make in-house visits for the purpose of language instruction. The visits had the added benefit of relieving some of the loneliness experienced by many of these secluded women.

It was not until the 1950s that St. Christopher House had its first Jewish staff member and first Jewish member on the board of directors. A significant development occurred in 1951 when John Braithwaite was hired as a boys' worker and became the first black staff member at a Toronto settlement house. He was the first staff member who had grown up in the surrounding community and had come to the house as a child. Braithwaite acquired his master's degree in social work from the University of Toronto and later became the executive director of North Shore Neighbourhood House in Vancouver.

By the 1950s St. Christopher House workers and some board members began to view the area's dilapidated housing as a serious social problem for many members of the house. Annual reports for the 1930s and 1940s tended to promote the idea that St. Christopher House was a friendly and welcoming place to visit with recreational and club programs for the whole family. In the 1950s questions were raised about just how beneficial the house's programmes were, when individuals and families had to return home to depressing and inadequate conditions. The 1958 annual report described the mood:

> Here is where rooming houses are filled with the sons of many lands seeking the promise of something better; where social tensions clash or harmonize as lonely people strive to feel they are part of something meaningful; where decaying housing is often left to the most needy; where transient workers have a temporary life until the season changes and a new job pulls them to another place.

As a response to the poor housing and generally impoverished conditions of the neighbourhood, St. Christopher House, in conjunction with other Toronto settlements and United Action for Slum Clearance, began active lobbying efforts. A number of meetings were held to discuss the proposed Alexandra Park redevelopment project. At the same time letters and appeals were sent to the city planning board about community housing needs. These appeals were reactive rather than proactive — made in response to a proposed redevelopment project rather than an active call for change — and represented the weakness of much of the social action history of Toronto settlement houses. However, considerable lobbying success was achieved in having traffic lights and one way street signs installed in the area, which contributed to a much safer environment. Another problem during this period was the increasing rate of juvenile delinquency. One youth was killed while taking part in a break-in at a dental supply shop on College Street in 1954. Eyebrows were raised at the house when two 14-year-old girls were arrested as prostitutes and four youths were charged with living off the avails of prostitution. It became all too apparent that holding classes and organizing basketball leagues was simply not solving the problems of troubled young people.

St. Christopher House attempted to pry a civic grant out of the city of Toronto to hire an additional youth worker. House worker Bill Leggatt told the city in late 1958 about "the problems of teenage narcotic addiction, pimping and prostitution, chronic unemployment of school drop-outs and habitual theft." This comment was reported in all the Toronto newspapers and brought immediate denials and sharp rebukes from area politicians and the police department; however it did lead to better funding for the house. Both the city and the Atkinson Foundation provided money to hire an additional youth worker and create a youth service project for school drop-outs. The settlement also paid heed to another group that had previously received scant attention — the elderly. Initially, seniors were hesitant to become involved, but by 1955 the Autumn Club had been formed with 38 members who met twice a week. The group soon settled into regular afternoons of bridge playing and attending films at local theatres. In 1957 Odeon and Famous Players Theatres agreed to provide free admission to members of the settlement's Autumn Club. As St. Christopher's programmes and services expanded so did its financial obligations. In 1946 the house's budget was $15,000; by 1960 it had increased to $100,000. In the late 1940s the two main sources of funding were the community chest of Toronto and the home missions board of the United Church in a ratio of two-thirds to one-third respectively. Indicative of a major change in funding was the receipt of a civic grant of $2,500 in 1953. By the end of the 1950s the city had succeeded the board of home missions as the second largest source of house income; with the decline in its financial support the church had much less say in the day-to-day running of the settlement. Throughout the 1950s there were few references to the church and its board of home missions at board meetings, a marked change from earlier years.

Attentive to the problems and emerging needs of the surrounding neighbourhood, St. Christopher House weathered the depression, the war and the post-war years as it reached out to those on relief, immigrants, juveniles in trouble with the law, and senior citizens. Its programming, staff and budget all dramatically increased. The ethnic composition of the community experienced a transformation from one that was almost exclusively Jewish and Anglo-Saxon in origin, to one reflecting a multitude of religions and nationalities. Over this period the staff — social work and child care — became increasingly professionalized reflecting the post-war trend for most social agencies.

UNIVERSITY SETTLEMENT — POST-WAR DEVELOPMENTS

In 1946 Frances Crowther, who had been head resident at University Settlement since 1934, resigned and moved to Los Angeles, where she was employed by the Episcopal diocese and worked with homeless men. Eventually, she moved to Victoria, British Columbia where she died in 1977. One of her biggest battles at the settlement occurred during her last year there and was over the issue of Sunday evening dances. All members of the settlement community — board, staff, club members and local clergy — were drawn into the dispute with what appeared to be unyielding sides quickly forming. "This seemingly mundane matter," wrote Hortense Wasteneys, "was indicative of the changes in mood, attitude and values which the depression and war years had helped to generate, particularly among the young. It is also illustrative of the difficulty of the established social order to adjust to the new values." The issue was simply that members of the teenage club wanted to institute Sunday evening dances. An articulate group, they buttressed their case with the argument that most could not entertain at home because their dwellings were too crowded and many had parents who were not receptive to friends being brought home. Throwing themselves wholeheartedly into the fray, the teenagers further advanced their case by pointing out that it was quite natural to want to be at the settlement on Sunday evenings since it was the one place they felt they belonged. Pursuing their case even further they pointedly asked what the difference was between listening to music or playing checkers on Sunday evenings (allowed activities) and dancing. Local clergy were diametrically opposed and drilled home the age-old argument that Sundays should be strictly for activities related to the church.

Aligning herself with the teenagers' position Crowther brought the matter to the attention of other local agencies including the Toronto Welfare Council. The head of the council, Bessie Touzel, told Crowther that having the controversy dropped in her lap had caused her no end of trouble with local churches, and now the Lord's Day Alliance was marshalling its forces for battle. Other settlements entered the dispute; Honorah Lucas, who had just assumed her new responsibilities as head resident at Central Neighbourhood House, collected information from the juvenile court on the number of juvenile offences occurring on Sunday. Her findings supported the teenagers' position that little was open to them on Sundays. The issue was finally laid to rest in February 1947 after Crowther left the settlement. The board reluctantly agreed to a compromise whereby Sunday dancing would be permitted for club members only after evening church services were completed. Grumblings about how unsatisfactory the resolution of the issue had been could still be heard among Toronto clergy into the late 1950s. "The whole affair regarding Sunday dancing might appear in retrospect to have been much ado about little," Wasteneys observed, "but in fact it did epitomize the generation gap that had been widened by the disruptive social influences of the depression and the War."

When Frances Crowther left the settlement in 1946, Mary Donaldson, a recent graduate of the University of Pittsburgh School of Social Work, was appointed as head worker. Her connection with University Settlement, however, stretched back to 1928 when she first joined the staff. The Pittsburgh school was a famous centre for the study of the new group work that was sweeping North American social work in the 1940s. The teaching there, Donaldson recalled, "saw group work — any kind of program — as a tool to help people grow with their peers." While at Pittsburgh she studied group work under two of its chief proponents, Gertrude Wilson and Gladys Ryland, the latter co-authored *Social Group Work Practice: The Creative Use of the Social Process* (1949), which served for many years as the textbook for the new group work ideas.

Donaldson's two years as head worker were somewhat troubled ones. There was considerable conflict with the board over new personnel policies and standards that she tried to introduce; in addition, new ideas about programme changes met with considerable resistance. In March 1948 the personnel committee of the board submitted a report outlining desired personnel policies and procedures that had been drafted by members of the committee, other staff and Donaldson. The board's initial reaction was negative and an amended version was brought back for a discussion one month later. Reluctantly, the board agreed to review the document clause by clause. Most clauses were accepted with little change; however, one encompassing the right to organize a union was resoundingly defeated. Addressing the annual meeting a week later the settlement's president, Hardolph Wasteneys, used the occasion to signal his decision to retire. He was distressed by the recently approved personnel standards and the more formal relationships between board and staff that would inevitably follow. "The action taken by the board at the last meeting," he sadly told his audience, "was a clear sign that it was time," for him to step down. "In this new order I could not feel at home." Warming to his theme Wasteneys gave full vent to his conception of social service work: "In a word it is through self-sacrificing love, not through concern for privilege or organization that the reward of success is gained in social work." Ultimately, the matter was resolved by a new watered-down version of the personnel statement hammered out by the board, staff and Wasteneys that seemed, publicly at least, to satisfy everyone. Wasteneys did not retire until 1953.

The crisis over the new personnel policies in 1948 was a critical turning point in the settlement's history. It marked the transition from the view of a settlement worker as altruistically helping others, to one of a professional worker with personal needs and rights. What was happening at University Settlement was simply reflective of a broader social trend that had been underway since at least the 1920s — the abandonment of a religiously based and idealistic approach to social service work and the adoption of one that was secular and technocratic.

Mary Donaldson, in line with her group work training, urged the staff to be much more permissive in their treatment of children. An approach that favoured the strict discipline of the classroom was replaced by one that encouraged the development of self-discipline through creative play and activity. Many board members were unhappy with this change of direction, particularly when damage occurred to settlement property. Dissatisfaction continued into the early months of 1949 when operating funds were found to be running a deficit of $1800. It was evident to most board members that Donaldson was woefully deficient in the basic skills of administration. Since it had been her intention to stay only two years when she took the job, a relatively amicable parting of the ways was arranged. After leaving Toronto, Donaldson spent a number of years in Pittsburgh settlement work and later retired to London, Ontario.

An important feature of settlement life in the 1940s was the increasing involvement of Toronto's black population. For many years black children and young black people had been in the clubs at University Settlement, but in the 1940s there was a growing feeling, according to Frances Crowther, that "it was all very well having blacks in the clubs but the settlement should also have them on the board and in the house." During Crowther's term as head resident she arranged for a member of the Home Service Association, an organization located on Bathurst Street that served as a kind of social settlement for the black population of Toronto, to become a member of the board at University Settlement. The first black resident at the settlement was Wilbur Howard, who later became the first black moderator of the United Church. Howard was born in Toronto and attended Victoria and Emmanuel colleges at the University of Toronto and was ordained as a United Church minister in 1941. For the next eight years he was boys' work secretary of the

Ontario Religious Education Council, which included most protestant denominations in the province. While occupying this position he was also, from 1944-1949, a resident at University Settlement. As a member of the settlement community Howard was one of the chief voices during the late 1940s that attempted to bring together the many ethnic groups in the neighbourhood. By all accounts he was a master at promoting less hostile and more positive inter-group relations.

After Donaldson left, a frantic search was on for a new head resident. The board was determined to find a person who would be more restrained in their enthusiasm for the permissiveness associated with the new group work ideas than Mary Donaldson. By July of 1949 the board settled on Kay Gorrie, a social worker with 25 years' experience, who, since 1943, had been executive director of Gordon Neighbourhood House in Vancouver. Gorrie grew up in a family with some radical leanings, and in 1936, while she was working at the Protestant children's home in Toronto, embarked on a trip to the Soviet Union with Margaret Gould of the child welfare council and Dora Wilensky, wife of Joseph Salsberg, a leading Toronto communist and herself head of the Toronto Jewish Family and Child Service. Gorrie and Gould were particularly interested in nursery schools and pre-school education in Russia. Joseph Atkinson of the *Toronto Star* advanced Gould $500 to write articles on the trip, which eventually appeared in book form. After their return Gould was hired as the first woman editor at the *Star*, and Gorrie gave at least one hundred talks about her experiences and early childhood education in a communist country.

On appointing Gorrie, the board expected her to rescue the settlement from the unfortunate Donaldson years and set three major goals for Gorrie to accomplish: stop the destruction of settlement property due to permissiveness, strengthen the settlement's relations with the university, and get rid of the day-care centre and restore the nursery school. It was Gorrie's deep rooted belief that "the war and the strong national feelings that came with it changed the role of the settlement. The need now is to provide an integrating factor in a community where vertical organization is strong and to give leadership in social action."

Hardolph Wasteneys was particularly anxious that the university and the settlement re-establish the closer ties that had characterized much of its earlier history. An unwavering apologist for the original settlement idea, Wasteneys pressed Gorrie on the point that the live-in residents ought to be university students. Under Donaldson, Wasteneys scornfully informed Gorrie, the settlement had come to resemble nothing more than a cheap boarding-house for clerical staff and social workers. Gorrie enthusiastically agreed that the university students ought to live at the settlement and put up notices around the campus offering inexpensive board in return for part-time work. This action bore fruit, and over the next several years a number of students from different departments came to live and work at the settlement.

Shortly after arriving Gorrie let it be known that she was opposed to day-care centres but not to nursery schools. In line with the common prejudices of the time, the board was fully sympathetic to this view; it and Gorrie were clearly of the opinion that a mother should look after her own children in the first few years of life. During World War II the ground floor of the junior house at 15 Grange Road had been converted to a war-time day nursery to enable women with young children to work in war-related industries. After the war, when the need for women to work was no longer so readily apparent, the nursery remained open. The original nursery school that had opened in the auditorium in 1929 had, by 1949, been closed. Gorrie was horrified to observe half-asleep toddlers stumbling along the corridors of the settlement dragged by over-wrought mothers hurrying to jobs. Finally, after expending considerable energy, Gorrie got the war-time day nursery (day-care centre) out and restored the nursery school. Gorrie carried on the debate on the evils of day-care in a radio broadcast where she locked horns with Florence Philpot of the Toronto Welfare Council. They had a bitter fight on the air but were friends in their private lives.

The geographical boundaries of University Settlement during the 1950s encompassed University Avenue, College Street, Spadina Avenue and the Waterfront. Kay Gorrie was remarkably successful in bringing new members into the house; from 1950 to 1954 membership doubled and attendance tripled, a credit to Gorrie's enthusiastic recruitment efforts. At least one-half of the 1500 members were children, and there were upwards of 40 nationalities represented. New members were pouring in so fast that, in 1953, the question was raised as to whether additional memberships should be restricted until more staff were hired. Tight budgets invariably made the acquisition of new staff difficult, and each year the settlement found itself chronically underfunded. A minor crisis occurred in 1952 when the settlement's budget committee approved expenditures for the coming year of $55,325, and shortly received word that the Toronto Community Chest had allocated a mere $42,500. Since staff pay increases had already been approved, Gorrie used some imaginative bookkeeping to earmark more money for salaries and less for items such as supplies. Largely through her own determination she was able to salvage a potentially disastrous situation.

The ethnicity of the neighbourhood underwent a notable change during the decade. Altering the composition were influxes of blacks, Japanese from the west coast and Jews and other displaced persons from Europe. Ethnic tensions ran high at times and considerable overt prejudice was evident with the derogatory term D.P. (displaced person) coming into common use. The problem of prejudice was fuelled in part by rising rates of unemployment and the apparent readiness of new Canadians to take work for lower wages and to work for longer hours. Family life could often be grim for these newcomers. Poverty and overcrowding were commonplace. Pockets of very poor housing characterized the social landscape below Queen Street; rent for a single room was typically $100 a month including a table, chair and cot. Many houses had from 15 to 20 occupants, often with four or five crammed into a single room. In addition to the excessive rents, rent controls were lifted and most of the housing was shabby and in violation of public health regulations. Peering into the backyards of these places one could observe piles of old tires, egg crates and packing boxes with little in the way of flowers or grass to relieve the dreary surroundings. Young children were exposed to crime and unseemly behaviour even when they came to the settlement. Grange Park was under constant surveillance by police as it was a notorious meeting place for alcoholics, drug addicts and prostitutes. With these impoverished social and economic conditions the involvement of settlement workers in the lives of these families and children was often of critical importance.

Attributing the squalid housing to years of neglect by landlords during the depression and war years, Gorrie took up the cudgels for those forced to live in these undesirable conditions. What particularly ignited her anger was the death of four people in a rooming house fire on River Street in 1953. She urged the board to send a pointed letter to city council setting out the case for increased subsidized housing; the board also wrote to the Toronto Welfare Council asking that they appoint a continuing committee to orchestrate action on the housing situation. The settlement was also involved with the department of architecture at the University of Toronto in canvassing social agencies in the area about housing problems. All these initiatives were a clear indication that Gorrie was keen to place a social reform stamp on the settlement's activities.

One of the mainstays of the settlement's program throughout its history had been the music school, which by the 1950s had become a well-organized conservatory of music and dance. The school was operating almost as a separate entity with its own director, registrar and 15 part-time teachers of violin, piano, singing, ballet and creative dancing. A special committee, set up in 1952 to examine the school, recommended that it be more integrated with the rest of the settlement's programs; accordingly, the director of the music school was made directly responsible to Gorrie for administration and management.

A controversial staff issue confronting Gorrie in the early 1950s was the question of whether staff should be required to live as residents at the settlement. There was a strong feeling among some staff that the board's wish to have new staff live in residence as a condition of employment could discriminate against married persons and those who simply preferred to live at home. In its defense the board maintained that to fully understand the philosophy of the settlement it was essential to spend time residing at the house. The staff needed to learn to empathize, it was argued, and this could only be accomplished through the experience of day-to-day living at the settlement. Gorrie diffused the bickering by suggesting that there were a number of ways for staff to learn the intricacies of settlement work without the necessity of residing on the premises.

Before she resigned in 1955, Gorrie became entangled in other disagreements with the board. Two professors from the school of social work, who were also board members, lined up against her and did not hesitate to make barbed comments about what they considered her inept handling of the budget. Contributing to the widening gap between Gorrie and faculty of the school of social work was her often-expressed view that, rather than training social workers, schools of social work in general were interested only in turning out pseudo-psychiatrists with vague Freudian notions drilled into their minds. In 1955 Gorrie departed and returned to Vancouver where she was offered two jobs, both of which she accepted on a part-time basis. The one position involved directing the affairs of North Shore Neighbourhood House, which was a social credit club, and the other was as director of International House at the University of British Columbia.

Taking over the reins from Gorrie in 1955 was Harry Morrow, the first man to hold the position since Dr. Norman Ware in 1915. He remained until 1966 after which he went to the University of Windsor to develop its school of social work. Morrow immediately put his mark on the settlement by requesting that his title be executive director rather than head resident; in addition, in a significant departure from past practice, he made it clear that he would not reside at the settlement. Morrow was the consummate administrator; he revised the constitution, clarified the terms of reference of the many committees, developed a much fuller statement of program policies and priorities, and produced a personnel manual for the staff. His vision of the settlement encompassed several related notions that he nurtured during his tenure as director: a community and neighbourhood centre, a locus for social research, a group work service unit and a music school. Throughout his years as director Morrow held to the view that University Settlement was part of a broad-based international movement for social progress, and he devoted considerable time and energy to national and international federations of settlements.

The most important achievement of Morrow's first years was overseeing the plans for a new building, which opened in April 1959 on Grange Road on the same site as the old quarters. The new University Settlement Recreation Centre was constructed with the aid of a grant of $665,000 provided by the city of Toronto. In securing these building funds a special agreement had been hammered out between the city and the settlement board in which the settlement relinquished ownership of the property while continuing to exercise total control over the day-to-day running of the settlement. Regrettably, with the opening of the new building, a long and venerable tradition of live-in staff and students came to an end because of new city by-law restrictions. On a more positive note University Settlement now boasted some noteworthy facilities: a well-lit art studio, a photography lab, woodworking shops, classrooms, lounges, a large gymnasium and swimming pool.

Morrow's fierce desire to build a recreation centre truly responsive to neighbourhood needs ultimately faced many difficulties in a community with rapid shifts and changes in population. In his first years he focused on European immigrants and established English classes and social clubs for many nationalities, including Italians, Germans and Hungarians. During Morrow's middle years as director, immigration to the neighbourhood slowed considerably while migrants from other parts of Canada arrived in ever-increasing numbers. The area was home to many multi-problem families requiring intensive social work services. By the mid 1960s large numbers of Chinese immigrants were moving into the district bringing many new challenges. Morrow had a remarkable ability to redirect the settlement's efforts to meet emerging needs and was able to inspire his staff to be ever-attentive to the daily concerns of those the settlement served.

Chapter Fourteen

From Settlement House to Neighbourhood Centre, 1960-1980

Described in broad terms the 1960s ushered in an interest in civil rights, citizen participation and an emphasis on community. By the middle of the decade the war on poverty in the United States and Canada had captured the imagination and enthusiasm of community activists. Settlement houses, or neighbourhood service centres as they were coming to be called, were viewed as one of the significant instruments for reducing or perhaps even eliminating self-defeating attitudes and behaviour on the part of the urban poor. A fundamental question asked by settlement workers was, "how can the poor be organized to press for relief from their poverty?". Storefront approaches to community change and notions of workers as social brokers began to surface. One document that had a pervasive influence on settlement workers in the United States and Canada was Arthur Hillman's *Neighbourhood Centres Today: Action Programs for a Rapidly Changing World* (1960), a study sponsored by the National Federation of Settlements and Neighbourhood Centres. This book, complete with case studies, fully explored the varying types of development that were emerging in the neighbourhood centre scene in the United States. Its seven chapters thoroughly surveyed ideas about citizen participation, service to multi-problem families, special youth services, inter-racial and inter-cultural programs, services for older adults, the relationship of settlements to the state, and social research and suggested that these were basic responsibilities of settlement activity.

While Hillman's account dealt exclusively with examples from the U.S. it had a marked impact on the Canadian settlements, which were just beginning to embrace some of the program areas described in *Neighbourhood Centres Today*. It was a benchmark in the understanding of settlement development and, coming as it did in 1960, its effects on the development of the Canadian settlement movement in that decade can scarcely be overestimated.

In 1960 University Settlement was just beginning to reap the benefits of its handsome new building provided by the city of Toronto into which it had moved the year before. The settlement was struggling to keep the spirit of a neighbourhood centre alive even while changing its name to the University Settlement Recreation Centre, in recognition of its fine new athletic facilities — a gymnasium and swimming pool unequalled in the entire downtown area. It was not coincidental, and in fact was a reflection of the influence of Hillman's analysis, that the 1960s saw University Settlement launch a major study of hard-to-reach youth and develop special youth services; the settlement also paid particular attention to multi-problem families and to racial difficulties.

Central Neighbourhood House, too, was at a turning point in its history. After the relatively quiet decade of the 1950s, in which order was restored after the stormy days of the late 1940s, Central Neighbourhood House, by the early 1960s, was ready to move forward into a new era of social research in cooperation with the School of Social Work at the University of Toronto. Central Neighbourhood House's copy of Hillman's *Neighbourhood Centres Today* was well thumbed, especially the chapter entitled, "Research as a Function of Settlements." Whether the seed of an idea was planted from workers pouring over that book, or whether Hillman's text simply reinforced the direction in which Central Neighbourhood House thinking already was moving cannot fully be determined; what is certain though, is that in the 1960s Central Neighbourhood House conducted six pivotal research studies — more than all other Toronto (and Canadian) settlements.

St. Christopher House did not have as definite a change of direction at this time; the flow of progressive ideas had moved steadily forward from the 1950s and through the early 1960s at a much more even pace. It too, though, launched several research studies dealing with school drop-outs and hard-to-reach youth. By the 1970s its various programmes had ripened to the point where *Neighbourhood Centres Today* could have been legitimately cited as the blueprint for its wide-ranging services; citizen participation, community development, youth services, inter-racial programs and services to older adults shared the spotlight with two nursery schools, a Portuguese information and counselling service, and cultural programs including art and dancing.

During the 1950s the city of Toronto experienced an alteration in the make-up of its population that had not been experienced since the great immigration waves of 1909-14. A good indication of the profound demographic changes underway can be ascertained from records maintained by the circulation division of the Toronto Public Library. In 1946 the division maintained a collection of 6070 books in foreign languages; by 1959 this collection had grown to over 22,000 volumes and a foreign literature centre at one of the downtown branches was completing its third successful year of service. About 2.7 million immigrants arrived in Canada between 1945 and the mid-1960s, with close to 25 per cent settling in Toronto. Metro Toronto's population was more than 1.6 million in 1961; five years later it had increased another 16 per cent. As James Lemon notes in *Toronto Since 1918: An Illustrated History* (1985), "the foreign-born population rose in the city from 31 per cent in 1951 to 42 per cent in 1961.... As for ethnic origins, the imprint of eastern and southern Europeans was clear by 1961....Italians quadrupled their numbers to 78,000, which was nearly 12 per cent of the city's population in 1961." Lemon writes that by 1961 "Toronto was well on its way to becoming the home of the largest concentration of 'ethnic' people in the country."

Throughout the 1960s the multi-cultural mix of Toronto became even more diverse. A principal reason for this was changes in 1962 to Canada's immigration policy, which abolished ethnic characteristics as determining suitability for entry. Those immigrants with particular skills considered useful to the increasingly complex Canadian economy were given priority treatment. As they had since their founding, the Toronto settlements played a key role in the relatively smooth transition of the city into a more cosmopolitan place.

UNIVERSITY SETTLEMENT, 1960-1980

During the course of its history the primary function of University Settlement had been to help immigrants to the downtown area adapt and adjust to life in Toronto and, by implication, Canada. An article in the University of Toronto student newspaper *The Varsity* in 1964 observed that, "these newcomers need to be shown what is expected of them and what they can expect in return. For example, University Settlement tries to make sure that none of these people are being misused or underpaid in their jobs...."

By the 1960s people migrating to Toronto from other parts of Canada in search of work increasingly occupied the attention of the settlement's workers; Maritimers in particular, as portrayed in Don Shebib's film *Goin' Down the Road*, flooded into the city in considerable numbers. There was a 40 per cent annual turnover rate of migrants in the University Settlement's neighbourhood, which resulted in almost continual change in the house's membership. Staff also came and went with considerable frequency in that highly transient decade as social workers with group work training were in great demand and often left for more attractive salaries elsewhere.

From 1959-63 University Settlement membership had grown to 3500; actual attendance at settlement activities and participation in programs often reached 15,000 a month. A study carried out in 1962 by the Social Planning Council of Metropolitan Toronto, successor to the Toronto Welfare Council, on the settlement's activities and organization, written by the council's research director John Gandy, offered a clear-eyed portrait of the settlement at the time. Not surprisingly, Gandy's review found that by far the largest majority of those participating in the settlement's programs lived in the centre of the city, many within easy walking distance. Fifty-six per cent of those active in settlement programs were male and 44 per cent female. The heaviest concentrations of activity were the music school, art centre and nursery school; each of these departments were always operating at capacity and had to limit enrolment. What the study unfortunately could not depict were the many intangibles of the house's work and accomplishments — the interpersonal relationships between leaders and members, the home visits and the day-to-day slogging of detached youth workers whose impact was impossible to quantify. It was evident that the settlement's long tradition of cooperative community work would need to continue into the 1960s. The council's study concluded by calling attention to the fact that the settlement's contribution to the life of Toronto "can be measured in the effectiveness of its service to the immediate neighbourhood in which it is located."

One issue that extended University Settlement's interests beyond the narrow confines of its own problems was how best to help the Home Service Association on Bathurst Street, an agency established in 1921 that offered service to Toronto's black population. University Settlement had been a pioneer in Toronto by welcoming blacks into integrated programmes: it had the first black resident, Wilbur Howard, in the 1940s; a black staff member, Ron Howze, in the 1950s; St. Christopher House was the first settlement in Toronto to hire a black staff person, John Braithwaite, in 1951; and appoint a black, Vyola Miller, to its board in the 1950s. While its record was impressive it was not completely unspotted. In 1956, after much soul searching and internal bickering, University Settlement decided not to allow a social evening for the great American black singer and political activist Paul Robeson to be held on its premises. The claim was made that this trying decision was based not on grounds of colour but rather out of a concern that the house's much-prized neutrality would be tainted because of Robeson's established and notorious left-wing political sympathies. Not everyone was convinced, and the incident cast some doubt on the settlement's genuine commitment to Toronto blacks. Despite these tensions University Settlement was, by the late 1950s, the closest of all the Toronto settlements to the Home Service Association; in no small way this bond had been cemented by George Tatham, a member of the boards of both organizations. Tatham, a University of Toronto geography professor and later the long-serving and popular dean of students at York University's Glendon College, was a person of generous inclinations and progressive views who had a particular knack for bringing people together.

In spite of an important record of accomplishments, problems confronting the Home Service Association were stacked up like cordwood. Toronto's United Community Fund indicated that it intended to cut off financial support unless an experienced body took over day-to-day operations. The social planning council made a plea to University Settlement to undertake this difficult and delicate task; somewhat reluctantly the settlement agreed to do this on a *pro tempore* basis. A University Settlement board committee was created to monitor the unfolding situation, and Edith Ferguson was appointed to act as executive director with the immediate responsibility of preparing a report with recommendations on the many difficulties plaguing the Home Service Association.

Working diligently, Ferguson presented her report to the University Settlement's board in April 1960. She had identified two fundamental but related problems. The association was trying to do too much by attempting to meet the needs of two different groups: the black community throughout Toronto and the largely Italian neighbourhood located in the vicinity of the settlement. By 1960 the area bounded by Spadina, Bloor, Manning and Dupont was a highly mobile one, often the second geographical stop on an immigrant's progress up the economic scale — 1. downtown districts; 2. north of Bloor Street; 3. farther north, east or west or to the newly developing suburbs. Very few blacks lived in the settlement's neighbourhood; in 1960 there were no black children in the Home Service Association's nursery school and only four out of a total of one hundred in the after school group.

The Home Service Association's initial purpose had primarily been to serve black families, although it never saw itself as restricting its services to one specific group. Its board had always been mainly black as had the director and other staff members. In 1960 it was estimated that the black population of Toronto was between 6500-8500. For many years there had been a strong concentration in the downtown area (bounded by Queen,

McCaul, College and Bathurst), the district served by University Settlement and St. Christopher House. By 1960 there was still a considerable concentration in the Spadina/College area. During the preceding ten to fifteen years many black families had moved and were now scattered throughout the city and its suburbs. Ferguson's report was careful to point out that Toronto's black population was far from homogenous. The two largest groups were native Torontonians and immigrants from the West Indies; a third, whose numbers had been steadily increasing, were from the U.S. and a fourth group consisted of a small number from Bermuda. As well, a small but growing cluster of black Nova Scotians was making its way to Toronto in the hope of improving their economic circumstances.

Ferguson's report examined the elements contributing to the tension and disharmony that existed among the various black groups and how the strain might be eased. During her inquiry into the problems of the Home Service Association and blacks, a great deal of pointed opinion was aired as to whether a separate organization for blacks should be maintained. No immediate or satisfactory solution to the problem seemed apparent to Ferguson, and for the remainder of 1960 University Settlement maintained a watchful eye over the operations of the Home Service Association. Later that year the association's nursery school was closed, a move which led Ferguson to resign at the end of the year and which was bitterly opposed by many in the black community. Other insensitive actions followed, and the scars from the unfortunate handling of the future of the Home Service Association were permanent.

Trouble was also brewing on another front. There had been many disturbing incidents at the settlement caused by rebellious and marginally criminal teenagers, which included a series of break-ins believed to have been committed by club members. In 1960-61 the concern for troubled youth was under constant review at board and staff meetings. Poverty and early school leaving, often by grade 8, were key contributing factors; it was becoming more and more difficult for those who did leave school to seek employment, and very few found permanent work that was suitable. To address this problem University Settlement established a youth project in 1961 that had as its main thrust detached street work with alienated youth, as the sociological literature was now calling it. In taking this action University Settlement propelled itself to the forefront of neighbourhood work — the project was the first of its kind in Canada. James Felstiner, who held degrees in law and social work, was appointed to head the project. Over the next four years Felstiner and others reached out to many troubled and distraught teenagers with considerable success. According to *The Varsity*, Felstiner's approach was to spend "long hours a week hanging out in restaurants and pool halls, walking the streets and alley ways near the settlement and visiting the boys' homes. The offer of the use of his car, a cigarette, or just a sympathetic ear earned him acceptance, and his uncritical accepting attitude towards the boys gained him their confidence and friendship." Felstiner later became a well-known family court judge in Toronto.

At board and staff meetings throughout his time as executive director (1955-66) Harry Morrow raised, on a regular basis, the problems of poverty, unemployment and public welfare. In 1961 he exhorted his staff to prepare some kind of statement for local MPPs on the growing affliction of youth unemployment; ultimately a committee was established to study unemployment and its effects on settlement members. Morrow's September 1963 report to the board discussed, at some length, the changing complexion of the settlement's neighbourhood. It was becoming much less a reception area, he observed, and much more a neighbourhood of very poor families. Many families were surviving on very low weekly incomes and struggling to keep themselves off welfare. Morrow informed the board that at Toronto city council there had been considerable debate about work-for-relief schemes for welfare recipients; this had stirred up deep-seated prejudices against those on welfare, with many members of the public being led to assume that everyone receiving city funds was shiftless. He reminded the board that one of the traditional roles of the settlement had been to interpret one group in the community to another; consequently, he proposed that the board draw up and release a statement "on the problem of poverty in our time." From Morrow's observations it was all too easy to forget about the poor, yet their plight was serious. As an example he referred to housing conditions on downtown Toronto's Widmer Street, which brought forth regular expressions of indignation from politicians and a somewhat sensational newspaper story, and yet, as he pointed out, conditions of run-down housing had existed on that particular street for at least 30 years. What disturbed Morrow was that no one in authority seemed in a hurry to do anything about the deplorable conditions in many of Toronto's subsidized housing tracts; regrettably, he concluded there were few positive signs of change in the air. Admitting that "this was a small fester in an affluent society, we ought to realize, nevertheless, that these pockets of poverty have the potential for real social problems in the future." Thirty years later his prognostications have proven correct.

Morrow brought up the matter again and instructed the board about the corrosive effects of poverty on people: "in periods of widespread prosperity some families still live on less than adequate incomes and their members suffer from the effects." Forced to tackle the issue again the board decided to distribute and be prepared to discuss the article "Our Invisible Poor" from a recent issue of the *New Yorker* magazine; it was becoming increasingly difficult to overlook the reality of a neighbourhood where 25 per cent of the inhabitants were estimated to be living below the poverty line. Not all board members tried to steer clear of the topic. Professor John Morgan of the school of social work at the university suggested, on more than one occasion, that tackling an intractable issue like poverty was beyond the capability of University Settlement, and he put forward the notion that all the Toronto settlements take some kind of collective action. Little ever came of these initiatives and the question of poverty served to demonstrate to anyone who cared to notice that there were limitations on the settlements' prospects for bringing about substantial social change.

In speaking to the Toronto Elizabeth Fry Society in November 1965, Mae Harman, supervisor of club programs for University Settlement, reflected on the formidable task of providing meaningful services to girls in the settlement's neighbourhood. "I think that girls are more wary of seeking and accepting help; they are taught to distrust and to protect themselves from advances," she explained. It was Harman's experience that when girls' difficulties were finally noticed they were often well into a pattern of promiscuity, and prostitution was often the result of years of neglect, loneliness and despair. It was the fate of many central city girls Harman had observed to adopt lifestyles learned from their mothers: "to bear the burdens of the family, have a lot of children and, perhaps, to be used and pushed around physically and, maybe, to be deserted." Harman confided to her listeners that it was one of her fondest wishes to bolster the self-image of the girls who came to the settlement enabling them to see that marriage could be more than that. She admitted that perhaps aspiring to a sense of fulfilment was a middle-class value, "but I'd like to wish it for all women, whether as wife or mother or career woman." She used the occasion to stress that practical services such as housing, health, legal aid and rehabilitation needed to be valued as much as the higher status case work method so revered by trained social workers.

By 1965 there was mounting pressure to reassess University Settlement's programs and priorities. Three distinct focal points were identified in the neighbourhood: older people, migrants from Eastern Canada and a large influx of Chinese. Meetings were held with representatives of the Chinese community and other groups to discuss the future of the district. Many more Chinese were using the settlement's facilities for regularly scheduled activities. In 1967 a Chinese speaking worker, Yin Chee Hung, was hired and in 1969 a Chinese information and interpreter service was set up along with the expansion of language and citizenship classes. At the end of the 1960s Chinese representatives began to serve on the board.

In June 1966 Harry Morrow resigned to accept a position as the director of the newly established school of social work at the University of Windsor. Only two applicants were seriously considered to replace him — Mae Harman and Ian Thomson, the then director of training, parks and recreation for the city of Toronto. Male board members strongly favoured Thomson and, despite misgivings by some that he was not a professional social worker, he was offered the position at $12,000 a year; to encourage her to stay Harman was invited to accept the position of assistant director at $9500 a year. Thomson accepted; Harman did not. She resigned at the end of 1966 to become the executive secretary of the Ontario Association of Professional Social Workers. University Settlement lost a worker who was vitally concerned with women's issues and struggles for equality.

Throughout the 1960s the board and the director firmly established community development as one of University Settlement's major themes. This thrust gained additional momentum in 1968 with the hiring of A. Dharmalingam (Dharma) to assess community needs and to promote stronger ties between the settlement and the neighbourhood. The basic approach was to form small neighbourhood groups on the block to fully air neighbourhood problems and to propose needed programs. In early 1969 Dharma outlined the key characteristics of the settlement's district for the board. The population of the area was about 10,400 living between University and Spadina avenues and Front and College streets. Of 1800 dwelling units two-thirds were occupied by tenants and the balance by owners. Slightly over 50 per cent of the population was Chinese with the two public schools having an enrolment of 80 per cent Chinese children; the area's separate school had an enrolment of over 80 per cent Portuguese, with most of these children being bussed to school from an area north of the settlement district. Average household income was $2400-$2500 per annum and there were pockets of relatively poor housing. Planned meetings with both homeowners and tenants were "primarily designed to acquaint the neighbourhood with current plans and projects in the area and to discuss their feelings and hopes in relation to their homes," Dharma informed the board. His report drew the board into a lengthy discussion regarding the difficulties the settlement was having relating to the Chinese community. Several members suggested that it was evident the settlement needed to move quickly to hire more Chinese staff, which in turn would serve to attract many more Chinese into the house's programs. In addition the time had clearly come to begin advertising services in Chinese. As further evidence that University Settlement was serious in its wish to foster improved relations with the Chinese community, a sign in Chinese was made for the front of the building.

By the beginning of the 1960s University Settlement's nursery school was in such demand, with larger numbers of women entering the workforce, that an afternoon program had been added. A serious difficulty occurred in 1968 when provincial legislation, following new federal requirements under the Canada Assistance Plan, made the application of a needs test necessary before financial assistance could be given for parents with children in nursery school programs. This resulted in a significant drop in enrolment at the settlement's nursery school. Many families who were slightly above the welfare level found it degrading to lay bare their financial status to obtain a subsidy for their children's attendance. A fair number of parents had placed their children in the nursery school because of special needs and not necessarily because they were working. In February 1968 ten of the forty-two families with children in the nursery school had withdrawn their children because of the new financial arrangements. Those adversely affected were in the $5000 income range, and were finding that the new legislation moved the nursery program into the category of a luxury that they could no longer afford. A brief for Ontario's minister of social and family services drafted by the director and board argued that the legislation gives "no recognition of the educative value of this form of pre-school where the children from a variety of backgrounds and income levels exchange ideas and expose themselves to different attitudes and values." As a result of many submissions making a similar case the Day Nurseries Act was altered later that year to again make it possible for those families who had been forced to drop out of the program to return.

Once securely ensconced in new facilities University Settlement's music program thrived as never before; upwards of 300 children, adults and seniors a year benefited from the pleasures of learning to play an instrument, sing and to give and attend recitals. Frederick Skitch, whose tenure as director of the music school stretched from 1949-1980, captured perfectly what the program was intended to accomplish: "the music school functions in the belief that all the arts, music included, are an essential part of life and living — that they reflect the quality of our living, and a participation in them strengthens the discipline by which we live and increases the enjoyment and meaning of our life."

By the end of the decade University Settlement had reaffirmed its general purpose of providing opportunities for people in the neighbourhood to achieve a more satisfying way of life. This general purpose could best be served through maintaining a partnership between the people in the neighbourhood and the settlement, by continually interpreting social and economic needs through responsible discussion, clarification of aspirations and the creation of planning groups and citizens' committees dedicated to the neighbourhood's development and improvement. Harry Morrow perhaps said it best when he described University Settlement as "not a charity but a means of helping people to help themselves, of giving leadership and self-assurance."

Two features in particular marked the work of University Settlement in the early 1970s: the growing influence of the Chinese community and organized efforts to block unwelcome development in the neighbourhood. More Chinese workers were hired by the settlement, particularly for positions as receptionists and community workers where face-to-face contact with the public was a factor; annual reports were now printed in Chinese as well as English; one-quarter of the children enrolled in the music school were Chinese; and the Metropolitan Toronto Chinese Golden Age Society, with a membership of 500, met regularly at University Settlement. In 1970 University Settlement participated in planning and organizing the first Chinese community conference at which dozens of resolutions were passed affecting the quality of life in the Chinese community. The Chinese information and interpreter service, from its establishment in 1969, was immediately flooded with requests for help by newcomers impeded by a language barrier and struggling to gain a foothold in an environment with few familiar landmarks.

At a board meeting in late 1970 an innovative proposal was brought forward by the program review and development committee for a centre, to be located at University Settlement, where all available data on the history and experiences of the Chinese in Canada could be assembled. One of the purposes would be to help "young Chinese to acquire a rich and stable identity, which would provide a base for scholarship and community understanding." The plan envisioned a collection of material from across Canada, which would be stored on microfilm. A budget of $10,000 was proposed and the board enthusiastically endorsed the proposal. The United Community Fund was asked to provide the necesary funds to set up the venture, and there the entire scheme ran aground. Undaunted the settlement pressed ahead with its promotion of Chinese culture; Chinese New Years' celebrations were, for example, now grand events with hundreds in attendance and considerable television and newspaper publicity. By 1974 Chinese cooking classes and Cantonese language classes for both Chinese and non-Chinese individuals, which provided further opportunities for those of different cultures to rub elbows with one another, were under way. The settlement's high profile with the Chinese community brought in its wake a number of racial incidents. One was a malicious letter circulated throughout the neighbourhood by the right-wing Edmund Burke Society asserting that University Settlement had allied itself with left-wing and pro-Peking groups, and it called upon the United Community Fund to reconsider its support of the agency in light of these undesirable political activities. Too experienced to fall for this red-baiting, the fund issued a positive statement in defense of University Settlement, which was published in local Chinese newspapers.

The transmission of ethnic culture through the University Settlement environment was, for Bill Stern who became executive director in 1973, one of the prime reasons for the settlement's existence. By 1971 the total Chinese population in Ontario was 48,000, and in Toronto almost 21,000; during 1970-73 Chinese immigration to Ontario increased at a dramatic rate; a total of 13,200 people from mainland China, Hong Kong and Taiwan moved to the province, the vast majority to the Toronto area. Typical of University Settlement's efforts to promote a more sensitive understanding of the Chinese element in the city was an intercultural seminar on the Chinese community sponsored by the Ontario Citizenship Bureau of the Ministry of Culture and Recreation in 1975. In spite of blustery early spring weather over 100 individuals showed up to hear Judge K. Wang of the provincial court's family division open the seminar with an historical overview of Chinese life in Canada.

In the early days Chinese men had come alone to work on the transcontinental railroad and had stayed on, finding employment mainly in laundries and small restaurants. They were barred by the prohibitive head tax, and later by the exclusionary clauses of the 1923 Chinese Immigration Act, from bringing their wives and families. With the more enlightened policies of the Canadian government, many more young people were now emigrating, often bringing with them a good knowledge of English. Judge Wang made a plea for more Chinese to become actively involved in public life in order to help overcome what was now more of a psychological disenfranchisement. Panel discussions followed on employment, youth and recreation, the aged, and health; all of these issues were united by a common theme of how best to ease the many tensions that the Chinese community experienced in these areas. Seminars and workshops held throughout the 1970s on the settlement's role in mediating and lessening ethnic conflict were a clear indication of its continuing resourcefulness in responding to a shifting neighbourhood and its long-standing commitment to nurturing neighbourly sentiment.

With its wider focus on community development and decreased emphasis on in-building group work and recreation, University Settlement was unwittingly drawn into the political realm in the 1970s, and strained relationships with local politicians developed. When one of the house's community workers presented a controversial brief to the metro transportation committee opposing the Spadina expressway, Alderman June Marks was quick to react. She questioned whether, in light of its new political role, University Settlement should continue to receive funding for its activities and programs from the city. Marks's ire was rekindled when the settlement's executive director Ian Thompson and other workers appeared before the city's building and development committee to support Chinese and other neighbourhood groups opposing proposals from the Windlass Corporation to construct a complex of high-density residential buildings between University Avenue and McCaul Street. As a supporter of the Windlass proposals and a member of the settlement's board (by virtue of her position as ward alderman), Marks was finding herself in an increasingly awkward situation and vented her frustration through lashing out at the house. Marks's criticisms drew a spirited response from former worker Mae Harman, and in a letter to the *Globe and Mail* Harman asked, "what social agency that dares to relate to its community and work with the people and their problems, their hopes and their desires, will be the next one to be threatened with lack of financial support?" Other letters went further in upbraiding Marks for her anti-community attitudes. In 1976 Ontario cabinet minister Allan Grossman charged that University Settlement had been taken over by a bunch of radicals when his request to hold a nominating meeting for his son, Larry, was turned down. The house had informed the irritated Allan Grossman that it had an explicit policy of not allowing political meetings to take place on its premises.

At the 1972 annual meeting the guest speaker was Colin Vaughan, former president of the Confederation of Residents and Ratepayers Associations and a prominent figure in the "stop-the-Spadina-movement." He talked of "the growing concern of citizens, particularly in downtown areas, about the forces which affect their lives and the mobilization taking place to ensure that they have a role in the decision making." These sentiments were exactly what had motivated University Settlement and the Grange Park community to become centrally involved in the hydro block issue.

In the late 1960s Ontario Hydro assembled (block-busted) a block of 42 houses in the middle of a low-rise, primarily Chinese neighbourhood just north of the Ontario Art Gallery, specifically the area bounded by Beverley, Cecil, Henry and Baldwin streets, with the intention of building a 13- to 16-storey transformer and switching station. Families were forced out and the houses boarded up, and the block soon showed all the grim signs of a neighbourhood destroyed. Massive public protest soon followed, and on the eve of the 1971 provincial election MPP and cabinet minister Allan Grossman announced that the Ontario Housing Corporation would take over the block for use as low-income housing, much more in scale with the neighbourhood.

A hydro block working committee was established with University Settlement community worker Kay Parsons serving as vice-chair. Various plans were drawn up, and by late 1973 all the pieces seemed in place to proceed with the necessary renovations for the houses. Delay was followed by delay, with the major sticking point being the cost of the land. Ontario Hydro had paid a highly inflated price for the land and the cost was passed on to the Ontario Housing Corporation (OHC). The per-unit land cost was $16,000 — $10,000 more per unit than Central Mortgage and Housing Corporation, which provided OHC's mortgage money, was willing to pay. Without a government write-down of the land cost, which the province would not consider, work on rehabilitating the houses could not proceed. Grossman and his colleagues were proposing some form of mixed development, with some private sales and only about 30 per cent of the land earmarked for low-cost public housing. This was a completely unacceptable solution to the working committee, which continued to insist that the low-income housing that one arm of the provincial government had taken away should now be fully restored by another arm of the same government, the OHC.

The issue continued to simmer away, and at the end of April 1975 about 100 residents marched on Queen's Park to protest the lack of action. Leather-lunged activists brandishing placards bearing slogans such as "Write Down Land Costs — Don't Write Off People," demanded to see Premier Davis and the now discredited Grossman. Ultimately an agreement was reached with Toronto's Non-Profit Housing Corporation to take over the boarded up houses and convert them to low-rental units, and city council agreed to give priority in tenant selection to former residents who had been displaced when Ontario Hydro first purchased the properties. The question of providing adequate rent supplements remained an unresolved bone of contention over the next several years.

After Ian Thomson left his post as executive director in 1973, a succession of directors and acting directors followed until A. Dharmalingham (Dharma) took on the post in 1978 and remained at the helm through the 1980s and into the 1990s. At the end of the 1970s the physical setting of the building had been greatly enhanced by a renovated lobby and a new lounge on the second floor. The day-care program had steadily assumed a place of importance in the house and almost 50 children, ranging in age from three months to five years, were looked after by a professional staff and parents who were strongly encouraged to participate. The music school, supported by a teaching staff of 20 qualified musicians, flourished; as did the usual array of club programs for all ages, which provided occasions for socializing and fostering a feeling of community. As the 1979 annual report stated, "the major concern of all aspects of the work of University Settlement is the development of a sense of community at the local level — and community is people."

ST. CHRISTOPHER HOUSE, 1960-1980

Although the formal connection between St. Christopher House and the United Church had been severed by the 1960s, when St. Christopher House was incorporated as an independent organization in 1963, the house still defined its work as "a readily distinguished type of Christian ministry." In celebrating its 50th anniversary in 1962, the board and staff drew inspiration from Graham Taylor, founder of the famous Chicago Commons Settlement, who had observed in 1919 that "the fundamentals of all true religion are 'vertical' and 'horizontal' — the fatherhood of God, and the brotherhood of man. Anything that comes within these concepts is wise and natural to teach in a settlement either formally or informally."

A great deal of St. Christopher House's time, attention and energy was taken up in the 1960s with evolving plans to vacate the old residence at 67 Wales Avenue in the Kensington Market area, where it had been located since its founding in 1912, and move to new quarters. Three main factors contributed to a growing feeling that a move was necessary. The first was related to the city of Toronto's 1956 twenty-five year parks plan, which recommended that community centres be established throughout the city. When, a few years later, the city built the $665,000 centre for University Settlement and yet another centre in Trinity Park, "the feeling of the board," Harriet Parsons wrote, "was that, if the new centres affected St. Christopher House to the extent that its services were no longer required, St. Christopher would not hesitate to move to a new location where their services were needed." A second factor was that space and maintenance problems could no longer be ignored. The five white houses joined together with architectural charm were rapidly deteriorating; termites and cockroaches had infiltrated, water pipes often burst, and the gymnasium roof was in a state of almost total collapse. The third factor was the proposed redevelopment of the slums of Alexandra Park in the area southwest of Bathurst and Dundas streets. The Toronto planning board recommended, as an integral part of its redevelopment blueprint for the district, that a recreation centre be a focal point for the residents. Shortly after, the social planning council, studying the need for a community centre, urged the planning board to build a new neighbourhood centre in the Bathurst and Dundas area that would incorporate, under one roof, basic community amenities such as group services, public health, counselling, a library and a day-care centre. It was also strongly recommended that since St. Christopher House had a long and distinguished history of serving the neighbourhood it should give up its present location and take over the operation of the proposed new centre.

This was music to the ears of those associated with St. Christopher House, and a future plans committee was set in motion, which eventually produced ten detailed studies on the settlement's future. Optimism reigned supreme when, in late 1966, Toronto city council's parks and recreation committee recommended that council "endorse in principle the desirability of erecting a major recreation and neighbourhood service centre in the triangle at Bathurst and Dundas streets to be owned and operated by St. Christopher House." It was also recognized that the provincial and federal governments would be asked to support these plans financially. Jubilation over this positive turn of events was short-lived.

During the next several years the problems related to bringing these plans to fruition multiplied: competition for the use of the triangle; changing city hall policies; the seeming impossibility of getting a definite commitment of funds from any level of government; the steady deterioration of the Wales Avenue buildings; and, perhaps most unsettling of all, internal uncertainties and differences of opinion as to what their own course should be. Ultimately St. Christopher House never assumed responsibility for the community centre in Alexandra Park where, by the end of the 1970s, the Scadding Court Community Centre was run as a separate organization. Instead, in 1973, St. Christopher House opened its new quarters at 84 Augusta Avenue. After this move the decentralization of many of the house's services, an approach adopted a few years earlier, continued as a permanent arrangement. Half the nursery school was now located in a church on Carr Street; the other half, along with the Portuguese interpreter service, shifted to the Kensington Community School. The Older Adult Centre had transferred to the Queen Street United Church (761 Queen St. W.). Remaining at the Augusta location were the administration, the music school, art classes, the youth and family service, and community development staff. In 1967 John Haddad, who had been the director since 1953, left and his place was taken by David Maben who had been the program director. In 1972 Jean Palmer took on the job for eight years; she came with fine credentials as a social worker and former director of the YWCA.

In the early 1970s a student at the school of social work at the University of Toronto questioned the wisdom of St. Christopher House decentralizing its programs to the extent that it had and whether it could continue to serve as a focal point of community involvement and community action. Through the years St. Christopher House had come to be known as a place to come for recreation, counselling, education or just a place to relax and warm up on a cold day. This place, it was feared, was now in the process of disappearing; no longer would it be one centralized visible agency in the community. These sentiments were voiced by many, and although the house developed many new approaches during the 1970s that responded to a changing neighbourhood, there were lingering doubts as to the wisdom of so many administrative rearrangements.

By the 1960s St. Christopher House was physically showing signs of age. Located as it was in a cramped, unfavoured district with its worn and broken floor, well-trodden red broadloom carpets and flaking grey paint, St. Christopher House continued to be an oasis in a large, impersonal city. It was not a formal social agency of chrome, glass and polished desks but rather a vibrant, earthy place. Defining itself now as a neighbourhood centre the house tried to be sensitive to the increasingly serious plight of inner city residents confronted by rapid urbanization, poverty and unemployment, and to a neighbourhood with more than its fair share of what social workers were now calling multi-problem families. St. Christopher House portrayed itself as a friend to the neighbourhood as well as bringing the emerging problems of school drop-outs and transient workers to the attention of the wider community. The staff did their utmost to maintain a friendly, relaxed atmosphere; one where, unlike many other social agencies, those seeking help did not have to wait for an appointment. An example of this occurred when a Hungarian woman, barely able to speak English, arrived on the settlement's doorstep having just fought off her landlord who had been sexually harassing her. The landlord had ordered her out of her lodging and she had nowhere else to turn; a staff worker at St. Christopher House found her a room, loaned her money and helped her move her belongings.

Community development work at St. Christopher House came of age in the 1960s. Community development is almost synonymous with settlement work; the emphasis is on the immediate neighbourhood and its people and how their civic consciousness-raising could ameliorate slums and grinding poverty. St. Christopher House brought this tradition forward when Charlyn Howze was hired in 1961 as the first designated community worker in Toronto. During the 1960s and the 1970s Howze, who died in 1968, and others inspired by her, encouraged and helped the community to organize autonomous groups to work actively towards a solution to neighbourhood problems. By the 1970s the term citizen participation was in widespread use, and it permeated every phase of the decision-making process at St. Christopher House and other settlements. This pronounced emphasis on community work marked an almost complete shift in focus from a purely building-centred approach to community involvement and community action in a great variety of ways — in the settlement, in the neighbourhood and in the larger community.

Far from turning its back on the day-to-day troubles and worries of individuals, St. Christopher House reached deep into the lives of its neighbours. On any given day the air literally vibrated with the comings and goings of many who found refuge in an otherwise uncaring society. Workers might turn their attention to a nervous and upset mother with slim resources, both financial and emotional, as she struggled to cope with a fractious three year old. Investigating the situation a worker might discover that there were no toys available for the child. St. Christopher House would then provide suitable equipment and involve the mother in a group where she could learn more about ways to relate constructively to her toddler. An old-age pensioner, feeling somewhat forlorn, would have his spirits lifted by a surprise birthday party; sad and lonely souls trying to cling to respectability on $13.00 a week unemployment insurance would find sympathy and help from a friendly English teacher. For St. Christopher House neighbourliness was not an outmoded idea, as the settlement envisioned itself "pushing out its walls and melting into the district."

Community work was the centrepiece of St. Christopher House's activities in the 1960s. The settlement provided a place for local groups to meet and begin exercising an independent voice and some measure of control over the development of their neighbourhood. Settlement workers would open channels with city departments and officials, thus drawing pressing neighbourhood needs to the attention of appropriate authorities. A greater measure of citizen participation, it was argued, would have valuable repurcussions: a greater sense of confidence and more tolerance towards those whose values and ideas differed from one's own; a discovery that participating in controversial social issues was an acceptable democratic principle; an awareness that banding together could aid in solving larger problems; the dawning realization that one did not always have to adjust to unsatisfactory conditions; and, most importantly, that social improvement often started with dissent. It was the job of the community worker to move out into the community and mobilize the capacities of people to solve many of their own difficulties and to create a satisfactory community life for themselves. Certainly by 1966 all these ideas had crystallized into a clear objective for community work at St. Christopher House. The house was now fixed in its resolve to deal with community problems through collective action, reform, the democratic participation of neighbours and self-help groups.

Spearheading community work at the house from 1961-67 was Charlyn Howze — "the Angel of Kensington," as she was affectionately called. Endearing herself to all she encountered, Howze was a person of slight build, indomitable courage and matchless integrity who gave her life to the Kensington area. By the sheer dint of her own industry and talent she almost single-handedly organized the Alexandra Park Residents' Association in 1963, and she continued to lend her most welcome support to the people of Alexandra Park through the various phases of urban renewal: initiation, planning, expropriation, demolition and renewal. All those who knew her attested that her tireless efforts, at considerable physical cost to herself, led to the establishment of close and harmonious relationships between city officials and residents of the area.

Howze was the moving spirit behind the Kensington beautification campaign of 1963. Concerned that the area was viewed by many in the city as an undesirable slum, 40 neighbourhood workers and Howze organized a door-to-door canvass to discuss with each family what part it might play in the neighbourhood. Much cleaning, painting and planting resulted; there were demonstrations of gardening and carpentry, and local schools held art competitions in which students drew pictures of the various beautification projects. The campaign closed with a flourish — a street dance, carnival and the awarding of prizes. One of the lasting benefits of this effort was the creation of a local committee to press the city for long-needed road and sidewalk repairs and for extra garbage collections. As a result of the overwhelming success of this first campaign others were organized, leading one observer to comment, "these community organization efforts seem to be reaping some startlingly good harvests. Among the members and their neighbours one can see new hope and enthusiasm, many ideas for self-help and clear signs of permanent change and improvement."

A fine example of the quiet but effective community work of Charlyn Howze was the manner in which she took on the local but urgent issue of traffic in the Kensington Market area in 1962-63. Congestion from traffic had become acute and extremely bothersome to residents; at the same time the city planning board was formulating rather elaborate plans for remodelling the area. Encouraged by Howze, two mass meetings of merchants were held at St. Christopher House out of which grew the Kensington Market

Businessmen's Association; the merchants latched on to the idea of approving a parking lot to be built by the city as a solution to the traffic problem and hoped they might be able to cajole local residents into accepting their solution. In the best community work tradition Howze also made contact with residents in the area, well aware that they might need some protection. Many of those contacted were not keen on the parking lot and, following a meeting of their own at the settlement also arranged by Howze, the homeowners made representations to the Ontario Municipal Board against the parking lot plan favoured by the Kensington Market merchants. Weighing the respective cases of the two sides, the board ultimately refused the city's request to purchase property for the lot. Throughout this period of conflicting views punctuated by bursts of bitter anger, Howze worked calmly and equally with the two opposing groups. She held firm to the view that any group in the neighbourhood should be able to organize around their concerns and entitled to a meeting place, assistance and expertise from the settlement. Her conduct in this issue firmly established her reputation as a person able to form relationships with people around their interests, with no axe of her own to grind. When Howze died in 1968 the city passed a resolution setting up a fund to purchase a piece of sculpture that was placed in Denison Square the following year to commemorate her enduring achievements as a community worker.

Another innovative thrust of St. Christopher House was the mounting of the first meals-on-wheels service in Toronto — services already existed in Peterborough, Brantford and Winnipeg — an idea that first surfaced at a board meeting in October 1964. A board member, who had been closely associated with starting a similar service in Great Britain in 1939, made a persuasive case that the steadily rising number of elderly in the city, who often went without a hot meal, was cause for concern. Enthusiastically embracing her suggestion, St. Christopher House set in motion the administrative mechanisms necessary for launching a Toronto meals-on-wheels program. A year later, with most of the stumbling blocks cleared out of the way, the service was up and running. A $5000 grant from the Laidlaw Foundation to cover the first three years' running costs was instrumental in launching the project. Initially eight elderly people were provided with a nutritious hot meal consisting of soup, juice, green salad, red meat or chicken, potato, vegetables, bread and butter, desert and milk. The meals were prepared by the Provincial Institute of Trades on Nassau Street and delivered by volunteers drawn primarily from women's groups associated with local churches. The program expanded rapidly and at the end of the first 18 months 30 elderly people were receiving home-delivered meals. By May 1967 nine other similar services had been developed throughout the city.

It was generally acknowledged that St. Christopher House was located in the middle of the most overcrowded, polyglot corner of Toronto, where it was not unusual for teenagers to equip themselves with knives; hence the vexing question of how best to combat juvenile delinquency often overshadowed other concerns. Many black youths in particular were driven to bleak despair by the racism they encountered daily and by what seemed a hopeless future stretching before them. In order to alleviate their somewhat baneful circumstances, St. Christopher House, in 1964, tried an unusual approach described by the Toronto *Globe and Mail* as "a drum beat beacon of black and steel." The idea, introduced by a young Trinidadian named Joe Brown who had successfully pioneered the method on New York's lower east side, was to have the black youths take out their frustrations and gain new confidence through participating in a steel drum band. Steel band music was of relatively recent origin, having gained popularity in Trinidad in the 1940s. The drums were created by hammering the tops of oil drums into tune, which were then played with rubber-tipped sticks producing a wide range of Afro-West Indian rhythms. Seen as a means of combatting delinquency the *Globe and Mail* observed that "boys who had the urge to strike out at society now beat rhythmically on steel drums instead." Brown's group was soon performing at church halls, Scout meetings and money-raising functions. The charismatic and impressive-looking Brown (he was 6'4") quickly became a hero to his youthful charges, and he used his influence to instruct them on matters of behaviour. His lessons on proper comportment were not always heeded, and one particularly embarrassing occasion for Brown occurred when the band played for more than 1200 people at a 1965 United Appeal luncheon in the crystal ballroom of Toronto's Royal York Hotel; the band stole the show and a considerable quantity of the hotel's silverware, which Brown later retrieved and returned. In his work with troubled teenagers Brown was propelled by a vision that regarded the universality of music as a means of uniting black and white. In a decade ripe for change, Brown's vision fit comfortably into the vision of St. Christopher House.

The launching of the federal government's war on poverty in 1964 and the establishment of the Company of Young Canadians (CYC) had a profound effect on the work of settlements across Canada, inspiring the development of many community projects with the assistance of federally funded volunteers. Speaking at a lunch in Toronto in 1965, Tom Kent, Prime Minister Lester Pearson's key advisor for the war on poverty, explained that the assault on poverty would be launched in three distinct programs: programs that the federal government could mount on its own, such as manpower mobility and the decentralization of industries to 35 designated areas; programs requiring federal and provincial co-operation, such as the Canada Assistance Plan, which would share basic welfare expenditures between the two levels of government; and local level involvement through the CYC working in conjunction with community-based agencies like St. Christopher House. Executive director of St. Christopher House John Haddad eagerly scrambled to assume a leadership role. When the legislation to establish the CYC was about to come before parliament he urged the Canadian Welfare Council to use their influence to have the bill include a provision for young, urban Canadians, who were not necessarily university graduates, that would enable them to qualify as volunteers under the terms of the proposed legislation. When the Canadian Association of Neighbourhood Services — an umbrella organization for settlements in Canada — established a national committee on poverty, Hadad assumed the role of chair. The committee maintained contact with the Canadian Welfare Council and the federal government and frequently forwarded suggestions as to the role settlements might play in the local wars on poverty. Ultimately many CYC volunteers fulfilled their contracts performing community work at St. Christopher House and other Canadian settlements.

After Haddad left in 1967, St. Christopher House's interest in the issue of poverty in the neighbourhood did not diminish. In 1970 the senate poverty committee, chaired by David Croll, discovered that St. Christopher House and its neighbourhood contacts provided an effective opening wedge to an understanding of the devastating effects of poverty in downtown Toronto, particularly among the Portuguese. St. Christopher House served as the meeting place where a number of organizations, including the Portuguese Canadian Congress, made representations to the committee.

In 1974 another battle against poverty was being waged out of St. Christopher House. Joan Clark, described as "a strong-minded, bright, outspoken lady who still bears the scars of a lifetime of poverty," was struggling to support herself, a fifteen-year-old son and five-year-old daughter on $262 a month from provincial social assistance, two federal family allowance cheques and $50 a month as a part-time community worker at St. Christopher House. After rent, food and telephone Clark found she had only $5 a week to spend on everything else. When the provincial government increased the basic welfare rates by 13 per cent in October 1974 Clark deemed it a paltry one. Clark was elected to head the recently organized Mother Led Union, which was fighting for increases that would be related to the cost of living. Born out of the frustrations of 35000 divorced, deserted, widowed and unwed mothers in Ontario attempting to raise their children on degrading welfare payments, the union was committeed to achieving a measure of power, something poor people felt they had never had. A year after its founding in 1974 the Mother Led Union had grown from four locals in Toronto to twenty-five, with groups in Ottawa, Sudbury, Chatham and Hamilton. The women who joined its ranks were disgusted with provincial officials who droned on about the nutritional value of peanut butter, powdered milk and day-old bread. Especially galling was the knowledge that their children would be better fed and dressed in a foster home. Issuing a direct challenge Clark declared, "if Premier Davis can't give natural mothers the same money he pays foster mothers, he can find foster homes for our children. They'll be better off." Unless something was done Clark threatened to lead a march of mothers and children on Queen's Park and leave the children there in an effort to press home to the government the seriousness of their demands: more money, the right to keep more of their part-time earnings and free day-care.

The Mother Led Union movement, centred as it was at St. Christopher House, laid the groundwork for women's activism and welfare rights in the years to follow. It served to jolt the complacent, if even for a brief moment, into recognizing that Ontario's system of social supports was painfully deficient and created a great deal of hardship and suffering. The union contributed to a growing awareness of the feminization of poverty as an ingrained feature of the Canadian social landscape and acted as a spur to a developing radical feminist movement in Canada.

In line with its enlarged community development thrust a separate unit was formed in the summer of 1974 to coordinate and promote community centred activities. Immersing themselves in intense discussions about the roots of inequality and the disadvantaged, St. Christopher House workers attached to the unit began to call into question many of the traditional methods and strategies of community work. While the earlier emphasis had been on community participation and self-help, these time-honoured notions were now seen to support and reinforce the widespread belief that individual inability and weakness were the primary causes of social problems. Therefore, high incidences of juvenile crime were attributed to parents not having the skills to raise their children adequately, and unemployment was seen as the direct result of individual laziness. This perspective was a barrier to be overcome by self-help, and programs at St. Christopher House stressed ways of motivating people to get involved, to get organized and ultimately to help themselves. Community workers at St. Christopher House now enthusiastically endorsed the belief that social and political structures were the fundamental cause of most social distress. A new agenda emerged from this revised social analysis to bring about changes in economic and social conditions through organizing the community to take a more radical posture concerning all social problems, even those that might at first seem to be individual in nature. This was an attempt to put into action sociologist C. Wright Mills's basic distinction between private troubles and public issues outlined in *The Sociological Imagination* (1959).

One particular project stemmed directly from this altered approach and was established in 1974. This initiative was intended to promote community development within the Portuguese community, particularly with women who were night cleaners in downtown office buildings, such as the large Ontario government complex at Bay and Wellesley streets, as well as service workers in hotels and restaurants. Most of these workplaces were unorganized, paid low wages and offered poor job conditions and uncertain job stability. The women felt powerless, having come from rural areas with little formal education and bound by traditional values including male-female relationships. Addressing the basic problem of illiteracy the St. Christopher House staff devised a threefold remedy: issue organizing, English as a second language and workshops. Considerable success was achieved in organizing Portuguese-speaking women around specific issues such as protesting the firing of a cleaner or demanding better working conditions. English classes were offered at the settlement, in the workplace and at home. However, community workshops in collaboration with other agencies met with more modest success as workers found it difficult to sustain long-term interest. Out of all these efforts a group called Cleaners Action emerged as a resource to immigrant women who not only worked as night-time cleaners and day-time domestics, but who had responsibility for home and children and were obviously struggling to hold themselves together under this crushing burden. Cleaners Action produced a newsletter distributed to downtown office workers that dealt with safety standards, employment practices, workers' rights and available services.

St. Christopher House also established a weekly women's support group for Portuguese women who were experiencing marital difficulties, which helped them explore concerns about child care, separation agreements and related health and legal questions. The Immigrant Women's Shelter Task Force, with St. Christopher House as a founding member, worked towards chiselling out plans for establishing an emergency shelter and resource centre in Toronto for battered immigrant women.

With the creation of the St. Christopher House Older Adult Centre in 1971, the house had risen to the challenge of reaching out to the growing number of seniors in the area. In a study carried out by settlement workers it was estimated that almost 12 per cent of the population being served was over 65 whereas the national average was 8 per cent. The major ethnic groups in the area were Portuguese, Ukrainian and Polish; the total number of residents whose mother tongue was not English or French was 60 per cent and the national average 12.9 per cent. The centre began working with older Portuguese people on a part-time basis in early 1973; later that year a federal government New Horizons grant enabled the centre to employ a full-time Portuguese worker. In October of that year total monthly attendance at the centre was 397, with Portuguese people comprising 34 per cent of the total. By July 1974 total monthly attendance was well over 1000 and the Portuguese element comprised 37 per cent. It was evident that the centre's services were in high demand. A report of the time identified three significant kinds of development that resulted from the centre's attention to the older Portuguese population: seniors had overcome fears related to community interaction in a new culture through a basic understanding of English, the recognition of street names and the ability to use street cars and telephones; a feeling of greater independence and an improved ability to effectively manage their personal affairs; and finally, a recognition of individual abilities and enhanced self-esteem. However, it soon became apparent that the centre's programs and socialization opportunities were not available to all older persons. Poor weather simply compounded the difficulties involved regarding transportation, and with snow and ice covering sidewalks during the winters many elderly were confined to their place of residence. Few senior citizens living in the area could afford their own car and even those that could were reluctant to use them in the winter; bus and streetcar stops were often blocks from their residences. Faced with the lack of proper weather shelters, overcrowded vehicles, high steps and schedules they could not understand, many seniors simply stayed home. The Toronto subway system with its long stairways, having no elevators and somewhat confusing transfer points made travel by public transportation unattractive for many of the city's elderly. Over the next few years efforts were made to overcome some of these transportation difficulties with generally happy results.

   The centre continued to offer activities in rugmaking, candlemaking, woodworking, painting, drawing, printmaking, ceramics, films, bowling, shuffleboard, cards and excursions as well as having a public health nurse available several times a week. By the end of the 1970s the centre at St. Christopher House was reaching out further into the community.

CENTRAL NEIGHBOURHOOD HOUSE, 1960-1980

In the 1960s Central Neighbourhood House, located at 349 Sherbourne Street, continued to serve the area bounded by Bloor, Queen, Yonge and the Don River, a district teeming with life and its concomitant frustrations and tensions. Central Neighbourhood House experienced challenges and setbacks in a city often thoughtless and raw in its political and social conscience. Nevertheless, the settlement held to its lofty goals of broadening people's experiences and continued to be a place that radiated happiness and laughter.

The settlement's neighbourhood, with a population of some 50,000, was an extremely heterogeneous area containing expensive high-rise apartments, rooming-houses, substandard housing, public and limited dividend housing (Regent Park and Moss Park), commercial areas, factories, shabby little stores and more solid sections of working-class housing all divided by major traffic arteries. This part of the city contained more than its fair share of social agencies, the red United Appeal sign was a familiar emblem on many streets, and many of the former stately residences now housed agency offices. This convergence of social agencies located close to a large number of people who needed their services was no mere accident. Redevelopment and talked-about development — the St. Jamestown apartments in the north-central part of the neighbourhood — had created a sense of uncertainty and unease. A large section of the population moved annually within the area, but few appeared to actually leave, viewing the district almost as a self-contained village. Residence in the district represented a downward trend to many families and apathy was a dominant characteristic; one report noted that "a somewhat static quality predominates rather than upwardly mobile strivings." The residents were still primarily Anglo-Saxon with small groupings of native Canadians, larger groupings of French Canadians and pockets of Germans, Chinese and blacks. The area was also experiencing a steady influx of families from the Maritimes, particularly New Brunswick. Disenfranchised youth clustered in the Jarvis/Dundas grid became a special concern of Central Neighbourhood House. Several restaurants in the area were frequented by bootleggers, prostitutes, other petty criminals and a disturbing number of teenagers. A 1959 report indicated that 42 per cent of a group of 137 teenage boys in Central Neighbourhood House's clubs had criminal records or were on probation. This nesting of vice in the south part of the district was seen as a constant threat to the neighbourhood's fabric of order. Certainly the area had an above-average share of social problems; although it contained 6 per cent of the city's total population, it had 11 per cent of all children's aid cases, 12 per cent of juvenile offenders, 19 per cent of welfare recipients, 34 per cent of the city's offences for drinking and 65 per cent of the older population of homeless and transient men.

Although traditional events — the Christmas "At Home," the spring fair, the fall rummage sale and bazaar, the weekly square dance — all continued into the 1960s and were well-received activities, Central Neighbourhood House struck out in some new directions in this decade. Helen Sutcliffe, who guided the house skilfully through the 1950s, had decided by 1960 that the agency ought to be given new life by draping itself in the mantle of social research. This would go a long way towards reviving its social reform tradition and help to channel its resources along more clear-cut lines; thus, Central Neighbourhood House distinguished itself from the other settlements by taking on a number of research/demonstration projects. The first of these was the school completion project, which was financed by the Junior League of Greater Toronto and ran from 1961-64. This project was launched as the high rate of school drop-outs continued to mount and it became increasingly necessary to reverse this trend. Workers at Central Neighbourhood House who had personal contact with many of the school drop-outs were only too aware that these young people were unable to hold a job, even ones requiring few skills, for more than a few months. The project was designed to find the best methods of keeping children in school as long as their academic potential indicated. As well as financing the undertaking the Junior League provided volunteers to visit the homes of project families, supervise and tutor homework sessions, provide instruction in clerical work and make posters. In order to implement the school completion project a combination of the social work methods of casework and group work were used in addition to specific programs in the house.

By the early 1960s the term multi-problem family was finding its way, with increasing frequency, into the reports of social agencies. It was generally accepted that a family would be deemed multi-problem if it exhibited many of the following characteristics: alcoholism, criminal acts, desertion or mental illness in the parent; criminal acts, mental illness or poor school adjustment on the part of the children; severe marital discord; economic deprivation or grossly inadequate housing; chronic cases of physical disability or death of either parent; or, as a result of three or more of the preceding factors, the family has been a chronic or intermittent dependent to the community for over three years.

When these criteria were applied to the 38 families involved in the project, 27 fell into the multi-problem category. One could picture the doleful effects on children of these unhappy combinations of deplorable circumstances. The project's researchers recorded:

During all their formative years these youngsters can be said
to be wanting and needing things, both material and otherwise,
that are beyond their grasp. They grow up seeing compulsory
attendance at school as just one more tie that fetters them to a
disappointing and unsatisfactory way of life. They leave school
at the earliest possible opportunity seeing the pay cheque as
the first step towards escape from want. Ironically, the kinds
of pay cheques these young people earn serve only to bind
them more securely to the kind of environment they hope to
escape.

One aspect of the project was the homework and tutoring programme.
Volunteers provided tutoring at Central Neighbourhood House, and it was
hoped that by holding the sessions at the house the importance of school
work would be elevated in students' minds. The homework sessions were
publicized by large, bright posters in the house, which stressed the value of
completing school in order to get a better and more secure job. A large,
attractive room, painted by volunteers and stocked with study lamps,
reference books, colourful maps, books and magazines, was set aside for
homework coaching. A deliberate attempt was made to keep the appearance
of the room as unlike a school as possible; there were no unwelcome
blackboards and children sat around small tables or sprawled on chesterfields
and lounge chairs. Afternoon sessions were held for younger students and
evening ones for the older pupils. Regular contact was maintained with
parents and, by all accounts, the program was a noticeable success as
attendance steadily increased, children experienced learning in a new light
and, most importantly, school performance markedly improved.

Home visits by project volunteers were another feature based on the
firm conviction that the home environment was a significant factor in early
school leaving — helping the family in what was often an emotional cauldron,
it was argued, would result in better school performance. Hunger, poverty
and the overcrowded conditions all acted as a drag on children's intellectual
progress. Project visitors were often the first link between the parents and
their child's school. Workers helped parents connect with other services,
arranged hospital visits and often accompanied nervous and reluctant parents.

Another thrust of the project was a series of group meetings for parents
held at the settlement to help them express themselves and to offer advice
and guidance on how to instill in their children the importance of attaining a
reasonable level of education. As the parents became comfortable they spoke
more freely about the absorbing problems they faced and about their hopes
and dreams for their children's futures. Central Neighbourhood House staff

stressed the interplay between a child's home and his or her performance at school, drawing on the venerable settlement tradition of seeking to create an association between school and neighbourhood. The staff believed that the most important outcome of the project was that many children, once identified as potential school drop-outs, could think more positively about themselves and improve their academic performance, thus gaining a greater measure of pleasure from their schooling. Parents were encouraged to understand the clash of values and ideas between the old and the new country and how this confusion adversely affected their children. After all, the original settlement residents were, more than anything else, educators.

Other similar initiatives were set in motion later in the decade. One, entitled the Extra Push Programme, was a set of summer activities geared to those children in senior kindergarten and grade 1 who had experienced difficulties the previous year adjusting to the school setting. Children would be involved on a daily basis in a small group programme where there would be an emphasis on the development of communication and socialization skills — the intention was to stimulate curiosity and broaden horizons. The children who were encouraged to enter the programme were considered culturally deprived and came from four local schools. Altogether 18 children participated in July, 1967. While the more affluent Toronto families transferred their living arrangements to the vacation areas north of the city, these inner-city children, who otherwise might have been hot and uncomfortable and acutely bothered by an awareness of their relative privation, enjoyed a daily round of activities and outings. A positive consequence of the programme was the opportunity it afforded settlement workers to get to know the parents, particularly the mothers, better. They would gather at the front of the house to pick up their children and the staff would engage them in casual conversation; often tea would be served. According to staff reports the children reaped considerable benefits. For many of the 18 young souls involved the summer of 1967 proved to be a heartening, relaxing and regenerating experience.

During that summer an outreach program for older children and teenagers was launched to prevent restless youths from pursuing less than wholesome activities during the summer holidays. These youths did not partake of established facilities as offered by the city parks and recreation department, community centres or libraries. Large numbers of these youngsters could be found in back alleys, school yards and other local hang-outs. The problem of alienated youth had preoccupied sociologists for a number of years, and part of the 1967 program at Central Neighbourhood House was aimed at just this disaffected and often antagonistic group.

Another approach took basic play equipment from street to street with the intention of locating kids who might then come to the house on a regular basis. Camping with a small select group of particularly unruly boys, introducing them to a different relationship with adults and taking away many of the props of their familiar city life was another component of the program, which continued to be offered in subsequent summers.

The arrival of an increasing number of native Canadians in the 1960s acted as a spur to the development of the Canadian Indian Family Project at the settlement. With encouragement from the board Helen Sutcliffe approached the provincial and federal governments as well as a number of foundations to fund a study of native people in the house's ambit. Ultimately her efforts bore fruit and the T. Eaton Foundation, the federal department of citizenship and immigration and Ontario's department of public welfare financed a two-year study of the problems faced by native families in an urban environment; it was expected that the study would demonstrate how a settlement could help these families cope with their difficulties. Many attached to Central Neighbourhood House were excited by this study, seeing it as placing the settlement on the threshold of new possibilities.

In 1962 native Canadians numbered approximately 190,000, with 45,000 residing in Ontario. Estimates for the number living in Toronto varied widely from 1200 to 6000, although Central Neighbourhood House's study convincingly supported the larger figure. Whatever the exact percentage, the largest number by far lived in Central Neighbourhood House's environs. In Ontario, native Canadians belonged primarily to two language groups; the Iroquois, which included the Six Nations Confederacy settled primarily in the St. Lawrence and Great Lakes basin, and the Algonquin, which included the Ojibway (often referred to as the Chippewa) and a smaller number of Cree living in the extreme northern fringe of the province. While the Ojibway were scattered throughout the province it was the northern Ojibway who comprised the bulk of emigrants to Toronto. Driven by a search for employment and a strong desire to break the poverty cycle, particularly for their children, the overriding motivation for emigrating to Toronto was economic. Increased educational opportunities were also a strong attraction.

The research at Central Neighbourhood House involved interviewing a select number of native families to ascertain the nature of their problems. It was the declared wish of the research staff that the results of the study be a springboard for action. The four key problems identified by the 30 or so participating families were ill health, poor finances, difficulty obtaining services from social agencies and bad housing. Project workers spent many hours combing the city in a desperate and usually futile hunt for better accommodation; however, more positive results were obtained in assisting families establish improved lines of communication with social agencies. This study was the first in Canada to explore the urban experience of native people and it enabled Central Neighbourhood House to maintain its pre-eminence among the Toronto settlements as the recognized leader in urban-based social research.

Allied to, but separate from, the Canadian Indian Project was a four-week certificate course offered by Central Neighbourhood House for those living on reserves. Its purpose was to train those involved in basic group and community work skills so they could, upon returning to their reserves, set up programs to respond to the social and recreational needs of their particular community. The first graduates enthusiastically headed north securely equipped to tackle the seemingly intractable problems facing their reservations in March 1964.

Toronto's social geography was altered by a substantial inflow of people from the East Coast, many of whom found the city unfriendly and unyielding. Plagued by low incomes and poor housing, gaining a foothold in the large metropolis was often a remote possibility. In an attempt to gauge the extent of their misery and their need, Central Neighbourhood House conducted an investigation following similar procedures used in the study of the native population. Interviews and questionnaires provided a glimpse of transplanted maritime life. Thus armed, Central Neighbourhood House's modern knights errant set about the task of encouraging families and children to attend settlement programs, make contacts with other local agencies for counselling and help search for jobs and housing. In addition, a committee comprising people from the East Coast operated to ease newcomers into their new environs.

Of all the house's research/demonstration projects none was as thoroughly prosecuted as the Unreached Youth Project for girls, which was conducted from 1964-66. Financial support from the United Community Fund of Greater Toronto facilitated the hiring of a project social worker who was hired to work with girls in the neighbourhood whose futures were, at best, cloudy. Seventy-two girls were involved and detailed case histories compiled. The overriding problem of the girls was their terribly negative self-image, their seeming lack of control over what happened to them, and feelings of anxiety and despair for their present and future prospects; invariably their families were caught up in cycles of destructive behaviour involving alcohol, drugs and prostitution. Poor school performance, promiscuity and distrust of adults were all shared characteristics. The methods employed to alter these patterns included individual contacts and counselling, group work in a small, club-like setting, and many referrals to other agencies.

One experiment that proved extremely successful was a weekly supper club, which had the appeal of sophistication. It had the added benefit of subtly introducing lessons on cooking and homemaking skills, still apparently seen in the 1960s as the most appropriate final destination for young women. The two-year project clearly demonstrated a need for detached youth services to become an integral part of day-to-day operations. Although not all the girls had responded positively, and some seemed simply beyond reach, it was observed in the project's final report that, "contrary to expectations, the 'unreached girl' can and will use the program." Enough evidence had been gathered to justify the claim that detached work, in combination with Central Neighbourhood House programs and the help of other appropriate agencies, could aid the process of broadening the girls' relationships with others and strengthen their positive feelings about themselves.

It was a matter of settled public confidence in Toronto in the 1960s that urban renewal and redevelopment would occur. The Regent Park public housing project of the late 1940s and early 1950s was an example of slum clearance that many Central Neighbourhood House residents feared would be attempted in the more northerly part of the district. In the 1960s Central Neighbourhood House was thoroughly immersed in this issue and provided leadership for many local groups struggling to make sense of the numerous urban renewal schemes that were cropping up like spring weeds. Urban planners had accepted, unchallenged, the notion that renewal of inner city decay was inherently good. A report by the city of Toronto planning board outlining proposed plans for improvement of the Don Vale district (the boundaries being St. James cemetery to the north, Gerrard Street to the south, Parliament Street to the west, and Parkland to the east) generated considerable interest at Central Neighbourhood House. Concern had been mounting for a number of years regarding the physical and social deterioration of the area in general. However, the main focus of the report was on the quality of housing, and the measures called for included: the acquisition and clearance of the most blighted housing with new public housing to be constructed in its place; the adoption and enforcement of a new minimum housing by-law; the encouragement of home-owners to take out loans to rehabilitate their houses; and major public works improvements. The release of the report and the passage of a new minimum housing by-law created apprehension among the residents of Don Vale about the future of their area, and a series of public meetings did little to allay their misgivings.

By 1966 the city had opened a site office with two community workers from Central Neighbourhood House to facilitate citizen participation and assist those whose lives might be uprooted by renewal. Major differences soon emerged over how much say residents would actually have as city planners' views of renewal and those of the area's inhabitants sharply diverged. Ultimately, with the capable assistance of Central Neighbourhood House community workers, the residents of Don Vale organized and challenged city officials on their approach to planning and citizen participation, which brought the project to a stalemate by December 1967. Throughout that year the air at meetings literally vibrated with tension as residents bombarded planners with tough questions about housing and rehabilitation standards, expropriation procedures, rehabilitation financing, tax increases, and the supposed economic advantages of private development.

From 1968 there was a marked change in the city's approach, and residents were able to persuade officials that the area's low-density zoning should be maintained and that plans for expropriation and high-rise development should be scrapped. A turning point in citizen participation in Toronto occurred on 20 November 1968 when city council approved, in full, the terms of reference of the Don Vale Working Committee, which had been formed earlier to represent the wishes of local residents. At the November meeting the working committee was officially recognized and empowered as the forum for citizen participation in the preparation of an overall plan for Don Vale. In addition, policy was set in place to ensure that no expropriation and no enforced rehabilitation beyond minimum housing standards would occur without government grants to cover all upgrading costs to residents. Throughout this process community workers from Central Neighbourhood House conducted social surveys of the area, thus providing yardsticks by which to measure the social quality of life in the district, answered hundreds of questions from anxious and overwrought residents, and acted as catalysts in promoting citizen participation.

Another urban renewal scheme that workers at Central Neighbourhood House joined with local residents in opposing was Trefann Court, the area bounded by Queen, Parliament, Shuter and River streets. The area had been occupied by low-income tenants for many years, with a large percentage of the dwellings owned by absentee landlords. The city's plans initially called for bulldozing the entire 24 acres, but with strenuous objections from residents' groups the city altered its tactics to one of slow attrition through letting the area deteriorate even further by not enforcing housing standard by-laws and then buying up the dilapidated housing. Central Neighbourhood House was a full participant in the democratizing of citizen involvement that the Trefann Court fight represented as Jim Lemon observed, "Pierre Trudeau's call for citizen participation in public affairs during an appearance in Nathan Phillips Square in June 1968 further pumped up enthusiasm." Neighbourliness, self-responsibility and community involvement were the distinguishing characteristics of Central Neighbourhood House as it emerged from the 1960s.

By 1970 Helen Sutcliffe had retired and Central Neighbourhood House had moved into a new building at 349 Ontario Street in the heart of Cabbagetowm, further south and east from the 17-room brick house on Sherbourne Street it had occupied for 40 years. Jeanne Rowles became executive director in 1970, and with her came a great deal of YWCA experience in Canada, Pakistan and Africa; she stayed in the position for six years. A great believer in the ethic of self-help, she promoted a number of community development initiatives during her tenure. By the time Central Neighbourhood House moved to Ontario Street the district was beginning to experience the Toronto phenomenon of white-painting — middle-class professionals were moving into the area, buying the Victorian houses cheaply, renovating them and, in the process, altering the traditional character of the neighbourhood. From the mid 1950s the area had become the last resort for many elderly people on skid row and low-income roomers who squeezed into the blocks surrounding the Regent Park, Moss Park and the St. James Town public housing projects. The most immediately visible group on Ontario Street were the old, knarled men and women with drinking problems who trudged up and down the street, often ending up in Allen Gardens at the corner of Sherbourne and Gerrard streets. For the new, up-scale neighbours the presence of so many indigent people was an unfortunate aspect of the area. The mutual disdain created by these two diverse groups living in such close proximity was one of the many simmering tensions confronting Central Neighbourhood House as it moved into the 1970s. The area was a sea of troubles characterized by poor housing, poverty, unemployment, a transient population of single adults, a high proportion of single parents and a large population of lonely, shut-in senior citizens. Undaunted, Central Neighbourhood House developed new programs and approaches in the 1970s to combat these seemingly intractable problems.

The Donwest Neighbours Group, a non-profit housing rehabilitation corporation, was established by a consortium of board members, friends and neighbours. It consisted of area home-owners, tenants and businessmen who were determined to enable residents to improve housing conditions in the area at reasonable cost. A substantial grant was obtained from the Central

Mortgage and Housing Corporation and from the federal government, through a L.I.P. (Local Initiatives Program) grant, to purchase 25 old houses, renovate them and make them available to low-income families. A distinguished architect, James Murray, designed and oversaw this work.

Another initiative sought to alleviate the problems of the unemployed. A number of previously unemployable individuals were put to work at Central Neighbourhood House and in the community as receptionists, workers for weekend programs, cooks at the nursery school, clerical workers and home visitors for shut-in seniors. The project was designed to help people overcome barriers to obtaining and keeping employment such as difficult personalities, child care arrangements and lack of specific skills. The scheme achieved only moderate success, but it did demonstrate that with encouragement a number of people who despaired of ever having income from work could be pleasantly surprised by their own industriousness.

Weekend drop-in programs were organized to provide opportunities for socialization of the area's single transients and skid-row denizens. For a brief period in 1973 a unique experiment with an overnight drop-in centre brought the city's night people to Central Neighbourhood House for a snack, a game of cards, roller skating or just the chance to sit and read. Those who came were not allowed to sleep since the intention was not to create another flop-house that might turn into a haven for kids wanting to leave home. In September 1972 the Dundas Day Centre — the outpatient or community psychiatry section of the Queen Street Mental Hospital — moved into quarters at the house, adding a further dimension to services offered. Out of concern for mothers and children in the nursery school the house arranged with Women's College Hospital to have a family practitioner on the premises once a week. In 1975 a food club began operating with the assistance of a L.I.P. grant; it operated on a pre-order basis with members bringing in their orders on a Wednesday or Thursday. Friday was 'market' day, and orders were made up by volunteers to be collected later in the day. High levels of quality were maintained and prices were generally 30 per cent lower than in food stores. On any given week approximately 40 households participated, including a number of shut-ins who had come to rely heavily on the club, which also arranged deliveries

The enthusiasm and the drive of Central Neighbourhood House was attacked by a harsh 1976 report, which had been commissioned after Jeanne Rowles resigned and the board was gearing up to strike a hiring committee for a new director. The report suggested that the decision-making process at the house was unclear and that there was little sharing of information. The board was criticized for being remote and causing souring relations with the community. When Paddy Ann Pugsley became executive director in 1977 she was described as a human dynamo who had clearly been hired to pump some adrenalin into the sagging reputation of the house. Closely identifying herself with the feminist movement, Pugsley had a social work degree and experience working in a psychiatric hospital and a neighbourhood house in England.

Under her stewardship the home help program, which was started a number of years earlier, expanded rapidly. Under the program Central Neighbourhood House paid a modest salary to people living in the community to act as home helpers for the elderly and handicapped; each helper had several clients who would be visited on a weekly basis and helped with cleaning, laundry, shopping, banking, transportation, income tax advice and referrals to other social agencies. Each recipient of the service shared a common need to be relieved of the loneliness and boredom that is so often the fate of the elderly. The overall goal was, of course, to offer a sound alternative to institutional care, and Central Neighbourhood House found itself in the vanguard once again in its efforts to promote community based service.

Pugsley's commitment to feminism gave a decided boost to the Opportunity for Advancement program at the house. Under the guidance of Central Neighbourhood House workers, sole-support mothers living on provincial social assistance came together for mutual support and friendship. Each mother was expected to make a realistic plan for her future, which might include academic upgrading, learning a new skill, joining an on-going group for self-development, seeking employment or participating in volunteer work. The program's attempts to help these women become more independent, to bolster their self-confidence and to widen their horizons were based on a solid feminist philosophy. Blending discussions of practical solutions with social analysis imparted to many a much greater degree of self-confidence and a new awareness that the difficulties they experienced in their daily lives were the product of an unjust, gender-biased social structure. In turn, this lifted the burden of self-blame and doubt that had plagued these women for most of their lives. The Opportunity for Advancement program, which was one of the first agency programs in Toronto to be guided by feminist ideas, stood as visible testimony to Central Neighbourhood House's long tradition of supporting the downtrodden.

PART 3

ASSESSMENTS AND CONCLUSIONS

Allan Irving,
Harriet Parsons
and Donald Bellamy

Chapter Fifteen

Assessments and Conclusions

The three Toronto settlements, St. Christopher House, Central Neighbourhood House and University Settlement have had a remarkable impact on Toronto during most of the twentieth century. They developed a wide array of services, including day-care, children and teen programming and programs for adult and senior citizens. In their many attempts to help new immigrants establish themselves in the city, the settlements organized nursery schools and well-baby clinics, pressured local politicians for better parks and playgrounds, ran language and citizenship classes, music schools, arts and sports programmes and carried out social research. In fact, one of the extraordinary accomplishments of the settlements has been the sheer range of programming and services offered over the years and the large number of people drawn into their orbit.

The three social settlements examined in this book have provided continuous service in downtown Toronto neighbourhoods for over 80 years to people of all ages, creeds and ethnic backgrounds. This has been achieved through periods of economic prosperity and depression, two world wars, changing patterns of immigration and changing social conditions and concepts. As the generalists of social service settlements proved to be trailblazers for many different kinds of services, services such as day-care, nursery schools, language classes, programs for seniors, which were later taken over by other more specialized institutions and often by government.

The settlements have been the training and testing grounds for countless social workers in Toronto and for most of their existence have been strong promoters of advanced education for social workers. In a more intangible but no less important sense, they created vast networks of interpersonal relationships among the people of the neighbourhoods and between them and the boards, staffs, students and volunteers involved in the settlements. Even today, having weathered the dramatic and far-reaching social changes of the 1960s and 1970s, they remain vibrant neighbourhood centres where people in their local communities continue to develop new ways of working together.

Canada, a latecomer to the social settlement movement, did not feel the full effects of the Industrial Revolution until long after Britain and the United States, and the urban and social reform movement that had been sweeping across the United States in the latter half of the nineteenth century did not really hit Canada with full force until the first decade of the twentieth century. The reform movement that followed industrialization and the growth of cities was a response to the myriad of social evils that sprang out of rapid social transformation. But in Canada there were few large cities before 1900, and even in 1910 when Toronto had passed the 300,000 population mark, farms were still located just north of St. Clair Avenue. By the 1890s small slums were beginning to develop in the downtown cores of Canadian cities, but they were nothing compared to the vertical, tenement-house slums of New York or the vast sprawling slums near the stockyards of Chicago. It is perhaps not surprising that in 1902 Mackenzie King remarked that social settlements like Hull House were not yet needed in Canada.

The great flood of European immigrants, which poured into the United States after 1850 and led directly to the founding of the first social settlements in the great American cities in the 1880s and 1890s, was not experienced in Canada until the early decades of the twentieth century. The first Canadian investigations into the new social settlement movement, which were launched at Toynbee Hall in the East End of London in 1884 and spread quickly to the United States in 1887, were made by Protestant clergymen anxious to see how the idea might be applied in Canada. They related their findings in Canadian church journals, and while they found much to praise, they also expressed shock at the lack of a religious ingredient and were surprised to find the staff often tinged with socialism. This reaction from the religious establishment delayed, for a number of years, the establishment of social settlements in Canada on the British and American model.

Other alternatives were attempted such as church institutes and missions with settlement-type programs. Like the first Canadian settlement, Evangelia, started by an American-trained YWCA worker Sara Libby Carson in 1902, these institutions had a strong religious flavour. These early experiments were soon laid aside, and the Canadian settlement house movement was launched with the establishment of University Settlement in 1910, Central Neighbourhood House in 1911 and St. Christopher House in 1912.

The view of settlement boards and most staff that their organizations ought to be a key instrument for instilling acceptable, middle-class habits and attitudes in the poor and in newcomers was a constant theme until at least well into the 1960s. Initially, there was the perceived threat of masses of unassimilated immigrants crowding into Toronto. In their work with new Canadians the Toronto settlements unwittingly acted, in part, as one of the many agents of social control present in any society. Only much later did the settlements begin to accord considerably more value to the cultural heritage that newcomers brought with them, and became more aware of the need to be uncommonly alert to the wishes of many immigrants to preserve their own traditions as they made their way in Canadian society. It could be fairly said that the settlements did more than any other service in Toronto during this century to foster and promote the conditions that enabled a multi-cultural city to emerge by the 1960s.

In October 1971, when the federal government proclaimed an official policy of multi-culturalism, little recognition was given to the fact that the main features of that policy had been carried out by the Toronto settlement houses since their inception. It would not be stretching a point to argue that the necessary preconditions and groundwork for these important developments had been laid by the three Toronto settlements over the previous 60 years.

The multi-cultural policy committed the federal government to providing support in four key ways: "the government will seek to assist all Canadian cultural groups that have demonstrated a desire and effort to continue to develop a capacity to grow and contribute to Canada, and a clear need for assistance, the small and weak groups no less than the strong and highly organized"; "the government will assist members of all cultural groups to overcome cultural barriers to full participation in Canadian society"; "the government will promote creative encounters and interchange among all Canadian cultural groups in the interest of national unity"; and "the government will continue to assist immigrants to acquire at least one of Canada's official languages in order to become full participants in Canadian society."

Even in the early years the settlements were institutions that welcomed immigrants of all nationalities into their programmes. Each of the three settlements encouraged the formation of specific ethnic groups within their overall programs in order to provide a secure and comfortable place for those who otherwise would have been adrift in a new and often intimidating city. While it is might be easy to describe the assimilation work of the settlements with immigrants as paternalistic, it should be recognized that many newcomers wanted exactly that — help in adjusting to Canadian society and the opportunity to move up in their new communities. As Judith Ann Trolander observes in *Professionalism and Social Change: From the Settlement House Movement to Neighbourhood Centres, 1886 to the Present* (1987), "in an increasingly fragmented city, the settlement house provided a meeting ground for different ethnic groups and for the well-off and the poor to come together, to bridge class differences, and to work together on resolving social problems."

The Toronto settlements, except for Central Neighbourhood House, devoted little energy to social reform and social change. Much of the philosophy behind the initial motivation for the establishment of the settlements put limits on social reform activities. Many of the leaders in Toronto's early settlement movement held fast to the belief that the economically and socially advantaged as well as the better educated classes had a moral obligation to assist the poor, immigrants and the less educated to personally improve their lot in life. In this way they could then contribute to the overall moral, social and economic improvement of society. In the case of University Settlement there was the additional high-minded view that university faculty and students could benefit from a period of living and working among the "lower-classes." This was all part of the ethic of social service and civic betterment that so inspired the young Mackenzie King and many other university students of his generation.

From the outset, broad-based urban social reform did not have a central place in the the settlements' stated objectives. Hortense Wasteneys observed in her fine history of University Settlement up to 1958, that "it would seem...that the majority of faculty members on the settlement board continued to be personally more interested in contributing to their students' social education than combating social problems and contributing to general civic improvement in Toronto at large." Even in the midst of the Great Depression the board encouraged the development of specific programs within the settlement as a response to the widespread suffering of the unemployed rather than any kind of social analysis that could have led to calls for state intervention. Although the Toronto settlements' work was largely premised on an approach that favoured friendship and personal service, there is little indication that these solutions to the deeply entrenched problems of urban Canadian society were ever viewed as ultimately inadequate.

One of the critical changes that occurred in the Toronto settlements, as elsewhere, was a gradual moving-away from the original settlement idea.

Initially, the Toronto settlements advanced a humane and creative vision of reconstructed local communities. In order to effectively accomplish this lofty goal they saw their mandate as embracing at least the following: tackling the problem of poverty, responding to the needs of immigrants, creating and maintaining a range of neighbourhood services, providing educational and recreational opportunities for people of all ages, cultivating the imagination and a sense of beauty, involvement in and encouragement of civic action to improve local conditions, and engaging in social research. As the early settlements enthusiastically pursued these aims a number of distinguishing characteristics appeared.

Of fundamental importance to the settlement ideal was the notion of residence; the more advantaged, well-to-do and educated would come to live, to settle, among a poor, immigrant community often in slum neighbourhoods. In this way they gained firsthand experience about the lives of the disadvantaged. The settlements offered help and often served as a kind of crisis centre where people could bring their problems, day or night, to a sympathetic ear. Inclusiveness was another guiding principle whereby the settlements served the whole neighbourhood, the whole family and the whole person.

The various strands of the social gospel movement, particularly as it gathered steam within the Presbyterian and Methodist churches, had a profound influence on the Canadian settlement movement. Many of the settlement leaders took spiritual and moral sustenance from this movement and were gripped by its linking of religion and social reform. A number of diverse conceptions of voluntarism also helped define the work of the settlements. First, since the people of the neighbourhoods came to the settlements of their own free will, free of coercion or obligation, their very attendance on this basis was a clear indication that the settlements were meeting real felt needs. Second, many of the program activities — recreational or educational — were conducted by volunteer workers who were young university students, which added a liveliness that otherwise might have been lacking. What these young and spirited volunteers lacked in experience and professional training they made up for with spontaneity and enthusiasm, establishing a real rapport with children and teenagers. Finally, the policy planning and funding of the settlements were in the hands of volunteer boards, men and women drawn from the upper and middle classes who served with a sense of *noblesse oblige*. During the course of the settlements' development there were some outstanding examples of personal devotion. Perhaps the most noteworthy examples were the commitments of Sir James

Woods to St. Christopher House and Walter Laidlaw to Central Neighbourhood House. Of course this elite control had negative aspects; for example, only much later was there local neighbourhood representation on settlement boards.

Neighbouring was seen as one of the most basic functions of settlement work. It involved neighbourly visiting on the part of staff and volunteers, fostering neighbourliness among people of diverse backgrounds through the communal atmosphere of the settlements, which would help break down barriers of race, nationality, religion, class and age. The settlements viewed themselves as having many prophylactic aims as well. It was an established principle of settlement practice that they could be a major social instrument for heading off trouble at the "top of the cliff," rather than sending "ambulances" to retrieve the remains of broken lives at the bottom. For example, athletic clubs for boys were seen as a deterrent to juvenile delinquency; carefully supervised social and recreational activities were an antidote to such unfortunate attractions as pool halls, saloons, public dance halls, lurid motion pictures and even such apparently harmless diversions as children playing in the street. The thought was that if children could be provided with wholesome recreation and activities of a generally uplifting nature, then the darker side of urban slum living could be warded off.

The flexibility and responsiveness of the settlements were critical to implementing their self-imposed mandate for the prevention of social problems. All three settlements exhibited a remarkable ability to modify and change their program emphasis to meet the evolving needs of their neighbourhoods. They even went as far as to move to a new location when there was a shift in the population or an area of greater need developed within the city. The overriding desire to"make good citizens" knit all these diverse and changing activities together. Many means were employed to this end: English classes for newcomers, talks on citizenship, self-governing clubs for boys and girls and clubs for immigrant women. Education was generally the main tool for the creation of responsible citizens, ready to live in a true democratic manner, and for the development of proper habits and social attitudes.

Early head residents placed considerable emphasis on the power of cultural events to positively affect the mind and spirit through beauty and joy. They had a deep-seated belief in the importance of aesthetic experiences in human development. It was no accident that all three settlements included music, drama, dancing, art and festivals in their programs. Over the years these cultural and artistic thrusts were at the core of what has made the settlements unique. In pursuit of these goals many well-known Toronto artists and musicians contributed to sustaining a lively interest in the arts among the children and adults who gathered weekly at the settlements.

Concern about poor social conditions was yet another preoccupation of the settlements. They all shared, in greater or lesser degrees, an uneasiness over the deleterious effects of poverty, bad housing, lack of proper sanitation, overcrowding and health problems. However, the ways that they confronted these problems varied considerably. All three made it their business to pinpoint social problems and to draw them to the attention of other social welfare organizations or civic authorities. In addition, there was general agreement on the desirability of conducting social surveys and of the usefulness of applied social research. Rarely though did they carry their social concern into definite action for social reform. Toronto settlements, and for that matter settlements elsewhere in Canada, were different from those in Great Britain or the United States; in those countries social settlements quickly established themselves as "spearheads of social reform." The Toronto settlements did exercise a continuing influence, though somewhat nebulous at times, on public opinion about the need for an improved range of social services. Canadian settlements were also much less involved with the labour movement or in regular discussions of political, economic and social questions. For example, Chicago's Hull House had four trade unions meeting there, two of which it had helped women workers to organize. Toronto settlements had no such connections. Toynbee Hall and Mansfield House in London's East End had "pleasant Sunday afternoons" where current topics including Marxism and socialism were discussed. The only comparable meetings in the early Canadian settlements were Mackenzie King's young men's group at St. Andrew's Institute in Toronto and the People's Forum at All People's Mission in Winnipeg during J.S. Woodsworth's regime. This difference remains a puzzle, but it may have had something to do with the lack of a strong reform tradition in Canada, a lack that historian Frank Underhill frequently bemoaned.

Perhaps the most arresting feature of the settlements throughout their history has been the predominance, at least when compared to other organizations, of women on settlement staffs. Social service work opened up careers for women at a time when a new group of relatively highly educated women were seeking outlets for their idealism and training. Settlement work offered a welcome opportunity to be of service to others. Many had been sheltered in their homes. University life and the idea of going to live in the slums had the allure of a certain sense of adventure. Living in residence too was pleasurable, often much freer than home and often simply fun. Low salaries in the early years acted as a deterrent to men.

Another factor that undoubtedly drew many women into settlement work was that much of the work involved women and children. It was widely accepted at that time that, of course, women had a natural affinity for this type of endeavour. Neighbourliness and mothering were considered typical elements of women's traditional domestic roles. Broadening these roles out into settlement work fit neatly with the maternal feminist movement of the early years of the century. All three Toronto settlements had women at the helm until well into the 1950s. The one exception was University Settlement, which for its first five years had three men as head resident. But after 1915 women at University Settlement served in this role until Harry Morrow took over in 1955. Central Neighbourhood House, from its founding in 1911, has always had a woman in the top staff position. A number of women who filled the post of head resident (later called executive director) such as Frances Crowther at University Settlement (1934-46), Beatrice Wilson at St. Christopher House (1943-53) and Helen Sutcliffe at Central Neighbourhood House (1949-70) served for long periods and were extraordinarily effective administrators. Their names and those of the many other women who people this history have now largely slipped from view, but their contributions are a vivid reminder that it was not just big businessmen and male entrepreneurs who created modern-day Toronto.

With the increasing professionalism that developed after World War II, the settlements underwent many changes that forever altered the nature of settlement work. Gone was the idea that had originally seemed so important, the concept of workers living in residence, and by the 1960s the settlement house had been replaced with the concept of neighbourhood centres. Recent trends have focused on a more democratic organization and operation of the settlements with an emphasis on citizen participation, self-help projects and neighbourhood improvement. Certainly by 1975 social agencies were struggling with the impact of the economic realities. By this time the settlements had come to rely more on government funding, which tended to be project-based and often put them on a treadmill pursuit of funds. These financial circumstances moved the management style to a more professional, business-based model with greater emphasis on added managerial layers often separated by specific expertise; for example, programming, fund-raising, public relations, information and office systems. All these rearrangements tended to alter the nature and general atmosphere of the houses. The project-driven approach necessary to survival meant assigning priority to politically popular programs currently eligible for funding. It had the subtle effect of pushing the houses in the direction of a more fragmented multi-service delivery rather than an integrated approach to their neighbourhoods.

Demographically there was the continual movement of people in the three neighbourhoods. The many attempts to save inner-city housing generated from philosophical sentiments of the 1960s were successful, but preservation of the integrity of the downtown core also made it more attractive to the affluent. The result was "gentrification" or "white-painting" of housing in traditional working-class and marginal neighbourhoods. This process brought old and new residents into conflict and the settlements were sometimes viewed as attracting undesirables to the upgraded residential areas. With the exception of subsidized housing, lower income residents, whether long-term residents or new immigrants, were forced outward from the city core often into the suburbs. Should the settlements follow these people to their new locations? Would the suburbanites welcome a neighbourhood centre being parachuted into their midst? Ultimately the settlements decided not to move and stayed in downtown Toronto.

By the 1970s the three settlements were caught in a swirl of cross-currents. Traditional idealism, which viewed settlement work as a vocation, came into conflict with careerism. The desire and the demand for greater citizen participation clashed with sophisticated corporate management trends, professional standards and the pragmatic urgency of current economic realities. Feminists were increasingly interested in group management of a participatory, non-hierarchical nature, while funding arrangements dictated movement in the direction of more specialization and hierarchy. Ethnic groups were more conscious of their rights within a multi-cultural framework and became more forceful in their dealings with social services.

But University Settlement, Central Neighbourhood House and St. Christopher House continue to make impressive contributions to Toronto's social and cultural life in the late twentieth century. They have helped thousands of new Canadians to find their place in a growing metropolitan and multi-cultural city. The key to their success has been their remarkable ability to combine continuity with change in the building of a better community.

APPENDIX

LOCATIONS OF THE THREE SETTLEMENTS

St. Christopher House
1912–1973:	67 Wales Avenue
1973–1985:	84 Augusta Avenue
1985–present:	53 Argyle Street and 761 Queen Street West

University Settlement
1910–1913:	467 Adelaide Street West
1913–1926:	95 Peter Street
1926–present:	15, 23-25 Grange Road

Central Neighbourhood House
1911–1919:	82-84 Gerrard Street West
1919–1928:	25-27 Elm Street
1928–1929:	12 Pembroke Street
1929–1970:	349 Sherbourne Street
1970–present:	349 Ontario Street

St. Christopher House

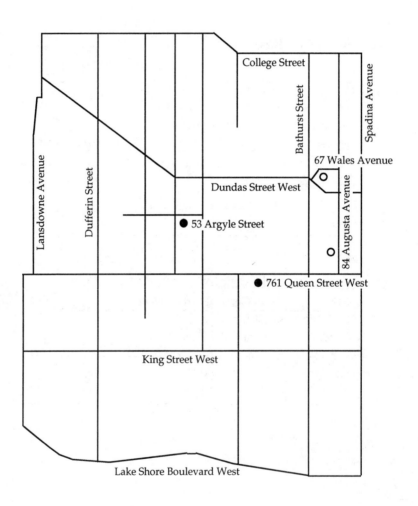

UNIVERSITY SETTLEMENT

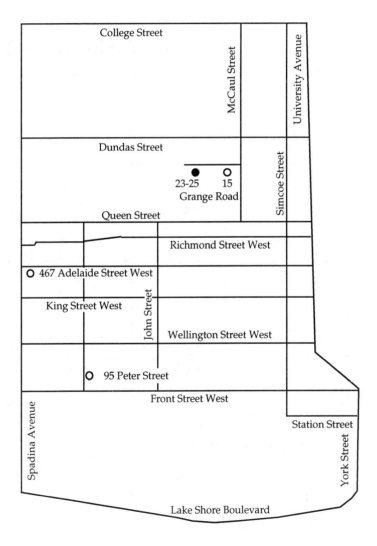

CENTRAL NEIGHBOURHOOD HOUSE

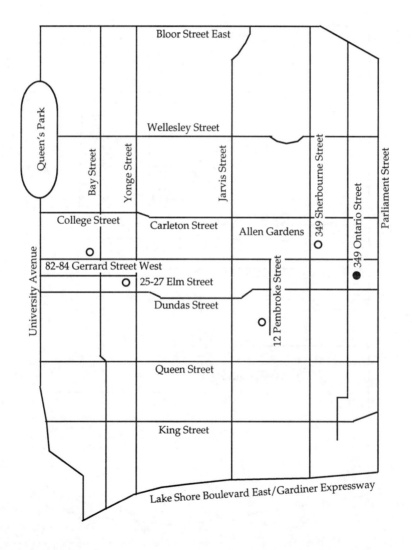

HEAD RESIDENTS/EXECUTIVE DIRECTORS

University Settlement

1910-1911:	James M. Shaver
1911-1913:	Milton B. Hunt
1913-1915:	Dr. Norman J. Ware
1915-1916:	Sara Libby Carson
1916-1917:	Ethel Dodds
1917-1918:	Hannah Matheson
1919-1921:	Marjorie W. Gregg
1921-1924:	Florence Campbell
1924-1928:	Myrtle Pascoe
1928-1933:	Olive Ziegler
1933-1934:	Edith Cook (acting)
1934-1946:	Frances Crowther
1947-1949:	Mary C. Donaldson
1949-1955:	Kathleen Gorrie
1955-1966:	Harry Morrow
1967-1973:	Ian Thomson
1973-1974:	William Stern
1974-1975:	A. Dharmalingham (acting)
1975-1977:	Philip Gandon
1977-1978:	Stuart Summerhayes
1978-:	A. Dharmalingham

St. Christopher House

1912-1917:	Helen Hart
1917-1921:	Ethel Dodds Parker
1921-1926:	Marion Yeigh
1927-1928:	Gwendolin Goldie
1928-1933:	Lally Fleming
1933-1934:	Anna Wilson (acting)
1935-1943:	Mina Barnes
1943-1953:	Beatrice Wilson
1953-1967:	John Haddad
1967-1972:	David Maben
1972-1980:	Jean Palmer
1980-:	Paul Zarnke

Central Neighbourhood House

1911-1915:	Elizabeth B. Neufeld
1915-1917:	Mary Joplin Clarke
1917-1942:	Helen E. Austin
1943-1944:	Elsie T. Bethune (acting)
1944-1945:	Mary B. Blakeslee
1945-1949:	Honorah Lucas
1949-1970:	Helen I. Sutcliffe
1970-1976:	Jeanne Rowles
1977:	Charlotte Maher (interim)
1977-1981:	Paddy Ann Pugsley

WORKS CITED

Abel, Emily K. "Toynbee Hall, 1884-1914." *Social Service Review* 53(4): 606-632.

Abel, Emily K. "Middle Class Culture for the Urban Poor: The Educational Thought of Samuel Barnett." *Social Service Review* 52(4): 596-620.

Acta Victoriana. XXXIII. October, 1909: 36 "The Students' Christian Social Union."

Acta Victoriana. XXXIII. December, 1909. Item on Mrs. Pankhurst's meeting at Massey Hall, Nov. 20, 1909: 198.

Acta Victoriana. XXXV. October, 1911: 27. Article on the YMCA, with description of the Social Union department.

Addams, Jane. *Democracy and Social Ethics*. With an introduction by Anne Firor Scott. Cambridge, Mass.: The Belknap Press of the Harvard University Press, 1964. (Original edition published by the Macmillan Company, New York, 1902.)

Addams, Jane. *Forty Years at Hull House*. New York: The Macmillan Company, 1935.

Allen, Richard. *The Social Passion: Religion and Social Reform in Canada 1914-28*. Toronto: University of Toronto Press, 1973.

Anderson, Alan B. and James S. Frideres. *Ethnicity in Canada: Theoretical Perspectives*. Toronto: Butterworths, 1981.

Archives of the Archdiocese of Toronto (generally referred to as the Catholic Archives). Contains Archbishops' papers, parish files, biographical files, etc.

Arnold, A.J. "Many Unskilled Become peddlers." *The Canadian Jewish News*, Feb. 21, 1975.

Associated Charities (Toronto). Partial statement concerning work of charity organizations on Associated Charities letterhead, 1908. In Toronto

Social Welfare Agencies file, Ms. 12, Rare Book Room, Thomas Fisher Library, University of Toronto.

Associated Charities (Toronto). "A Need Recognized." Pamphlet, 1911. In Toronto Social Welfare Agencies file, Ms. 12, Rare Book Room, Thomas Fisher Library, University of Toronto.

Associated Charities (Toronto). Annual Report, 1909, 1911. In Toronto Social Welfare Agencies file, Ms. 12, Rare Book Room, Thomas Fisher Library, University of Toronto.

Bain, Ian. "Poor Boy Pioneered Children's Aid Work." Newspaper article found in the Central Neighbourhood House Archives; name and date of paper missing, but written after Bain's thesis of 1955.

Bain, Ian. "The Role of J.J. Kelso in the Launching of the Child Welfare Movement in Ontario". MSW thesis, University of Toronto, 1955.

Baker, Walter. "Profiles 8: John Joseph Kelso." Canadian Welfare, vol. 42, no. 6, November-December 1966.

Barnett, Henrietta. The Beginnings of Toynbee Hall. In Towards Social Reform, by Henrietta and Samuel Barnett, 1909 (in Pacey's Readings).

Bator, Paul Adolphus. "Saving Lives on the Wholesale Plan: Public Health Reform in the City of Toronto, 1900 to 1930." 2 vols. Ph.D. thesis, University of Toronto, 1979.

Berger, Carl. The Sense of Power: Studies in the Ideas of Canadian Imperialism, 1867-1914. Toronto: University of Toronto Press, 1970.

Berger, Carl. The Writing of Canadian History; Aspects of English-Canadian Historical Writing: 1900 to 1970. Toronto: Oxford University Press, 1976. For biographical information on Adam Shortt and analysis of his contribution to Canadian historiography see pp. 21-30; for same regarding O.D. Skelton, see pp. 47-52.

Beveridge, (Sir) William H. Power and Influence. London: Hodder and Stoughton, 1953.

Bibliography of College, Social, University and Church Settlements, 5th edition. Compiled by Caroline Williamson Montgomery for the College Settlement Association. Chicago, 1905.

Bridle, Augustus. "The Drama of the Ward." The Canadian Magazine, vol. XXXIV, no. 1, November, 1909.

Brown, Robert Craig and Ramsay Cook. Canada 1896-1921: A Nation Transformed. Toronto: McClelland and Stewart Limited, 1974.

Bryce, George P. Biographical folder in the United Church Archives.

Burnet, Jean with Howard Palmer "Coming Canadians:" An Introduction to a History of Canada's Peoples. Toronto: McClelland & Stewart Inc., 1988.

Canada. *Census of Canada.* for 1901, 1911 and 1921. Ottawa: King's Printer.

Canada. *Sessional Papers, 1909, No. 14 Department of Interior,* Report of the Chief Medical Officer (Dr. Peter Henderson Bryce,) Ottawa, May 14, 1908: 69-137.

Canadian Conference of Charities and Corrections. *Proceedings.* Issues of the published proceedings of the conference have been consulted for the years 1899, 1900, 1901, 1903, 1905, 1909-1911, 1913, 1916 and 1917.

Carson, Sara Libby. "How Settlement Work Began." *The Presbyterian Record,* June, 1915: 245.

Carson, Sara Libby. "The Social Settlement" — address given at the Social Service Congress of Canada, Ottawa, 1914 and published in the Report of the Congress.

Carson, Sara Libby. Official documents:

Will, dated March 19, 1928.

Probate of Estate, Court of Probate, District of Woodbury, Woodbury, Conn. 1929-1934.

Death Certificate, Dec. 29, 1928, issued by the Department of Health of The City of New York, Bureau of Records.

The Catholic Church Extension Society. History, a typescript of highlights in the Catholic Archives, Archdiocese of Toronto.

The Catholic Register. In 1909, re-named *The Catholic Register and Canadian Extension.* (Referred to in footnotes as Register). Microfilm of The Catholic Register at St. Michael's College Library. The index to the register, available at the reference desk, presents an annotated table of contents of the Toronto and Canadian material, arranged chronologically.

Charities Commission. Reports on institutions, 1911-1923. In Toronto Social Welfare Agencies file, Ms. 12, Rare Book Room, Thomas Fisher Library, University of Toronto.

The Christian Guardian (Methodist). Available in the United Church Archives.

The Christian Guardian. Editorial, "In the Slums of 'Toronto the Good.'" May 26, 1909.

The Christian Guardian. Editorial, "Students' Social and Evangelistic Movement." Aug. 31, 1910: 6.

The Christian Guardian, Mar. 4, 1914. Item re the First Annual Report of Wesley Institute, Fort William, p. 19.

"A Christian Social Settlement." *The Outlook,* vol. 68, July 20, 1901: 660.

City of Toronto Municipal Archives. "Events and Factors in the Advance of Public Health Measures in Toronto, 1866-," a typewritten document listing events chronologically.

City of Toronto. *City Council Minutes*, 1907 to 1911. Mayors' inaugural addresses in Appendix C.

City of Toronto. Reports of the Medical Officer of Health to the Toronto City Council, Feb. 1, 1909 to Nov. 2, 1910. (In *City Council Minutes*.)

Clark, S.D. *The Developing Canadian Community*. 2nd edition. Toronto: University of Toronto Press, 1968.

Cleverdon, Catherine L. *The Woman Suffrage Movement in Canada*, with an introduction by Ramsay Cook. Toronto: University of Toronto Press, 1974 (original edition 1950).

Coit, Stanton A. The Neighborhood Guild Defined, 1982. In *Readings in the Development of Settlement Work*, ed. L.M. Pacey. New York: Association, 1950.

Copp, Terry. *The Anatomy of Poverty: The Condition of the Working Class in Montreal, 1897-1929*. Toronto: McClelland and Stewart, 1974.

Corelli, Rae. "The Ward." *Toronto Star*, 1964.

Craig, Gerald M. *The United States and Canada*. Cambridge, Mass.: Harvard University Press, 1968. Chapter 12, "Canada's Century Looming, 1897-1914."

Creighton, Donald. *Canada's First Century: 1867-1967*. Toronto: Macmillan of Canada, 1970.

Davis, Allen F. *Spearheads for Reform: The Social Settlements and the Progressive Movement, 1890-1914*. New York: Oxford University Press, 1967. (The Urban Life in America Series).

Dawson, Robert MacGregor. *William Lyon Mackenzie King: A Political Biography, 1874-1923* (vol. I of a series.) Toronto: University of Toronto Press, 1958.

Denison, Flora MacDonald. "The Open Road to Democracy." *Sunday World* (Toronto), May 14, 1911. An article about the founding of Central Neighbourhood House, which includes a reference to Jane Addams' address to the I.C.W. meeting in 1909.

Department of Health, Toronto. *Report of the Medical Health Officer Dealing with the Recent Investigation of Slum Conditions in Toronto, Embodying Recommendations for the Amelioration of the Scenes*. Toronto, July 5th, 1911 (usually referred to as the Hastings Report).

Di Stasi, Michael. "Fifty Years of Italian Evangelism: The Story of St. Paul's Italian United Church, Toronto." Toronto, 1955. Provides early history of the Toronto Methodist Italian Mission and its branches, as well as of their amalgamation as St. Paul's Italian United Church. (Copy in St. Paul's folder, United Church Archives.)

Encyclopedia Canadiana, Toronto: Grolier Limited, 1975.

Falconer, Robert Alexander. "The University Spirit," *The Varsity* (Toronto), Oct. 10, 1908: 2. This was President Falconer's first address to the students of the University of Toronto in Convocation Hall, Oct. 1, 1907.

Falconer, Robert Alexander. The Robert Alexander Falconer Papers (commonly referred to as the Falconer Papers) — chiefly correspondence during his presidency of the University of Toronto. Held at the University of Toronto Archives.

Federation of Settlements (Toronto). Minutes Book, 1918-1952. In the Toronto Association of Neighbourhood Services (TANS) Archives, at the Municipal Archives, City Hall, Toronto.

Firth, Edith G., ed. *The Town of York 1815-1834.* Toronto: University of Toronto Press, 1966.

Florinsky, Michael T. *Russia: A History and an Interpretation.* 2 vols. New York: The Macmillan Company, 1947. 12th printing, 1967.

Forsey, Eugene A. *The Canadian Labour Movement, 1812-1902.* Ottawa: The Canadian Historial Association, Historial Booklet No. 27, 1974.

Fraser, Brian J. "The Moral Crusaders: The Men and Ideas of the Presbyterian Social Gospel, 1896-1914." Ph.D. thesis, York University, 1983.

Fraser, Donald T., (Mrs.). Interview with Harriet Parsons, April 3, 1974.

Fred Victor Mission Annual Reports (UCA):

1900 *Lights and Shades of City Life: The Story of the Work of Fred Victor Mission, Toronto.*

1901 *Sunshine and Shadow: The Story of a Year's Work in the Fred Victor Mission, Toronto.*

1905 *The Streets and Lanes of the City: Another Year's Work.*

1906 *These Twenty Years, 1886-1906: The Growth and Work of the Fred Victor Mission.* Includes the following:

"How it Originated," by Mrs. M.T. Sheffield.

"These Twenty Years," by Bertle Edward Bull.

"Our Present Work," by Rev. J.D. Fitzpatrick.

"Work Among the Children", by Rev. Thomas McKay.

1908 *The Story of Our Work by Our Workers: Annual Report of the Toronto City and Fred Victor Mission Society of the Methodist Church.*

1909 *Forward: The Story of Our Work by Our Workers: Annual Report .*

Fred Victor Mission. Sixteen-page pamphlet issued with the beginning of the new mission in 1894. Includes, "How the Mission Started," by B.E. Bull, President of the Toronto City Missionary Society of the Methodist Church. (FVM)

Glazebrook, G.P. *The Story of Toronto.* Toronto: University of Toronto Press, 1971.

The Globe and Mail (Toronto), July 18-24, 1895 — gives an account of the Pan-American Congress of Religion and Education, including Jane Addams' address.

Grant, John Webster. *The Church in the Canadian Era; The First Century of Confederation.* Toronto: McGraw-Hill Ryerson, 1972. Vol. 3 of *A History of the Christian Church in Canada,* ed. John Webster Grant.

Harney, Robert F. "The Italian Community in Toronto, 1900-1950." Unpublished study, circa 1975 (copy given to author by Dr. Harney.)

Harney, Robert F. (ed.) *Gathering Place: Peoples and Neighbourhoods of Toronto, 1834-1945.* Toronto: Multicultural History Society of Ontario, 1985.

Harney, Robert F. and Harold Troper. *Immigrants: A Portrait of the Urban Experience 1890-1930.* Toronto: Van Nostrand Reinhold Ltd., 1975.

Hart, Helen L. "Evangelical Social Settlement Work." *The Presbyterian Records,* June 1915: 255.

Henderson, Charles Richmond. *Social Settlements.* New York: Lentilhon & Company, 1899.

"History of Canadian Settlements" file in the Baldwin Room, Metropolitan Toronto Reference Library. Contains the working papers on which Mary Jennison's "Study of the Canadian Settlement Movement" was largely based. Deposited in the Baldwin Room by Mrs. G. Cameron Parker, Chairman of the Committee on the History of Canadian Settlements, after the project as originally planned broke down (about 1965).

The History of Memorial Institute. Typewritten page in folder on "Federation of Settlements," Ms. 12, Box 2, Rare Book Room, Thomas Fisher Library, University of Toronto. No date, but history only carried to founding of Institute in 1912, so presumably prepared about that time.

Hogg, Carol Stanton. "Mildmay Institute." History of Canadian settlements file, Book B (Baldwin Room, Metropolitan Toronto Reference Library.)

Home Garden Settlement, vol. 1, no. 1, March, 1911. Official publication of the settlement, 405 East 116th Street, New York, N.Y.

Horne, Edward (Rev.) Biographical file in the United Church Archives. Contains copy of obituary published in the *Acts and Proceedings of the 68th General Assembly of the Presbyterian Church in Canada, 1942.*

Horowitz, G. *Canadian Labour in Politics*. Toronto: University of Toronto Press, 1968.

House of Industry. *House of Industry — 99th Annual Report, 1935-36*. Also a folder on House of Industry history. Both in Toronto Social Welfare Agencies file, Ms. 12, Rare Book Room, Thomas Fisher Library, University of Toronto.

Howes, Ruth. "Adelaide Hunter Hoodless." In *The Clear Spirit: Twenty Canadian Women and Their Times*, ed. Mary Quayle Innis. Toronto: University of Toronto Press, 1966.

Innis, Mary Quayle. *Unfold the Years: A History of the Young Women's Christian Association in Canada*. Toronto: McClelland and Stewart Ltd., 1949.

The Italian Methodist House of Toronto — a four-page folder (written about 1914) in the Toronto Italian Methodist Mission file, United Church Archives.

The Italian Mission of the Methodist Church: Directory of Services — a four-page folder (about 1907) in the above file.

Jennison, Mary. "Study of the Canadian Settlement Movement" (ca. 1967). Unpublished manuscript for the book originally sponsored by the Committee on the History of the Canadian Settlements. A copy is in the OISE Library, Toronto. Chapter II, "The Chain of Presbyterian Settlements," pp. 83-97.

Johnson's Universal Cyclopaedia. 8 vols.New York: A.J. Johnson Company, 1895. Items on Canada, Toronto and Winnipeg.

Jones, Andrew and Leonard Rutman. *In the Children's Aid: J.J. Kelso and Child Welfare in Ontario*. Toronto: University of Toronto Press, 1981.

Kealey, Greg, ed. *Canada Investigates Industrialism*. Toronto: University of Toronto Press, 1973.

Kelso, J.J. "Neglected and Friendless Children." *Canadian Magazine*, January, 1894: 213-16. Reprinted in *Saving the Canadian City*, ed. Paul Rutherford. Toronto: University of Toronto Press, 1974.

Kelso, J.J. Directory, *Charities of Toronto, 1910-11*, including Benevolent and Social Reform Agencies. Toronto: William Briggs, 1910.

Kelso, John Joseph. "Can Slums be Abolished or Must We Continue to Pay the Penalty?" Toronto, n.d. (probably 1909 or 1910). Pamphlet, illustrated.

Kelso, John Joseph. "Some First Principles of Social Work." Written in 1909, but printed in 1913 in the 21st Annual Report of the Superintendent of Neglected and Dependent Children. An offprint copy is in the Kelso Papers, PAC, vol. 6.

Kelso, John Joseph. The John Joseph Kelso Manuscript Collection (commonly referred to as the Kelso Papers). Ottawa: Manuscript Division, Public Archives of Canada. Includes autobiographical files, correspondence, diaries, subject files, notes and drafts, notebooks, scrapbooks, newspaper clippings, broadsheets and reports.

Kelso, Martin M. "J.J. Kelso — biography — 1864-1935." Typescript in J.J. Kelso Papers, Mss. Collection 115, Rare Book Room, Thomas Fisher Library, University of Toronto.

Kelso, Martin M. Interview by Harriet Parsons, Feb. 18, 1975.

King, W.L. Mackenzie. The Mackenzie King Diaries, 1893-1931. Toronto and Buffalo: University of Toronto Press. Microfiches. (Film F K54 K54, History Section, Metropolitan Toronto Reference Library.)

King, William Lyon Mackenzie. "Foreigners who Live in Toronto." Two articles in Mail and Empire (Toronto), Sept. 25 and Oct. 9, 1897.

King, William Lyon Mackenzie. "In Chicago Slums — The Work of Hull House Among the Poor." Globe and Mail (Toronto), Jan. 16, 1897.

King, William Lyon Mackenzie. "The Story of Hull House." The Westminster, Nov. 6, 1897.

King, William Lyon Mackenzie. A series of four unsigned articles in the Mail and Empire (Toronto):
   "Crowded Housing, Its Evil Effects" — Sept. 18, 1897.
   "Toronto and the Sweating System" — Oct. 2, 1897.
   "Foreigners who Live in Toronto" — (two articles) Sept. 25 and Oct. 9, 1897.

King, William Lyon Mackenzie. Industry and Humanity — A Study in the Principles Underlying Industrial Reconstruction. Toronto: Thomas Allen, 1918. A recent reprint edition published by the University of Toronto Press has a perceptive introduction by David J. Bercusson.

Klein, Maury and Harvey A. Kantor. Prisoners of Progress: American Industrial Cities 1850-1920. New York: Macmillan Publishing Co., Inc., 1976.

Knox Archives, Knox College, Toronto. Contains archival material of the Presbyterian Church in Canada to the present, various Presbyterian journals, etc.

Knox, William John (Rev.). "Settlement Work in Chicago." The Presbyterian, April 6, 1904: 139.

Knox, William John (Rev.). "How to Organize a Brotherhood." The Presbyterian, Oct. 7, 1908: 362.

Knox, William John (Rev.). "The Presbyterian Brotherhood." The Presbyterian, March 18, 1909: 327.

Lappin, Bernard W. "Stages in the Development of Community Organization Work as Social Work Method." Ph.D. thesis, University of Toronto, February, 1965.

Lasch, C. ed. *The Social Thought of Jane Addams*. Indianapolis: Bobbs-Merrill Company, Inc., 1965.

Leiby, James. *A History of Social Welfare and Social Work in the United States*. New York: Columbia University Press, 1978.

Lemon, James. *Toronto Since 1918: An Illustrated History*. Toronto: James Lorimer & Company, 1985.

Lewis, Victor George. "Earlscourt, Toronto — A Descriptive, Historical and Interpretative Study in Urban Class Development." M.A. thesis, University of Toronto, 1920. Not only provides a history of the Earlscourt Methodist Church, but compares the Earlscourt church and neighbourhood with Central Neighbourhood House and the Ward.

Lippert, Frieda E. "Christodora House Settlement." *The Commons*, vol. VI, no. 64, November, 1901: 11.

Local Council of Women of Toronto. *Nothing New Under the Sun: A History of the Toronto Local Council of Women*. Toronto, 1978.

Mallon, J.J. "Toynbee Hall: Past and Present." *Britain Today*, No. 100, August and September, 1944. In *Readings in the Development of Social Work*, ed. L.K. Pacey. New York: Association Press, 1950.

Massey, Hart A. Letter to Mrs. M.T. Sheffield, Oct. 21, 1893.

McCurdy, J.F., ed. *Life and Work of D.J. Macdonnell, Minister of St. Andrew's Church, Toronto, with a Selection of Sermons and Prayers*. Toronto: William Briggs, 1897.

McGillicuddy, Owen Ernest. *The Making of a Premier: An Outline of the Life Story of the Right Hon. W.L. Mackenzie King, C.M.G.* Toronto: The Musson Book Company Limited, 1922.

McNaught, Kenneth. *A Prophet in Politics: A Biography of J.S. Woodsworth*. Toronto: University of Toronto Press, 1959.

Melville, Kate. "An Eastside Settlement." *The Westminster*, October 14, 1899: 429.

The Methodist Church (Canada). *Journal of Proceedings of the Eighth General Conference of the Methodist Church, 1910*. Contains "The Quadrennial Reports: The Methodist Missionary Society."

The Methodist Young Men's Association and the Italians — a 12-page pamphlet in the Toronto Italian Methodist Mission file, UCA. n.d., but published about 1905 or 1906 when the Mission was starting its work.

Middleton, Jesse Edgar. *The Municipality of Toronto: A History*, vol. II. Toronto: The Dominion Publishing Co., 1923.

Millman, Mary. Interview with Harriet Parsons, June 21, 1976.

Mills, Alexander. "Mission to the Italians." *The 1905 Annual Report of the Fred Victor Mission Society*: 24-26.

The Missionary Society of the Methodist Church, 83rd Annual Report, 1906-07. Includes Report of J.S. Woodsworth, Superintendent of All Peoples' Mission, Winnipeg.

The Missionary Society of the Methodist Church (Canada). *Methodist Missions at Home and Abroad, Annual Report, 1908.*

Mitchinson, Wendy L. "Aspects of Reform: Four Women's Organizations in Nineteenth Century Canada." Ph.D. thesis, York University, 1976. (microfiche.)

Mitchinson, Wendy L. "The YWCA and Reform in the Nineteenth Century." *Social History: A Canadian Review*, vol. XII, November 1979: 368-384.

Morgan, Henry James, ed. *Canadian Men and Women of the Time: A Handbook of Canadian Biography of Living Characters*, 2nd edition. Toronto: William Briggs, 1912.

Mutchmor, James Ralph (Rev.). Biographical file in the United Church Archives.

Nijenhuis, Herman (ed.) *Hundred Years of Settlements and Neighbourhood Centres in North America and Europe*. Utrecht: International Federation of Settlements and Neighbourhood Centres, 1986.

O'Connor, Patricia J. *The Story of Central Neighbourhood House 1911-1918.*

O'Connor, Patricia J. *The Story of St. Christopher House 1912-1984*. Published by the Toronto Association of Neighbourhood Services as part of the series *Good Neighbours: A History of the Toronto Settlement House Movement 1920-1985.*

Our Lady of Mount Carmel Church. Parish file in Catholic Archives, chiefly correspondence relating to the founding of the Italian church in 1908.

Pacey, Lorene M., ed. *Readings in the Development of Settlement Work*. New York: Association Press, 1950.

Paris, Erna. *Jews, An Account of Their Experience in Canada*. Toronto: Macmillan of Canada, 1980.

Parker, Ethel Dodds "The Story of St. Christopher House." *Friends to Thousands*. 50th Anniversary booklet, 1962.

Parker, Ethel Dodds. "Religion and Early Social Work in Canada." Paper prepared for a conference entitled "The Social Gospel: Religion and Social Reform in Canada," at the University of Saskatchewan, Regina Campus, March 21-24, 1973.

Parker, Ethel Dodds. Interviews by Harriet Parsons, Guelph, Ontario, July 20, 1974 and Feb. 9, 1976.

Parsons, A. Harriet. "The Role of J.J. Kelso in the Canadian Settlement Movement". Unpublished research paper, 1977. (Copy in the Baldwin Room, Canadian History Department, Metropolitan Toronto Reference Library.)

Pidgeon, George C. "Dr. John G. Shearer: Christian Soldier." *The Presbyterian Witness*, vol. LXXIV, no. 15, Mar. 10, 1921: 9-10.

Pimlott, J.A.R. *Toynbee Hall: Fifty Years of Social Progress, 1884-1934*. London: J.M. Dent and Sons, Ltd., 1935.

Piva, Michael J. *The Condition of the Working Class in Toronto, 1900-1921*. Ottawa: University of Ottawa Press, 1979.

The Presbyterian, Feb. 13, 1908, p. 195. Editorial entitled "A Great Opportunity." Concerning immigration boom and economic crisis of 1907-1908.

The Presbyterian, June 4, 1908. Editorial on Mrs. Humphry Ward's address at the Evangelia Settlement concerning playgrounds for children in congested districts.

The Presbyterian, vol. XIV, no. 26, July 1, 1909. "Impressions from the International Council."

The Presbyterian. Articles, editorials and announcements relating to city problems and the Presbyterian Church's response in 1911:

    "Facing the City Problem," Feb. 9.

    "The Problem of the Immigrant," March 10.

    "Moral and Social Reform and Evangelism," March 30.

    "Christianity in Relation to Present Day Social Problems," March 30.

    "To Rescue the Perishing" (redemptive homes), May 25.

    "The Problem of the City," June 1.

    "The Problem of the City — Its Solution," June 8.

    "The Civic Cancer" (slums), Aug. 3.

    "Board of Social Service and Evangelism," Sept. 14.

Presbyterian Church in Canada. *Acts and Proceedings of the General Assembly of the Presbyterian Church in Canada 1911*. (United Church Archives).

Presbyterian Church in Canada. *Acts and Proceedings of the General Assembly, 1907-1943*.

    Some reference to the Jewish work may be found in the *Acts and Proceedings* themselves, but most of the material on the Jewish missions appears in the Appendices: under the Foreign Mission reports until 1912, the Home Mission reports until Church Union in 1925, and thereafter under the General Board of Missions. The *Acts and Proceedings* up to 1924 are available at either the United Church or Knox College Archives; from 1925 on, at the Knox Archives only.

Presbyterian Church in Canada. Board of Home Missions and Social Services. United Church Archives (PCC GA 38 B65) — Box 2, File 19. Includes Board papers and miscellaneous items from 1907-1922. Of special interest in this study is a report on institutional work among the foreigners of Western Canada," which includes information on the steps leading up to the foundation of Robertson Church and Burrows Avenue Mission, Winnipeg, prior to the launching of the Presbyterian Chain of Settlements.

Presbyterian Church in Canada. Board of Moral and Social Reform. Box in the United Church Archives (PCC GA 34 B5-6). Includes Minutes, reports and correspondence of the Committee on Temperance and other Moral and Social Reforms, 1907, the Board of Moral and Social Reform, 1908-1910, and the Board of Moral and Social Reform and Evangelism, 1910 (Sept. to Nov.).

Presbyterian Church in Canada. Board of Social Service and Evangelism. Box in United Church Archives (PCC GA 34 B6). Includes pamphlets, some correspondence of Dr. J.G. Shearer and program for a proposed British Columbia Social Service Congress in 1916.

Presbyterian Church in Canada. *Mission to the Jews, First Annual Report, May, 1909 (UCA)*.

Presbyterian Church in Canada. PCC Board of Foreign Missions files on Missions to the Jews in the United Church Archives (PCC GA41 B6 J). Includes folders on:

> Mission to Jews in Palestine, 1889-1898; 1908-1912 (correspondence).
>
> Mission to Jews in Canada, 1908-1920 (correspondence, committee minutes, reports, etc.).
>
> The Archives provides a finding aid to the latter file, entitled "Jewish Mission Work in Canada, 1907-1925, The Presbyterian Church in Canada."

Reinders, Robert C. "Toynbee Hall and the American Settlement Movement," *Social Service Review* 56(1): 39-54.

Report of the Social Survey Commission, Toronto. Presented to the City Council, Oct. 4th, 1915. Copy available in the Municipal Archives, City Hall, Toronto.

Rhind, F.H. Interview with Harriet Parsons, Jan. 14, 1977.

Riasanovsky, Nicholas V. *A History of Russia*, 2nd edition. New York: Oxford University Press, 1969.

Ross, Murray G. *The Y.M.C.A in Canada: Chronicle of a Century*. Toronto:

Ryerson Press, 1951.

Royce, Marion V. "The Contribution of the Methodist Church to Social Welfare in Canada." Master's thesis, University of Toronto, 1940.

Royce, Marion V. *Eunice Dyke, Health Care Pioneer*, Toronto: Dundurn Press, 1983.

Rutherford, Paul, ed. *Saving the Canadian City: The First Phase 1880-1920. An Anthology of Early Articles on Urban Reform.* Toronto. University of Toronto Press, 1974.

Rutherford, Paul. "Tomorrow's Metropolis: The Urban Reform Movement in Canada, 1880-1920." In the Canadian Historical Association's *Historical Papers, 1971.*

Sangster, Margaret E. "Christodora House." *The Congregationalist,* vol. 84, March 2, 1889: 304.

Scott Mission. *Who? When? Where? — A Brief History of the Scott Mission,* an illustrated folder giving a capsulated account of the evolution of the mission from the founding in 1908 of the Presbyterian Mission to the Jews (later named the Scott Institute) down to the Scott Mission of 1975.

Scudder, Vida Dutton. *On Journey.* New York: E.P. Dutton & Co., Inc., 1937.

Shaver, J.M. "The University Settlement." *The University Monthly,* February, 1911: 113.

Shaver, James M. Biographical folder in the United Church Archives. Contains "Life Sketch of Mr. J.M. Shaver," written by himself in 1923; also record of his church appointments, and a brief mimeographed biography.

Shaw, Rosa L. *Proud Heritage: A History of the National Council of Women of Canada.* Toronto: Ryerson Press, 1957.

Shearer, John G. "The Call of the City to the Church." *The Presbyterian,* June 29, 1916. Describes Settlements and some city missions under jurisdiction of the Board of Home Missions and Social Service; Robertson Institute, Winnipeg; Chalmers House, Montreal; and Hebrew Christian Synagogue, Evangel Hall and St. Christopher House, Toronto.

Shearer, John G. Letter from Shearer to J.J. Kelso regarding the Board of Social Service and Evangelism's Report entitled "The Problem of the City," May 22, 1911. (Kelso Papers, PAC, vol. 1).

Sims, Mary S. *The Natural History of a Social Institution — the Young Women's Christian Association.* New York: Woman's Press, 1936.

Social Service Commission Report dealing with the origins, duties, growth and work since November, 1912. 1921.

Social Service Council of Canada. *Social Service Congress, Ottawa, 1914: Report of Addresses and Proceedings.* Toronto, 1914.

Social Welfare, vol. XI, no. 5, February, 1929. "Sara Libby Carson," p. 113 – an obituary reprinted from *The Woodbury Press,* Woodbury, Conn.

Speisman, Stephen A. "The Jews of Toronto: A History to 1937." 2 vols. Ph.D. thesis, University of Toronto, 1975.

Speisman, Stephen A. Interviews by Harriet Parsons, Jan. 8, 1975 and Jan. 18, 1982.

Speisman, Stephen A. *The Jews of Toronto: A History to 1937.* Toronto: McClelland and Stewart, 1979.

Splane, Richard B. *The Development of Social Welfare in Ontario, 1791-1893: A Study of Public Welfare Administration.* Toronto: University of Toronto Press, 1965.

St. Christopher House. *St. Christopher House Silver Jubilee, 1912-1937.* 25 years of service and achievement.

Stapleford, Frank. *After Twenty Years: A Short History of the Neighbourhood Workers Association.* Toronto, 1938.

Star Weekly, Aug. 3, 1912, picture section, p. 3. "In a Church Playground," photograph of playground at Memorial Institute, with caption.

Strauss, Marina. "Bathhouse Awash in Deficits," *Globe and Mail* (Toronto), Feb. 12, 1980: 4.

Strong-Boag, Veronica Jane. *The Parliament of Women: The National Council of Women of Canada, 1893-1925.* Ottawa: National Museum of Man (Mercury Series) 1976. History Division Paper No. 18.

Sutherland, Neil. *Children in English-Canadian Society: Framing the Twentieth Century Consensus.* Toronto: University of Toronto Press, 1976.

Teireira, Richard. "The Roman Catholic and United Churches' Progress with the Italian Community of St. John's Ward, 1885-1920 and 1951-1961." Unpublished paper, Apr. 8, 1983 (copy on deposit in the Catholic Archives).

Thompson, Gordon. "Gipsy Smith in Toronto, Massey Hall, May 8th to May 24th." *The Christian Guardian,* March 24, 1909: 10.

Toronto City and Fred Victor Mission Society of the Methodist Church. Annual Reports:

> *Forward: The Story of Our Work by Our Workers,* 1909.
> *Making History, 1886-1911,* 1911.
> *The Messenger,* 1912.

Questionnaire forms for the Students' Christian Social Union

Report of Toronto Visitations. A few filled-in forms from the 1909 survey are preserved in the Fred Victor Mission file in the United Church Archives.

Toronto Methodist Italian Mission. *Second Annual Report*, printed in the 1907 annual report of the Fred Victor Mission Society, pp. 32-34.

Toronto Methodist Italian Mission. *Third Annual Report*, printed in the 1908 annual report of the Toronto City and Fred Victor Mission Society, pp. 40-42.

Toronto Playgrounds Association. *Playgrounds — What Toronto is Trying to do for its Children*. Toronto, 1910. Booklet includes historical sketch of founding of the Toronto Playgrounds Association and its work to 1910, written by J.J. Kelso.

Toronto Social Welfare Agencies, Ms. 12 (2 boxes) in the Rare Book Room, Thomas Fisher Library, University of Toronto. A collection of pamphlets, reports, letters, etc., dealing with early Toronto charitable and welfare agencies.

Toronto Star. Clippings of article about Fred Victor Mission by David Jones, n.d.

Toynbee, Arnold. *The Industrial Revolution*. Boston: Beacon Press, 1966. First published in 1884.

Toynbee, Arnold. *Lectures on the Industrial Revolution in England, Popular Addresses, Notes and Other Fragments*, (together with a short memoir by B. Jowett, Master of Balliol College, Oxford). London: Rivingtons, 1884.

Trofimenkoff, Susan Mann. Review of Strong-Boag's "The Parliament of Women." In *Social History: A Canadian Review*, vol. XI, May 1978: 238-239.

Trolander, Judith Ann. *Professionalism and Social Change: From the Settlement House Movement to Neighbourhood Centres, 1886 to the Present*. New York: Columbia University Press, 1987.

Trotter, Frances. Interview by Harriet Parsons, July 4, 1983.

Turnbull, J.A., D.D. "What does Associated Charities Mean and What is its Object?" Address given to the Canadian Club of Toronto, Nov. 8, 1909. Reprinted in *Saving the Canadian City*, ed. Paul Rutherford. Toronto: University of Toronto Press, 1974.

Underhill, Frank H. "King, William Lyon Mackenzie," biographical entry in *Encyclopedia Canadiana*, vol. 5, 1972 edition. Grolier of Canada.

United Church Archives. Toronto. Contains archival material of the Methodist and Presbyterian churches in Canada up to 1925, and of the United

Church of Canada from 1925.

University of Toronto. *University of Toronto Calendar, 1909-1910.*

"The University Settlement — Secretary's Annual Report." *The University Monthly,* June, 1911: 379-380.

Varsity, vol. XXIV, no. 8, Dec. 1, 1904: 131. "The College Girl" column by Miss P.A. Magee describes the work being done at Evangelia House.

Varsity, Nov. 26, 1909: 3. "YMCA Notes."

Victoria University. *Calendar of Victoria University, Faculty of Theology,* 1909-1910 and 1910-1911.

Wald, Lillian D. *The House on Henry Street.* (1915; reprint, with an introduction by Helen Hall) New York: Dover Publication, Inc., 1971.

Wallace, Elisabeth. "The Origin of the Social Welfare State in Canada, 1867-1900." *The Canadian Journal of Economics and Political Science,* Vol. XVI, August 1950: 383-393.

Wallace, Elisabeth. *Goldwin Smith: Victorian Liberal.* Toronto: University of Toronto Press, 1957.

Wallace, Elisabeth. Interview by Harriet Parsons, July 5, 1985.

Wallace, Malcolm (Mrs.). Interview by Harriet Parsons, July 4, 1974.

Ward Graphic. Single-issue tabloid newspaper published by Central Neighbourhood House, Inc. 1918. Contains article, "Central Neighbourhood House: The Story of Its Origin and Establishment — Its First Workers — The Stated Objects of Central Neighbourhood House," p. 4.

Wasteneys, Hortense. "A History of the University Settlement of Toronto, 1910-1958." Ph.D. thesis, University of Toronto, 1975.

Waters, F.W. (Rev.). Memorial Institute, a brief description of the Institute's history, 1912-1943, in "History of Canadian Settlements" file, Book B (Baldwin Room, Metropolitan Toronto Library).

Weinfeld, Morton, William Shaffir and Irwin Cotler, eds. *The Canadian Jewish Mosaic.* Toronto: John Wiley & Sons Canada Limited, 1981.

Wesley House, vol. 1, no. 5, May-June 1909. Official publication of the settlement, 212, East 58th Street, New York, N.Y.

Wiebe, Robert H. *The Search for Order: 1877-1920.* New York: Hill and Wang, 1967.

Wilson, Elizabeth. *Fifty Years of Association Work, 1866-1916: A History of Young Women's Christian Associations in the United States of America.* New York: National Board of the Young Women's Christian Associations of the United States of America, 1916.

Women's Missionary Society of the Presbyterian Church in Canada. *Annual Report, 1914-15* (Knox Archives).

Woods, Robert A. and Albert J. Kennedy, eds. *Handbook of Settlements.* New York: Russell Sage Foundation, Charities Publication Committee, 1911.

Woods, Robert A. and Albert J. Kennedy. *The Settlement Horizon: A National Estimate.* New York: Russell Sage Foundation, 1922.

Woods, Robert Archey. *The Neighborhood in Nation-building: The Running Comment of Thirty Years at South End House.* (Boston and New York: Houghton Mifflin, 1923; New York: Arno Press and the *New York Times*, 1970).

Woodsworth, James Shaver. *My Neighbour: A Study of City Conditions and a Plea for Social Service*, with an introduction by Richard Allen. Toronto: University of Toronto Press, 1972. Originally published in 1911 by The Missionary Society of the Methodist Church, Canada.

Woodsworth, James Shaver. *Strangers within Our Gates, or Coming Canadians*, with an introduction by Marilyn Barber. Toronto: University of Toronto Press, 1972. Originally published in 1909 by the Missionary Society of the Methodist Church, Canada.

World (Toronto), Apr. 18, 1901. "Forty in a House — Most Congested Portion of the City is in Centre Avenue." Article concerning overcrowding in the Ward.

World (Toronto), Oct. 14, 1907: 2. "Earl Grey Here Today to Open Evangelia Home — Building at Queen and River streets to be dedicated by Governor-General."

World (Toronto), Oct. 18, 1907. "Mr. Kipling on Immigration," an editorial.

Young Men's Christian Association of the University of Toronto. *Fifth Annual Report, 1908-1909.* Toronto: The University Press (Probably not published until 1910). The report of the City Mission Committee (George P. Bryce, convener) contains the information on the Hayter Street Mission works.

Young Men's Christian Association of the University of Toronto. *Fourth Annual Report, 1907-1908* (published until 1909). As quoted by Hortense C.F. Wasteneys in her Ph.D. thesis, "A History of the University Settlement of Toronto, 1910-1958," University of Toronto, 1975.

Young Women's Christian Association (National). Papers. Public Archives of Canada, Ottawa. Minute Book – National Executive Committee – 1895-1905 (first minute book).

Young Women's Christian Association (Toronto). Papers. Archives of Ontario. Toronto YWCA – Minute Book, 1897-1904.

Zeidman, Alex. Director of the Scott Mission. Brief interview by Harriet Parsons, Mar. 20, 1984, on founding of the Scott Mission by his father, Rev. Morris Zeidman.

Ziegler, Olive Irene. *Woodsworth, Social Pioneer*. Toronto: The Ontario Publishing Co. Ltd., 1934. Foreword by Dr. Salem Bland.

NOTE ON SOURCES

The main source for the three chapters in Part II is the large collection of material — annual reports, newsletters, publicity brochures — assembled by Harriet Parsons during her research for the book from University Settlement, Central Neighbourhood House and St. Christopher House, her extensive and detailed handwritten research notes based on the papers of the three settlements which were most useful. During the time she was carrying out her research, these papers were still housed at each of the settlements; subsequently the settlement papers were transferred to the City of Toronto Archives. The Parsons' material and notes used to write the chapters in Part II are currently in the possession of Allan Irving and Donald Bellamy at the Faculty of Social Work, University of Toronto and may be examined there.

The following two unpublished papers by Harriet Parsons were used extensively in this part as well: "Highlights of Community Development at St. Christopher House" and "The Metamorphosis of St. Christopher House, 1955-1976" (copies of these two documents may be obtained from Allan Irving).

As part of her research for this book Harriet Parsons carried out a number of interviews and wrote them up in a most detailed and thorough manner; these were used throughout Part II by Allan Irving and copies of Harriet's transcripts are in his possession and may be consulted by contacting him. A list of the Parsons' interviews follows: Jean Palmer, September 12, 1974; Beatrice Wilson, September 19, 1974; James Walker, October 10, 1974; John Braithwaite, September 16, 1975; Louis Zimmerman, September 17, 1975; Mina Barnes, September 13, 1975; Eugenia Berlin, September 2, 1974; Mary C. Donaldson, July 24, 1977; Dr. Wilbur Howard, June 30, 1976; Frances Crowther, September 9, 10, 1975; Kathleen Gorrie, August 5, 1974; Honorah Lucas, April 18, 1975; William Leggatt, December 20, 1974; William Stern, March 7, May 23, September 22, 1974; Helen Sutcliffe, no date; Olive Ziegler, no date; Edith Cook Vinnels, no date; Muriel Boyle, no date; Kay Kato Shimizu, no date; and Harry Morrow, no date

Four graduate student papers written in the 1986-87 academic year under the direction of Allan Irving by Irv Kideckel, Pamela McCann and Ellen Pomer based on the Parsons' research notes were extremely helpful in reconstructing these years. These four papers are in the possession of Allan Irving and may be consulted by contacting him: Ellen Pomer, "A Powerhouse of Social Reform?: Central Neighbourhood House, 1930-1959;" Irv Kideckel, "St. Christopher House, 1930-1960;" Pamela A. McCann, "University Settlement, 1930-1960;" and Pamela A. McCann, "University Settlement, 1960-1970."

Three excellent booklets written by Patricia J. O'Connor and published in 1986 by the Toronto Association of Neighbourhood Services provided good overviews of each settlement: *The Story of St. Christopher House, 1912-1984*; *The Story of University Settlement, 1910-1984*; and *The Story of Central Neighbourhood House, 1911-1986*

In the same series the booklet, "The Story of the Toronto Settlement House Movement, 1910-1985," by the late Elspeth Heyworth provided a good general overview.

Index of Names

INDEX OF SUBJECTS